AIRBORNE ASSAULT

Patrick Stephens Limited, a member of the Haynes Publishing Group, has published authoritative, quality books for enthusiasts for more than twenty years. During that time the company has established a reputation as one of the world's leading publishers of books on aviation, maritime, military, model-making, motor cycling, motoring, motor racing, railway and railway modelling subjects. Readers or authors with suggestions for books they would like to see published are invited to write to: The Editorial Director, Patrick Stephens Limited, Sparkford, Nr Yeovil, Somerset, BA22 7JJ.

AIRBORNE ASSAULT

PARACHUTE FORCES IN ACTION, 1940-91

Bruce Quarrie

PSL

Patrick Stephens Limited

First published in 1991

British Library Cataloguing in Publication Data
Quarrie, Bruce *1947—*
    Airborne assault: parachute forces in action, 1940-1991
    1.   Parachute units, history
    I.   Title
    356.166

    Library of Congress catalog card number 91-71108

    ISBN 0-85059-807-9

Patrick Stephens Limited is a member of the Haynes Publishing Group P.L.C., Sparkford, Nr Yeovil, Somerset, BA22 7JJ.

Printed in Great Britain by J. H. Haynes & Co Ltd.

Contents

Dedication

This book is dedicated to the memory of my dear and greatly missed
friend Bryan Philpott

Introduction

Paratrooper! The very word is evocative of military prowess, conjuring up an image of the perfect warrior descending from the skies to inflict death and confusion on his enemies. Yet paratroops are ordinary men, trained in extraordinary skills but still the same flesh and blood with the same hopes and fears as the rest of us. Despite this obvious fact, there is a cachet attached to the paras which ranks their members alongside fighter pilots and submarine aces and bestows upon them a romanticism which the men themselves would be the first to disavow.

The concept of the paratrooper is not new, and as early as 1784 Benjamin Franklin raised the question of how a country could adequately defend itself against an airborne army. The idea continued to fascinate speculative writers and military thinkers long before it became a practical proposition, and one contemporary illustration from the time of the Franco–Prussian War of 1870-71 shows huge balloons packed with troops and guns descending upon an enemy fortress. There were proposals during the First World War to drop troops by parachute behind enemy lines to break the stalemate of trench warfare, but these came to naught and it was not until the 1930s that the paratroop concept, alongside those of glider-borne and air-landed forces, came to maturity.

The German use of airborne troops in the conquests of Denmark, Norway, Belgium and Holland spurred the British and Americans to develop their own units which eventually grew to the size of several divisions and were used in all the decisive campaigns of the European war from November 1942 onwards, as well as more sparsely in selected operations in the Far East. Subsequently, paratroops have been used in many other campaigns, not always in their true role but as élite infantry or as helicopter-borne 'airmobile' forces. The reason paras are often selected for the most critical and dangerous missions is a result of several factors. First, every para is a volunteer. Second, the intensity of his training and the extraordinary demands made on his physical and mental sinews make him particularly resilient under combat stress. Third, the knowledge that he is a member of an élite body of men whose battle honours include Arnhem and Bastogne, Cassino and Crete, Goose Green, Grenada and a host of others inspires an *ésprit de corps* second to none.

Yet there are doubters. There are those who say that paratroops are an expensive luxury and that all their achievements could have been accomplished by ordinary 'line' infantry or amphibious commando forces. Such detractors will point out that not once has a major airborne operation (excluding small-scale raids and hostage rescue missions) succeeded without the support of a follow-up by land or sea. They will say that when paras were most successful, as at Salerno in 1943 or during the Rhine crossing in 1945, they were 'merely' employed as a mobile reserve. There is a lot of truth in these allegations. A number of airborne operations were, or nearly would have been, disasters without more conventional backup, and that includes the battle of Crete which forms the subject matter of Chapter 1. But — and it is a big but — such detractors conveniently forget that in an equal number of cases operations could not have succeeded so swiftly (if at all) without the presence of airborne troops to seize vital airports, bridges and other tactical features before the enemy could respond effectively. Surprise, speed and shock are the three factors which win battles with minimum casualties, and these are what the paras practise and capitalize upon.

In recent years airborne forces have come to form the rapid deployment reserve of most major countries, ready to fly anywhere in the world at scant hours' notice. After President Saddam Hussein of Iraq invaded neighbouring Kuwait in August 1990, it was unquestionably the United States' swift deployment of the 82nd Airborne Division to Saudi Arabia in operation 'Desert Shield' which caused the dictator to shelve his plans to overrun that country as well. A single division could not, of course, do more than delay an army of a million men plus thousands of modern tanks, but the speed of the American response imposed a psychological check prior to the arrival of stronger air, sea and land forces from America and several other nations. If ever vindication of the value of airborne troops was needed, August 1990 provided it.

Full details were still not available at the time of writing, with the war in the Gulf only just concluded, so a more in-depth account of operation 'Desert Sabre' will have to await a second edition of this book. Briefly, the deployment of the 82nd as the spearhead of Lt-Gen G. Luck's XVIII Airborne Corps stopped Saddam Hussein in his tracks. The Corps' other three divisions – 101st Airborne, 1st Cavalry and 24th Mechanized – followed rapidly. Then came Vice-Admiral S. Arthur's 1st and 2nd US Marine Corps Divisions; and Lt-Gen F. Franks' VII Army Corps (1st Infantry and 1st and 3rd Armored Divisions). The American units were backed up by contingents from Britain (1st Armoured Division, commanded by Maj-Gen R. Smith) and France (6th Armoured Division, commanded by Gen M. Roquejeoffre). Additionally, Saudi Arabia deployed three task forces under Lt-Gen Prince Khaled-bin-Sultan; Egypt a division under Gen M. al Halaby; and Syria a task force under Maj-Gen A. Habib. Moroccan and Pakistani troops were also involved, as were elements of the small Kuwaiti army. Overall commander of the allied coalition forces in the Gulf was Gen Norman Schwarzkopf, who told his troops 'we are going to kick their butts'.

And, of course, they did. As the months of preparation dragged by and it became obvious that the United Nations' economic embargo and blockade were not going to force Saddam Hussein to pull out of Kuwait, Schwarzkopf began planning operation 'Desert Storm'. Just before midnight on 16 January 1991 the first waves of allied bombers swept into Iraq. For the next month they would pummel Iraqi airfields, air defences and missile sites – particularly the mobile Scud B launchers – before turning their attention to Saddam Hussein's ground forces. The attacks, in wave after wave by day and night, destroyed a large part of the Iraqi war machine. They also had a staggering effect on the morale of the Iraqi troops, many of them already exhausted after eight years of war with Iran. Saddam Hussein was given every chance to pull out of Kuwait but in the end, on 24 February Schwarzkopf launched the ground phase of the war, operation 'Desert Sabre'. And once again the paras were to the fore.

The bulk of the 82nd Airborne Division was based deep in the desert in western Saudi Arabia, alongside the French 6th Armoured Division on the coalition's left flank. The majority of the Iraqi forces were either in Kuwait or eastern Iraq, south of Basra. Schwarzkopf, by masterly deception, had persuaded Iraqi intelligence that the main blow would be an amphibious assault by his Marines, but in fact this was a feint. The main blow actually fell in the centre of the line, the armoured and mechanized divisions sweeping in a broad left hook to trap the Iraqi forces in the east, which included the vaunted Republican Guard. Elements of the 82nd flew into Kuwait City ahead of the Marines plus the Egyptian and Saudi forces who would complete the liberation of the country – though not, unfortunately, until Saddam Hussein had set fire to over 500 oil wells, producing a black pall of pollution. It was the action of a demented child – 'If I can't have them, neither can you'.

On the left flank, the balance of the 82nd was airlifted in just west of Salman, where they were speedily joined by French tanks racing across the desert. This established a blocking position both to prevent Iraqi reinforcements being sent east and similarly prevent the troops in that part of the country from escaping towards Baghdad. The helicopter-borne troops of the 101st Airborne followed through on the right of the 82nd, establishing an air base at Nasiriyah, on the river Euphrates. Exactly 100 hours after it had begun, operation 'Desert Sabre' was over and Iraq's army had surrendered. It was a remarkable demonstration of speed and precision, a victory of firepower and, just as importantly, of willpower. And once again, the paras had done their bit with panache and skill.

In this book I have tried to cover every major and most minor instances of airborne assaults over the half century from 1940 to 1991. Technical details have been kept to a minimum but those interested will find information in the appendices on the principal parachutes, transport aircraft and gliders used. It should be noted that I have given contemporary place names first and their correct or more modern spellings in parentheses afterwards, where appropriate. People's names and ranks are given in full wherever possible, although in a few cases such information has unfortunately eluded me. The idea throughout has been to make this as reliable a reference source as possible while at the same time remaining, I hope, readable. I have tried not to play favourites, or to assign to the airborne forces of any nation an exaggerated importance beyond what is rightfully due. I have, I believe, corrected a number of errors and omissions which have crept into other publications, and if I have made any of my own they are my sole responsibility and not those of the people who have helped in my research.

Among those are the editors of The Parachute Regiment journal *Pegasus* and the curator of the Parachute Regiment Museum, Aldershot; Mr Hans Teske and other members of the *Fallschirmjäger* old comrades' association; the editor of the French Foreign Legion magazine *Le Képi*; Mr Edwin P. Hoyt; Mr Gavin Cadden; Mr Robin Scagell of Marshall Cavendish for his permission to quote extracts from *Images of War*; my old friends Paul Beaver, Terry Gander and Martin Windrow; John and Diane Moore of Military Archive and Research Services (whom I shall never forgive for giving the task of writing the script of their video *Airborne Assault* to my other old friend Bill Gunston and saddling me out of the blue with *Amphibious Assault* in its place!); and the staffs of the Imperial War Museum, London, the Bundesarchiv in Koblenz and the Bildarchiv Preußischer Kulturbesitz in Berlin. Also Mr E.R. Chinnery, Mr Marcel Comeau, Mr Larry Cormier, Mr Derek Glaister, Col W.S. Hathaway, Mr Chris Mason, Mr George Rosie and Mr Roland Thick. If I have inadvertently forgotten anyone, my sincere apologies.

Bruce Quarrie
Wellingborough, August 1991

Rank abbreviations used in the text

Pte	Private
L/Cpl	Lance Corporal
Cpl	Corporal
L/Sgt	Lance Sergeant
Sgt	Sergeant
Uffz	Unteroffizier
Flt Sgt	Flight Sergeant
S/Sgt	Staff Sergeant
Sgt-Maj	Sergeant-Major
Obfw	Oberfeldwebel
Lt	Lieutenant/Leutnant
Oblt	Oberleutnant
Capt	Captain
Flt Lt	Flight Lieutenant
Hpt	Hauptmann
Maj	Major
Sqn Ldr	Squadron Leader
Lt-Col	Lieutenant-Colonel
Wg Cdr	Wing Commander
Obstlt	Oberstleutnant
Obst	Oberst
Col	Colonel
Gp Capt	Group Captain
Brig	Brigadier
Brig-Gen	Brigadier-General
Maj-Gen	Major-General
Lt-Gen	Lieutenant-General
Gen	General

1

Mediterranean inferno

'A huge red cloud of dust hung over the airfield. Within 15 minutes my *Kette* [formation of three aircraft] was all set to go with a crew of eight paratroopers. The Junkers Ju 52s rolled forward. The rope was secured and the dust from the first wave of aircraft had not settled when the signal came to start. The overloaded DFS 230 glider rumbled along clumsily behind the towing aircraft and wouldn't leave the ground. Slowly we were pulled into the air.'

Obfw (Flt Sgt) Walter Wachter was a glider pilot in the 7th *Flieger* (Airborne) Division whose men would be among the first to land on the Mediterranean island of Crete on 20 May 1941. Already a veteran who had piloted a glider during the audacious attempt to cut off Allied troops in Greece by seizing the Corinth Canal earlier in the year (*qv*), Wachter knew this operation was going to be rather different because the Australian, British, New Zealand and Greek troops in Crete were fully alerted. What neither he nor anyone else in Germany appreciated was the strength of the Allied forces on the island, which intelligence reports had grossly underestimated.

'Everyone was lost in his own thoughts. We flew past the Peloponnese — the open sea lay before us. We had now reached our unhooking height. It was a peaceful flight in the first light of dawn. Suddenly the towing aircraft to our right drew ahead of us, trailing a rope but no glider. We now had 20 men. Too few.

'We could see a lot of mushroom-shaped smoke clouds — the bombers were at work, preparing the ground. There were smoke clouds coming from the anti-aircraft guns. At intervals I could make out the lie of the land — it was bloody narrow and steeply inclined. A few bushes and trees and hedges were blocking the landing area. We were soon very close to the landing point but too high. On the left of our landing site was a dry stream bed running north to the beach. We had to move very swiftly — we couldn't present any target for the AA guns. Everything was happening so fast now. After a few manoeuvres, there was the ground before me. Apparently no machine-guns. Then they opened up. They rattled out as we were a few feet from the ground, but there were not only hedges, there were terraces with hedges on top of them. We flew across them and away, almost touching down — one, two, three terraces — then smash, into a bush. The left wing struck a tree and broke off. The glider rocked and stayed still. The crew were unscathed — we all climbed out.'

Wachter was lucky. The third glider smashed into a terrace and all its occupants were severely injured. Later in the day, though, he was wounded by small-arms fire and subsequently evacuated back to a hospital on the Greek mainland. For his achievement he was awarded the Iron Cross First and Second Class.

The German invasion of Crete, codenamed *Merkur* ('Mercury') was a gamble which paid off, although at such heavy cost that Hitler afterwards forbade any further large-scale airborne operations, restricting the *Fallschirmjäger* (paratroops) to an ordinary infantry role and only permitting small-scale airborne raids for limited objectives. One significant result of this was that the Germans never invaded Malta, which would have given them control of the eastern Mediterranean and crippled the Allied effort in North Africa. But before examining the Cretan operation in more detail, we have to backtrack before the war, to April 1939 when Britain and France guaranteed aid to Greece if the country was attacked. When that attack came it was not, however, from Germany, but from Italy, whose Fascist dictator Benito Mussolini was determined to create a new Roman empire throughout the Mediterranean. The Italian army had already occupied Albania and in October 1940, following the German occupation of Romania, Italian troops invaded Greece. The small but tough Greek army fought back with such ferocity despite its lack of modern equipment that the Italians were not merely checked in their tracks but by mid-December had been driven halfway back to Tiranë, the capital of Albania. By this time, too, a small British Empire expeditionary force of 7,500 men had arrived from Egypt and British troops had also occupied Crete to safeguard the important naval base of Suda (Soúdhas) Bay.

At the beginning of 1941 more Allied reinforcements began arriving. This move had been the subject of delicate negotiations because the Greek government insisted on all or nothing — either a force strong enough to repel a German invasion or none at all, because a weak force might simply tempt the Germans who were already sending troops and tanks out to Libya to bolster the Italian army there. As it happened, the worst Greek fears were realised. The British promised Maj-Gen Bernard Freyberg's tough 2nd New Zealand Division, the 1st Armoured Brigade and Lt-Gen Sir Thomas Blamey's 6th Australian Division. This would have constituted a total of 57,000 men — still far short of the 100,000 the Greeks had asked for — but in the event only the New Zealanders, a few tanks and a few battalions of Australians had been landed when Germany struck.

It is often said that, as in North Africa, Hitler's motives were simply to pull Mussolini's chestnuts out of the fire, but in fact they were far more pragmatic. With plans well advanced for the invasion of Russia, the dictator could not accept a strong Allied presence on his southern flank. Moreover, it was vital to protect the Ploesti oilfields in Romania from attack by RAF bombers based in Greece. On top of this Hitler had finally run out of patience with the Yugoslav government headed by Prince Regent Paul, which had persistently refused to join the Axis. He issued an ultimatum on 25 March and Paul at last reluctantly agreed. Not for long, however. The very next day a military junta overthrew the government, placed the under-age King Peter II on the throne and repudiated the agreement. In a rage, Hitler ordered German forces to prepare for a joint invasion of both Greece and Yugoslavia on 6 April, the former codenamed *Marita* and the latter *Strafe* ('Punishment').

Yugoslavia's small, antiquated army crumbled with barely a fight and German forces were able to advance directly southwards into Greece to link up with other troops coming from Bulgaria to the east. Salonika (Thessaloniki), Greece's second city, fell after only three days and the Greek army itself was in total disarray with most of its strength still concentrated against the Italians in Albania. The commander of the Allied expeditionary force, Gen Sir Henry Maitland Wilson, conducted a valiant defence along the line of the river Aliákmon, but finding his flank threatened by the German success in Yugoslavia was forced to fall back, first to a line straddling Mount Olympus then to Thermopylae, scene of the epic battle between the Spartans and Persians in 480 BC. Even this proved inadequate and when Greece formally surrendered on 22 April Wilson ordered his forces to retire into the Peloponnese whence they would be evacuated by sea from Kalamata.

Their route would inevitably take them across the narrow neck of land west of Athens bisected by the steep-sided Corinth Canal, and the Germans saw a perfect opportunity to cut them off before they could be evacuated. The 2nd *Fallschirmjäger* Regiment under Obst (Col) Albert Sturm was rushed from Bulgaria to the Greek airfield of Larissa and at 05:00 on 26 April the first aircraft took off, six gliders carrying 54 parachute engineers from the regiment's 6th Company under Lt (2nd Lt) Hans Teusen preceding the 272 Junkers Ju 52 trimotor transports carrying the remainder of the regiment's two battalions (I/ and II FJR 2). The gliders — including that piloted by Walter Wachter — landed either side of the sole bridge across the canal, only one of them cracking up against a pillar. The engineers raced out and despite heavy fire from the retreating Allied troops, succeeded in removing the demolition charges which Maitland Wilson had intended to set off once all his men were across. Then the parachutes of I/ and II/FJR 2 began to blossom at some 350ft (100m) above the dusty landscape.

Just at this point a stray shell from a Bofors gun may have landed in the pile of explosives which the engineers in their haste had simply dumped in a heap. Nobody to this day knows for certain what caused it, but a huge explosion rent the early morning air, destroying the bridge. There is even a story that a couple of British officers set it off by firing their rifles into the mound! Nevertheless, the engineers, whose ranks had been decimated by the blast, rapidly built a temporary replacement bridge further south, where the canal banks were lower. Some 10,000 Allied troops, caught on the north side of the canal between the 1st *Fallschirmjäger* Battalion and the 1st SS Motorized Infantry Division *Leibstandarte 'Adolf Hitler'* which was pressing at their heels, entered captivity. On the Peloponnese side the 2nd Battalion captured a further 2,000, but the bulk of Wilson's force — some 43,000 men (50,732 including patriotic Greek soldiers who refused to acknowledge their government's surrender) — were successfully evacuated by the Royal Navy, about 16,000 of them being shipped to Egypt and the remainder to Crete. (These figures are often confused, 43,000 being given as the total number of Allied troops evacuated and 16,000 as the number sent to Crete, leading to quotes of 23–28,000 as the Allied contingent on the island in May. I believe my own figures to be correct but would welcome further substantiated comment.)

The subjugation of Yugoslavia and Greece was not enough for Hitler, because RAF Wellington bombers could still reach Ploesti from the three airstrips on Crete. Even before the Greek surrender, on 21 April he had agreed to the audacious plan proposed by Gen Kurt Student, commander of XI *Fliegerkorps* (airborne corps), to take the island by means of a combined aerial and amphibious assault. The principal forces available to Student were the 7th *Flieger* Division and the *Luftlande-Sturm* (air-landing assault) Regiment plus a number of smaller units. The third major component of the corps, the 22nd *Luftlande* Division, was in Romania preparing for the invasion of Russia and could not be detached, and in its place Student was given Gen Julius Ringel's 5th *Gebirgs* (mountain) Division, tough troops well suited to fighting in the rugged Cretan terrain but completely untrained in air-landing operations.

To support the operation Student also had the co-operation of Gen Freiherr von Richtofen's VIII *Fliegerkorps*. The total number of aircraft available was 502–532 Ju 52 transports, 72–80 DFS 230 gliders, 150–205 Ju 87 Stuka dive-bombers, 228–280 Ju 88 and Do 217 bombers, 90-119 Messerschmitt Bf 109 single-engined fighters and 90–114 Bf 110 twin-engined *zerstörer* (destroyers). In addition there were about 40–50 reconnaissance machines. (The number of aircraft vary widely in German, British and American sources and probably reflect different reporting of numbers available [ie, listed] and numbers operational [ie, not undergoing maintenance and repair]. Up to about 100 gliders were actually available but there were insufficient qualified pilots to man them all.) Despite these numbers, there were not enough aircraft to land the paras in a single wave, so the assault had to be staggered and only after at least one airstrip had been secured could the mountain troops be delivered. Against this air-borne armada, the Allies had only seven out of 35 aircraft left after the constant German bombing, and even these were evacuated to Egypt the day before the invasion took place, denuding the island totally of aerial defence. Unfortunately too, a plan to mine Máleme airfield proposed by Maj F.M.H. Hanson of the Royal Engineers was not acted upon. As will be seen, this could have been decisive because Máleme was the key to control of the island.

The combined force of 22,040 paras and mountain troops which would be landed were opposed, not by the 5,000 or so Allied troops predicted by German intelligence but by *41,840* — 30,000-odd Australians, British and New Zealanders and 11,000 Greeks, all under the overall command of the pugnacious Maj-Gen Bernard Freyberg. The odds were therefore against a German success from the beginning, because normally an assault against prepared positions requires a three-to-one superiority before success is almost assured. (British paras were to secure a victory against even heavier odds 41 years later, on another island many thousands of miles away.) Moreover, it was obvious to Freyberg even without assistance from the 'Ultra' cryptanalysts at Bletchley Park, where the Germans would concentrate their attacks, for the three airfields and the naval base were the inevitable prime targets. However, Freyberg's troops were sadly lacking in heavy equipment because most of it had been abandoned in Greece. They only had 49 field and anti-aircraft guns salvaged by cannibalization, six slow-moving Matilda tanks armed with 2pdr guns which could only fire solid armour-piercing shot — useless against infantry — and 13 little Vickers light tanks armed solely with machine-guns. German equipment by comparison was more modern and more suited to the conditions, although the importance of these factors should not be exaggerated.

Gen Student's plan for the attack concentrated on the north flank of the 160 by 40 mile (256 by 64km) island where the three airstrips were strung like beads along the coast road either side of Suda Bay, overlooked by the town of Caneá (Khaniá). Freyburg, of course, had concentrated his forces in approximately brigade-sized formations around these features, for to have kept them all in the western half of the island would have run the risk of revealing the Ultra secret to the enemy. Thus, although outnumbered overall, the Germans could create pockets of local superiority at key points.

(To digress briefly, the Ultra secret did not begin to become public knowledge until nearly 30 years after the war and many details are still obscure. To simplify a long and fascinating story, in the summer of 1939 agents of Polish, French and British intelligence succeeded in stealing an example of the latest German 'Enigma' device. These machines were in effect paired typewriters with three reels or spools in between them which automatically encoded signals for radio transmission, signals which could not be decoded without another Enigma and a key to the current code. The latter was cracked by a primitive mechanical computer, one of which was needed to run through all possible three-letter combinations for each reel, and throughout the war scientists at the top secret decoding centre at Bletchley Park in Buckinghamshire were able to make almost instantaneous translations of German radio traffic. This was something of a double-edged sword, however, because if the Allies showed they knew too much about German troop movements and intentions, German intelligence would smell a rat and change the system, perhaps even continuing to use Enigma to broadcast false information.)

Because there were insufficient aircraft to transport four regiments of paratroops in a single airlift (at full strength a regiment comprised 3,206 officers and men), the attack had to go in two waves spread between the four initial objectives. Assault Group West, commanded by Maj-Gen Eugen Meindl, had Máleme airfield as its objective. This comprised the bulk of the Assault Regiment less the 1st and 2nd Companies of the 1st Battalion which were attached to Assault Group Centre on their left (eastern) flank. This, the strongest of the three groups, was commanded by the CO of the 7th *Flieger* Division, Lt-Gen Wilhelm Süssman. It consisted of the three battalions of the 3rd Regiment, 7th *Flieger* Division, (I/, II/ and III/FJR 3) under Obst Richard Heidrich (the later hero of the German defence at Cassino), plus the two companies of the Assault Regiment, the divisional Engineer Battalion and a machine-gun company.

Süssman would be reinforced by two battalions of Obst Alfred Sturm's 2nd Regiment (I/ and III/FJR 2) after the Ju 52s had dropped the first wave and returned to Greece to refuel. Assault Group Centre's task was to drop either side of Suda Bay to capture Caneá and the airstrip at Retimo

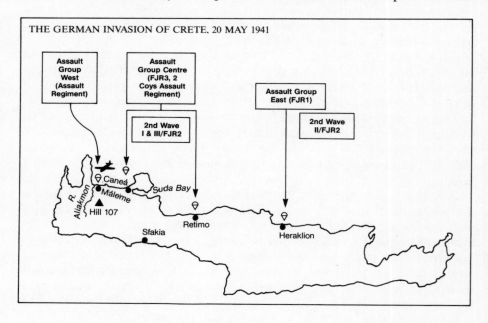

THE GERMAN INVASION OF CRETE, 20 MAY 1941

(Réthimnon). Finally Assault Group East comprised Obst Bruno Bräuer's 1st Regiment (I/, II/ and III/FJR 1) plus II/FJR 2 which would also be dropped in the second wave, its task to capture the third airstrip at Heraklion (Iráklion). Julius Ringel's *Gebirgs* Division could not be airlifted in until at least one airfield had been captured, so the Assault Regiment's rapid seizure of Máleme was essential to success. The remainder of the mountain division, including the Artillery Regiment, would travel by sea in ancient Greek fishing boats known as 'caiques' escorted by the almost equally ancient Italian destroyers *Lupo* and *Sagittario*.

This expedient, determined by the lack of transport aircraft in the first place plus anticipated losses, proved a disaster, for the first convoy of 25 vessels escorted by *Lupo* was intercepted by the Royal Navy during the night of 21/22 May and 10 ships were sunk leaving only 52 survivors from two of the *Gebirgsjäger* battalions (II/GJR 85 and III/GJR 100). The remainder scattered and fled. The second convoy escorted by *Sagittario* was ordered to turn back and although Royal Navy warships spotted it, they were too low on ammunition to pursue. Even though the *Luftwaffe* (German Air Force) took its revenge over the next couple of days, sinking or badly damaging several British warships including Lord Louis Mountbatten's HMS *Kelly*, the German losses at sea seriously jeopardized the success of operation 'Mercury'.

Confusion. Confusion and fear. Confusion and noise. Confusion and blood, filth and death. Whatever the circumstances, in the dust under a blazing sun, in the mud under an endless downpour, in the permanent dusk of a snow-filled sky over dirty grey snow on the ground, one feature remains permanent on any battlefield. Confusion. The so aptly called 'fog of war'. The neat maps with their carefully drawn arrows, circles and symbols bear little or no relation to the situation experienced by the combat soldier on the spot. Even in exercises and manoeuvres where every stage of the 'battle' is choreographed, the overwhelming impression is still one of confusion. As it was on Crete, so a battlefield ever shall be. Objectives are not taken on schedule. Reinforcements do not arrive when or where they are supposed to. Supposedly undefended areas turn out to be bitterly contested, and vice versa. What looked flat on the map is rugged. What appeared to be a commanding hill turns out to be a mere pimple. Even afterwards, reconstructing exactly what happened when and where, with which and to whom, is worse than re-assembling any jigsaw or Rubik's Cube. The private soldier only sees a tiny portion of his personal hell. Field officers see a little more and the generals yet further, but whether you look at the detail or the overall picture which emerges in the inevitable historical post mortem, neither conveys that terrifying lost feeling which every soldier experiences, that numbing confusion and often paralysing indecision. So it was on Crete, where things seemed to go wrong for the German paras almost from the word 'go'.

Karl Eisenfeller was lost. The 19-year-old private from FJR 3 had, like many of his comrades, been accidentally parachuted a considerable distance from the designated point. The problem was how to rejoin his unit. Abandoning even his helmet in the fierce heat, he approached a scruffy and anonymous cluster of houses, clutching his automatic pistol. The first thing he saw was two dead paras lying in the road in a pool of blood. The next was a woman, washing her clothes, who screamed loudly. Bypassing her house, Eisenfeller approached the village where a number of young Cretan men were standing around. Trying not to show his fear, he begged a drink of water and departed, his spine crawling in anticipation of a bullet in the back. 'Luckily', he says, 'they only shot when I was quite a way down the road and they missed'. Many other German soldiers were less fortunate. Cretan partisans mutilated and killed at least 135 paras from the Assault Regiment alone, women as well as men using knives, garottes and shotguns, and the bodies of many more were never recovered. The savage reprisals are, for once, almost understandable even if they cannot be condoned.

'I found good cover in a little stream which led through this valley', Eisenfeller continued, 'then headed off to the right, up into the hills. I met a comrade who wanted to get water from the stream. He told me about a group of soldiers — he thought they must have been British, and if I carried on, I'd run straight into them. After a while we threw a few hand grenades, but it was probably too late for next instant a machine-gun fired at us from what seemed to be point-blank range.' His companion dived into cover and scurried away, but Eisenfeller says 'I made an error. I ran towards the hills, heading for a small sheep shed which stood right against the hill. As I ran, I looked down and it seemed as if the earth was moving under me. My enemies had spotted me and shot off all their guns at me. When I reached my goal, I couldn't believe that I'd come through unscathed. But then I thought, "Now I'm in a trap — and I might not get out!"

'There was another way in from the other side and I felt that at any minute the enemy would come and mow me down. I didn't dare run through such fire again. They shot at the entrance, as if to remind me they'd not forgotten me. So I decided to wait until it was dark and to crawl out very quietly in the opposite direction. The way was now firmly imprinted in my mind and I waited until it got really dark. It came off OK and in a short time I was being asked by one of our sentries for the password. I didn't know it. I'd been away the whole day. I called out, "Don't shoot, I'm Eisenfeller from 2 Company". I could then walk forward with my hands up and they said "My God, man, it *is* you!".'

Like Walter Wachter, Karl Eisenfeller was one of the lucky survivors. Unknown to him, his commanding officer, Gen Süssman, had been killed alongside most of his staff when his glider crashed shortly after take-off, while Gen Meindl, CO of the Assault Regiment, had been so badly wounded that tactical command at Máleme had to be assumed by the commander of the 2nd Battalion, Maj Edgar Stentzler. Similarly, temporary command at Caneá was taken over by Obst Richard Heidrich. These breakdowns at the top of the command hierarchy compounded the confusion even further, particularly since the news took time to filter back to Kurt Student in Athens because the radios of the time were not terribly reliable.

The Allied defenders on Crete had been awakened at daybreak by the usual morning strafing attack by Messerschmitts, and when the fighters departed the men were stood down. This meant that large numbers of them were away from their slit trenches when the bombers arrived some 20 minutes later, wave after wave of Ju 88s and Do 217s pummelling their positions. Later came the terrifying shriek of the sirens mounted beneath the wings of the evil gull-winged Stuka dive-bombers. Normally easy targets for fighters, on this occasion the Ju 87s had a field day. Vast clouds of dust and smoke enveloped and choked the men on the ground. Then came the gliders, dropped just off the coast by their ungainly Ju 52 towing aircraft, eerily descending with just a swish of air like gigantic birds of prey.

First on the ground at Máleme was a company of 90 men under Oblt (Lt) Alfred Genz who landed just after 07:00 in a hail of small-arms fire, and although anti-aircraft fire was both sporadic and erratic, there were many losses amongst the gliders, particularly in bad crash-landings. They were rapidly followed by the rest of the 1st Battalion of the Assault Regiment (I/LLStR) which was commanded by Maj Walter Koch, one of the heroes of Eben Emael (*qv*). Some of these landed right on top of positions occupied by companies of the New Zealand 22nd Infantry Battalion and many of the *Fallschirmjäger* were chopped down as they tried to get out of their aircraft. Nevertheless the assault troops quickly subdued the anti-aircraft defences on the west side of the airfield, seized the sole metal girder bridge over the dried-up river Tavonritis and dug in along its banks under murderously accurate fire from 'C' and 'D' Companies of the battalion. Koch himself received a minor head wound, and there were dozens of more serious casualties.

II/ and IV/LLStR landed more or less without incident south and west of the airfield although there were further losses from bad landings; it was while trying to link up with the 1st Battalion, ducking from pillar to pillar beneath the bridge, that Gen Meindl was wounded. Most of III/LLStR landed to the east of the airfield, coming under such torrential fire from the reserve New Zealand 21st and 23rd Battalions that within minutes two-thirds of their number (over 400 men) were casualties.

The biggest stumbling block preventing capture of the airfield was the fact that the New Zealanders controlled the high ground, Kavkazia Hill (also known as Point 107), and the paras expected a counter-attack at any moment. The two British Matilda tanks assigned to the airfield which appeared during the afternoon proved a paper tiger, though; the turret of one would not traverse and it had to retire, while the other bogged down in the soft sand of the river bed and had to be abandoned.

Despite the failure of this attack, on which the CO of the 22nd Battalion, Lt-Col Andrew, VC, had placed high hopes, the Assault Regiment knew it had serious problems. By midday Walter Koch realized his men were just about stretched to their limit. The bulk of the airfield remained in New Zealand hands and there were strong, as yet uncommitted, reserves to the east. Nor had matters fared much better around Caneá.

First on the ground here was Maj Ludwig Heilmann's III/FJR 3 which landed in scattered groups to the east of Galatas. Many men were injured through bad landings amongst the rocks, others fell into a reservoir where their heavy kit dragged them straight to the bottom, and still more descended right in the middle of Australian positions where those who had not been killed by small-arms fire while they helplessly drifted towards the ground were rapidly captured. By nightfall Heilmann's battalion had been reduced to little more than company size. I/ and II/FJR 3 were somewhat luckier. Hpt (Capt) Freiherr Friedrich-August von der Heydte's 1st Battalion managed to land close together near the local Agya Prison, a useful strongpoint which was soon turned into their headquarters, but they encountered very heavy opposition from Greek and Australian infantry as they approached the village of Perivólia and for the time being were unable to advance any further towards Caneá and Suda. (Von der Heydte, incidentally, had caused colleagues a good deal of amusement a few days earlier by casually walking into an Athenian bookshop and buying a *Baedecker* guide to the island. 'Oh,' said the guileless salesgirl, 'you're going to Crete then?' So much for security!) Finally, Maj Derpa's 2nd Battalion landed southwest of Galatas and rapidly joined up with them, while Heilmann's survivors straggled through under cover of darkness that night.

Back in Greece there was almost equal confusion as the Ju 52s returned to their airfields to refuel and pick up the troops for the second wave. The dust of their original departure was barely settling as they landed, stirring it all up again, and then the fuel had to be manually loaded from jerry cans — a hard task at the best of times, exacerbated by the harsh heat of the summer sun. These two factors delayed the departure of FJR I and II for Retimo and Heraklion, but due to a breakdown in communications the bombers which should have immediately preceded them went in at the originally scheduled time, giving the defenders plenty of time to prepare for the now inevitable arrival of the paras.

Hpt Gerhard Schirmer, a Knights Cross winner from the 1940 campaign in the West, was a member of Hpt Erich Pietzonka's II/FJR 2 assigned alongside FJR 1 with the capture of Heraklion as part of the second wave.

'My battalion was to be assigned 48–50 Ju 52s. Because of the terrible dust on the airfields, the order of the units who were to jump was changed, and I was now the first. I didn't get my eight aircraft as planned – only four. That meant that I had to leave more than one complete company behind. But we were lucky – we were the first to jump in the area of Heraklion, and where we jumped there was hardly any defensive fire.

'It wasn't long, however, before the first attacks came, principally from the New Zealand and Australian forces. The western edge of the town was magnificently defended by the English. There was an ancient 10-metre high town wall in which there were few gates, and it was impossible to get in. Next day we attacked again. This time we succeeded in getting into the town along the coast, but the counter-fire was so heavy we had to pull our forces back again – it was impossible to reach the airfield. Very heavy fighting ensued. The English attacked – we counter-attacked – it was a period of uninterrupted fighting.'

The remainder of FJR 2 dropped at Retimo. Uffz (Sgt) Martin Pöppel, a veteran of the Norwegian and Dutch campaigns the previous year – and the most junior man of the regiment to have won the Iron Cross 1st and 2nd Class – was a member of the Machine-Gun Battalion, his own No 2 Company being attached to Maj Hans Kroh's 1st Battalion (I/FJR 2). In his exciting book *Heaven and Hell: The diary of a German paratrooper* (Spellmount 1988), he recalls dozing on the two-hour flight to Crete, waking up to check that the static line attached to his parachute was securely clipped to the jump line, then the aircraft was over the coast and the men began tumbling out of the Ju 52's door. Pöppel landed in an olive tree, somersaulted to the ground, and was immediately struck, not by a bullet, but by the heat. At this time no tropical uniform had been issued and the men were in full temperate climate kit complete with bulky jump smocks. Many of them immediately started shedding items of clothing for comfort, abandoning everything except their helmets, weapons, ammunition and water bottles. The savage white glare of the sun was a constant enemy to both sides and dehydration a serious problem.

The battalion formed up and began to move towards Retimo either side of the coast road, some of the men actually wading through the sea, glad as the evening cool began to settle over the island. By daybreak on the 21st they were in position to attack the vineyards on the hill overlooking the airfield. In the grey light of dawn they stormed the Allied position. It was no good, Pöppel records: 'People are getting hit all around us, and the air is full of their cries and groans of pain. We're forced to withdraw from this hill of blood and so fail to achieve our objective. Firing continues on both sides. We manage to find some cover on the rear slopes, then move quickly to a white house where we can care for our wounded.'

Hpt Wiedemann's 3rd Battalion (III/FJR 2) with Obst Albert Sturm in overall command had fared no better. On the first day they took the high ground overlooking the east of the airfield, but were driven out by an Australian counter-attack in the morning and forced to establish a defensive perimeter in and around an olive oil factory, where Maj Kroh's

1st Battalion joined up with them after their own retreat. For the moment there was no hope of taking either Retimo or Heraklion — the defences were simply too strong. Everything rested on the battle still raging around Máleme and Caneá.

At Máleme the Assault Regiment had an unexpected stroke of luck. Lt-Col Andrew, unable to communicate with his brigade headquarters and failing to see any signs of the reinforcements he had asked for, at about 22:00 on the 20th had taken the decision to withdraw 'A' and 'B' Companies of the 22nd Battalion back from their commanding position on top of Point 107. At this time he had also lost contact with 'C' and 'D' Companies and apparently believed they had been virtually wiped out. In fact, although tired, thirsty and with many wounded, they were still hanging on with determination and only withdrew themselves when they realized their flank support had disappeared and that they were in danger of being cut off. Thus, when the Germans cautiously started patrolling up the slopes of the hill in the morning of the 21st, they found to their joyful amazement that the New Zealanders had inexplicably departed. Meanwhile, a solitary Ju 52 flown by Hpt Klete had touched down, disgorged its cargo of ammunition and medical supplies, taken aboard as many wounded as it could carry (including Meindl), and hastily taken off again despite fire from Allied troops still holding parts of the eastern airfield perimeter.

Then, early in the afternoon, the remaining two companies of II/LLStR landed and, thus reinforced, the regiment finally succeeded in clearing the airfield. Shortly afterwards Obst Hermann-Bernhard Ramcke arrived to replace Gen Meindl. This tough and resourceful officer soon summed up the position and established a cordon against a counter-attack which did not come until the night of the 22nd/23rd, partly because Freyberg considered himself overstretched and partly because he lacked reliable intelligence as to the exact situation at Máleme. Ramcke meanwhile received more reinforcements during the afternoon of the 21st when Ju 52s carrying the first 550 men of the 5th *Gebirgs* Division began to arrive as well. Unfortunately the small 1,000yd (600m) airstrip was unsuited for such a flow of traffic and soon became congested, with aircraft colliding into each other in the dust-laden air and having to be manhandled off the runway before others could land.

With Máleme in his hands, Ramcke could concentrate on sending aid to FJR 3 at Caneá. Throughout the 22nd a constant stream of Ju 52s poured into the airfield, disgorging thousands of mountain troops, most of whom were promptly send eastward. At Heraklion, the CO of FJR 1, Obst Bruno Bräuer, was relieved to receive instructions that the capture of the airfield was no longer necessary. All his Group East had to do was block the coast road and surrounding hills to prevent the Allies sending reinforcements west towards Retimo, where the two battalions of FJR 2 had been thrown out of their olive oil factory into the hills to its east. Unknown to them, though, because the Australians, British, Greeks and New Zealanders were still pouring heavy fire into them, by the 24th General Freyberg had decided that with Máleme firmly in German hands following the failure of the night attack on the 22nd/23rd (conducted with great gallantry by the New Zealand 21st and 23rd Battalions, reinforced by companies from other units which included fearsome Maori warriors), 5 Brigade in retreat and Caneá under siege, the defence of Crete was no longer feasible. One of his biggest problems was that the *Luftwaffe* and *Regia Aeronautica* (Italian Air Force) enjoyed almost total aerial supremacy, making daylight counter-attacks hazardous in the extreme. Another factor which influenced him was that, also on the 24th, Bräuer's men actually succeeded in storming and taking an artillery battery which was causing them trouble, and next day captured the hill overlooking Heraklion airfield from the west. Despite orders, Bräuer was determined to take FJR 1's original objective but had to give his men a rest first.

All was set for the attack on the 27th — the same day that Caneá finally fell and Freyberg ordered evacuation of all Allied forces by sea from Sfakia and Timbakion on the south coast — when Bräuer's men were relieved by the first *Gebirgsjäger* troops to push this far east, having taken Retimo, retaken the oil factory from the Australians after a fierce struggle, rescued FJR 2 and, using captured British vehicles, had pushed on to Heraklion as quickly as they possibly could. The small and demoralized garrison which Freyberg had left as a rearguard on the airfield did not stand a chance. To all intents and purposes, apart from mopping up, the battle for Crete was over. Freyberg succeeded in evacuating some 17,000 men, mainly through Sfakia, before the Germans captured the port on the 31st. The Allies had lost 4,000 killed, 2,500 wounded and 11,800 taken prisoner. But German losses, particularly among the paras, had also been high: 3,250 dead and missing and 3,400 wounded. As a recognition of their achievement, all the men who had taken part were subsequently allowed to wear the embroidered gold and white '*Kreta*' cuff title on their sleeves.

2

Ploughshares into swords

The basic idea of the parachute evolved as a lifesaving device but the concept of airborne troops to drop upon the unsuspecting heads of enemies beneath the clouds is as old as the story in Greek mythology, when the winged horse Pegasus carried the warrior Bellerophon into battle against the dragon Chimæra. Later, during the Renaissance, Leonardo da Vinci sketched a hollow pyramid with a man dangling on a rope beneath it, but the first practical parachutes did not emerge until shortly before the First World War. By this time the use of balloons as aerial reconnaissance and artillery spotting platforms had been well established, the first re-corded instance in actual warfare being by the French as early as the battle of Fleurus in 1796, only three years after the Montgolfier brothers' first man-carrying hot air balloon flight. But, with the advent at the beginning of the 20th century of heavier-than-air craft carrying small arms and, later, machine-guns, tethered observation balloons became hideously vulnera-ble and their almost suicidally brave crews began sustaining unsupport-able losses over the Western Front.

Parachutes, as toys, had existed for centuries, modelled on parasols, and by the end of the 18th century animals were being dropped by parachute from balloon baskets as entertainment for spectators. The first man courageous enough to try one himself was a Frenchman, Monsieur A.J. Garnerin, who made demonstration jumps from a hydrogen balloon over Paris and London in 1797 and 1802 respectively. Following this, progress was slow and it was not until after the American Civil and Franco–Prussian Wars, some time during the 1880s, that the concept of a parachute with a limp canopy evolved — ie, one without rigid spokes to hold its shape during descent. From 1887 onwards, when Tom Baldwin made the first recorded jump with a 'chute of this type in view of an enthralled crowd in San Francisco, parachutists became popular as fairground attractions in America, intrepid balloonists jumping from their baskets and allowing their weight to pull their canopies free from the containers which were firmly tied to the wickerwork. Then, after the

Wright brothers proved in 1903 that sustained powered heavier than air flight was possible, it was not long before the idea of using parachutes with this novel form of transport was tested. A man called Albert Berry made the first recorded jump from an aeroplane, a Benoist biplane with a 'pusher' propeller, over Jefferson Army Barracks in Missouri on 28 February 1912. But the equipment was cumbersome, the parachute being housed in a rigid container beneath the aircraft so that the aviator had to clamber out of the cockpit on to the wheel struts before jumping. This was fine for demonstration purposes but hardly of much use as a life-saving device in an emergency.

Charles Broadwick, an American carnival parachutist, is generally regarded as the inventor of the modern parachute. Just prior to the beginning of the First World War he designed and demonstrated a parachute which was actually worn on a flier's back, sewn in a canvas bag into a reinforced coat. A length of rope connected the back of the bag to a wing strut on the aircraft, and when the aviator baled out this automatically pulled the canopy out of the pack. Thus was born what has subsequently become known as the 'static line' method of parachuting, as opposed to the 'ripcord' method which did not come until 28 April 1919 when Leslie Irvin *(qv)* demonstrated his own freefall design to United States Army Air Service officers.

With the latter type of design, choosing when to pull the cord and open the 'chute is left to the parachutist himself. This is the technique universally used by skydivers, both military and civilian. With a static line, however, instead of a ripcord a length of thin but strong rope or wire leads from the parachute pack with a snap fastener on its end which is clipped to a rail or another hardpoint in the aircraft. When you jump out of the aircraft door, the static line jerks taut and automatically opens the parachute for you. This obviates the risk of 'freezing', when a jumper is so paralysed by exhilaration or fright (the two are often indistinguishable) that he fails to pull the ripcord before he hits the ground. The static line has further military advantages in that relatively inexperienced parachutists can be safely dropped from a lower height, eliminating time in the air during which they are vulnerable to ground fire; and it means that the men in each 'stick' (one aircraft's load) will hit the ground fairly close together.

In Europe, a designer called Everard Calthorpe devised the first practical parachute — nicknamed 'Guardian Angel' — for the British Army during the First World War. Canisters suspended from the balloon shrouds each contained a parachute, with a rope and a clip suspended from it. When the occupants of the balloon basket felt they were in danger of being shot down, they clipped the rope to a harness around their bodies and jumped, relying on gravity to pull the parachute out of its container and allow them to float clear before the thousands of cubic feet of hydrogen gas above them exploded. Pilots and other crew members of powered aircraft in the Royal Flying Corps and Royal Naval Air Service were not, however, issued with parachutes because it was felt that such an escape route could have encouraged cowardice in the face of the enemy (an irrational argument if ever there was one — did giving a sailor a life-jacket encourage him to jump ship?)! Although the Germans started issuing parachutes to their pilots in May 1918, British and American flyers did not begin to get them until just before the war's end, in September of that year.

In the meanwhile, other military uses had been discovered for the parachute, not as a lifesaver so much as a weapon of war. The French, Italians and Russians all dropped reconnaissance and sabotage teams behind Austro-German lines in 1916–18, and these two roles have subsequently become an important part of paratroop forces' duties. Parachutes were also used on several occasions to drop supplies into beleaguered garrisons, with limited success due to the low load-carrying capability of First World War aircraft. Little notice was taken of these developments in either Britain or the United States, although the controversial American Gen William 'Billy' Mitchell did put forward a plan in 1918 to overcome the German garrison in Metz by dropping battalions of paratroopers behind their lines. Like so many of Mitchell's ideas which have only received proper acknowledgement since his death in 1935, the suggestion was ridiculed at the time. Nevertheless, after the war pioneering work in training parachute troops continued both in Italy, where the first training school was established in 1925 and the first exercise held two years later, and in Russia after the civil war. Britain and America would not really sit up and take notice of the potential of parachute troops until after the sweeping German successes in Norway, France and the Low Countries in 1940, although the RAF did form an experimental Parachute Flight at Henlow in the 1920s.

In Germany, following the Treaty of Versailles in 1919 the army was restricted to a mere 100,000 men and all development of military aircraft, U-boats, artillery and tanks was prohibited. Ever ingenious, the Germans soon found ways and means around these restrictions. Gen Hans von Seeckt, commander of the *Reichsheer* (army) from 1920 to 1926, created a paramilitary force under the cover name *Arbeitskommando* ('Labour Commando') which practised drill and marksmanship. Other unofficial organizations such as the *Freikorps* ('Free Corps') and *Stahlhelm* ('Steel Helmet'), comprised of disillusioned veterans, continued to bear arms and formed a malleable nucleus for the growing ranks of Adolf Hitler's SA 'brownshirt' bodyguard in the 1920s. The police were also armed and even equipped with a small number of armoured cars, and would similarly form a trained reserve for the army if and when restrictions were lifted. The national airline, Lufthansa, trained aircrew, and basic flying instruction was given in gliding schools — gliding at the time being an increasingly popular hobby throughout Europe. The *Deutsches Forschungsinstitut für Segelflug* (German Gliding Research Institute) instigated a research programme into high aspect ratio gliders, ostensibly for meteorological investigations, and this would ultimately lead to the DFS 230 which was first demonstrated in 1937 *(see Appendix 2)*. Even before this, however, there had been a number of other developments.

From 1921 onwards the Soviet Union — which was not a signatory to the Versailles Treaty — allowed German troops to practise their skills in Russia, far removed from prying eyes, in return for the Germans providing instructors and technicians to help modernize both the Soviet armed forces and Russian industry. If this seems strange, it must be remembered that both Germany and the new Russian state were considered pariahs by the rest of Europe, on top of which Germany at the time had a socialist government.

German military observers were particularly impressed by a Soviet exercise in 1931 featuring a parachute drop by the Leningrad-based 1st Paratroop Landing Unit. Admittedly, Russian methods were still primitive. The paras themselves crouched like stuntmen on the aircraft wings and after pulling their ripcords, allowed the slipstream to open their parachutes and drag them clear! The Tupolev TB-3 (ANT-6) aircraft themselves could only fly at 60mph (96km/h), barely above the stall, or the men would have been blown off before reaching their dropping zone. Among the observers at this event were the former First World War fighter ace Hermann Göring, who had attached his star to that of Adolf Hitler and his *National-Sozialistische Deutsche Arbeiterpartei* (NSDAP, National Socialist German Workers' Party); and Obst Kurt Student, an infantryman who had flown in the First World War but had subsequently rejoined the army and hence had dual experience on which to formulate his own ideas of airborne forces. He is, in fact, generally regarded as the 'founding father' of all modern parachute formations.

In 1932 Göring was elected President of the *Reichstag* and a year later, after the triumph of the Nazi Party and Hitler's appointment as Chancellor, he was given a cabinet post and the job of head of the Prussian police force, by which time Student also had a new task as director of Air Technical Training Schools. After Hitler began repudiating the Treaty of Versailles and re-arming Germany in 1935, Göring became head of the *Luftwaffe*. And having witnessed further Russian airborne manoeuvres later in the same year, during which 1,000 parachutists seized their objective and defended it while another 2,500 men were air-landed, Göring determined to create a parachute regiment of his own. He already had in the paramilitary Prussian *Landespolizeigruppe* (Provincial Police Group) *'General Göring'*, a nucleus from which to work, and incorporated this into the *Luftwaffe* in October the same year. In January 1936 Göring called for volunteers to form the first battalion of a new regiment, the *Fallschirmjäger* Regiment *'General Göring'*.

By this time the Soviet Union, in contrast, had expanded the original paratroop force raised in Leningrad in time for the 1931 demonstration and trained no fewer than 30 battalions of paratroops organized in three brigades, the 201st, 204th and 214th, while parachuting was fast becoming a Russian national sport. They were used in combat near Petsamo in

November 1939 at the start of the Winter War against Finland and subsequently during the occupation of Bessarabia in 1940, but without a great deal of success due to poor co-ordination with ground forces. This was to emerge as a perennial problem for airborne forces in general. Poland and Romania were also experimenting with parachute troops and would have their own training schools and fledgeling units at Bydgoszcz and Pantelimon respectively before the outbreak of war in 1939. Similarly, France had opened a parachute training school at Avignon-Pujaut in 1935. Polish and French paras who escaped the German occupation and joined the 'Free' forces in Britain would later make a substantial contribution to the Allied war effort.

The first battalion, some 600 men, of the German 1st *Fallschirmjäger* Regiment was commanded by *Luftwaffe* Maj Bruno Bräuer. Not to be outdone by the air force, the army also began raising its own first parachute battalion in 1936 under Maj Richard Heidrich, a War College instructor. All jump training was carried out at a new central school at Stendal which fell under Kurt Student's direction.

At this time there were two rival schools of thought about the correct deployment of airborne troops. The army favoured using them in sufficient strength to seize key objectives ahead of the advancing *Panzer* (armoured) divisions as an essential ingredient in the *Blitzkrieg* ('lightning war') concept, a doctrine also advocated by Student. The air force, on the other hand, saw their principal usefulness as saboteurs behind enemy lines to disrupt communications and sap their opponents' morale. In the event, of course, both tactics would be employed with varying degrees of success.

Meanwhile, wrangling continued about who should have jurisdiction over the German airborne forces. In July 1938 Bräuer's 1st *Jäger* Battalion was detached from the *'General Göring'* Regiment as the cadre for a new formation to be known as the 7th *Flieger* Division under Kurt Student, by this time a Maj-Gen. The division would incorporate all parachute, glider and air-landing troops then in the *Luftwaffe*. (The parent regiment continued to remain in existence, eventually growing to the size of a full division and ultimately a corps, *Fallschirm-Panzer Korps 'Hermann Göring'*, although only a minority of its personnel were parachute-qualified and it was used exclusively in the ground role.) Then, at the beginning of 1939, Heidrich's army battalion was, at Göring's insistence, incorporated into the *Luftwaffe* by order of the OKW (*Oberkommando der Wehrmacht* or Armed Forces High Command), swapping its field grey uniform for air force blue-grey and its army-style parachute badge for the air force one.

Regardless of a man's origins, training for the all-volunteer parachute force consisted of the same three months' basic instruction in drill and weapons' handling, with a great deal of physical exercise and long route marches culminating in the final 16-day parachute course. To quote new recruit Martin Pöppel, the course was 'unbelievably hard, but basically fair. It passed quickly even if only because we were drilled so hard from morning to night that we never got a moment to think.' Jump training has not changed much in 50 years and involved learning how to fall, how to exit the aircraft in the right manner, and how to pack parachutes, for after his first jump every *Jäger* packed his own 'chute. After six qualifying jumps singly, in groups, from different heights and in different weather and visibility conditions, each man was awarded the coveted winged eagle badge to signify graduation. German parachutes themselves were based on the Italian Salvatore design *(see Appendix 1)*.

The two original battalions, plus an air-landing battalion commanded by a Maj Sydow, constituted the 1st *Fallschirmjäger* Regiment (FJR 1) with its headquarters at Tempelhof in Berlin. Later, in June 1939, authorization was given for the raising of a second regiment. Bräuer, now a Colonel, was given command of FJR 1 and Heidrich, with the same rank, of FJR 2. Army pride was soothed by its own retention of the 22nd *Luftlande* Division, an ordinary infantry division trained in air-landing techniques and tactics and commanded until 1942 by Lt-Gen Graf Hans von Sponeck. Part of this division, and a couple of battalions from the 7th, took part in the invasion of Poland, but not in the airborne role, for the existence of a German parachute force was being kept secret for the time being. Next year, however, the Allies would have cause to remember the remark made by the Soviet Marshal Mikhail Schtscherbakov to France's Marshal Henri Pétain during a pre-war tour of the Maginot Line: 'Fortresses like this,' he said, 'may well be superfluous in the future if your enemy . . . parachutes over them'.

3

By air to battle

Sirens wailed and flares burst in the misty early morning air as the crackle of automatic weapons broke the silence of what promised to be a scorching early summer's day. It was 05:20 on 10 May 1940 and nine DFS 230 gliders had just landed out of the blue on top of the supposedly impregnable concrete and steel Belgian fortress of Eben Emael. They carried 55 German paras of Assault Section *Granit* ('Granite') commanded by Oblt Rudolf Witzig — 55 men against a garrison estimated to be 1,200-strong! However, the fort's rapid capture was essential to the German Blitzkrieg through Belgium into France for, whereas the Maginot Line could simply be bypassed, Eben Emael commanded the confluence of the river Meuse (Maas) with the Albert Canal southwest of Maastricht, and the three bridges at Veldwezelt, Vroenhoven and Kanne. If the Germans failed to capture these bridges and get their Panzers across the canal quickly, the whole plan for the invasion of the West masterminded by Gen (later Field Marshal) Erich von Manstein would be put in jeopardy.

The Manstein plan was a masterpiece of both audacity and simplicity. While conventional German forces invaded neutral Holland to draw French and British forces north to the Dyle Line, the largest concentration of Panzers would sweep unexpectedly through the rugged and heavily forested Ardennes and across the Meuse to end up in the Allied rear and sweep to the Channel coast, cutting off the bulk of the French army and British Expeditionary Force from their lines of communication and trapping them in an enormous vice. Speed and surprise were the key words to the operation, and the parachute and glider-borne troops were to play a vital role in both Holland and Belgium.

Despite an alert at 00:30 following reports of German troop movements to the east, the Belgian defenders in Eben Emael and behind the Albert Canal were complacent. The 'Phoney War' had dragged on for over six months with nothing bar the occasional aircraft sighting to suggest that a state of war actually existed; besides, the closest point of the German frontier was nearly 15 miles away (24km), across the southern 'bulge' of

Holland, and the garrison in Eben Emael confidently expected plenty of warning of an attack. So complacent were they that, of the fort's normal garrison of 1,200, some 500 were either on leave or billeted in local villages and farmhouses. Eben Emael, the Belgian authorities thought, could hold out almost indefinitely against anything except the heaviest air and artillery bombardment. They did not reckon on gliders landing on top of their 'impregnable' fortress, although why they could not have foreseen the possibility is a mystery because German airborne troops had been used to capture targets in Denmark and Norway the previous month.

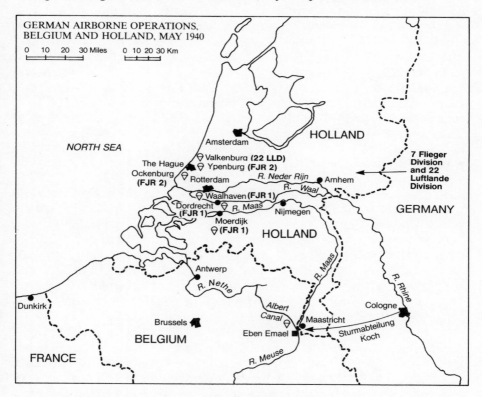

GERMAN AIRBORNE OPERATIONS, BELGIUM AND HOLLAND, MAY 1940

The forces involved here on 9 April 1940 were the five companies of Hpt Erich Walther's I/FJR 1. Oblt Walther Gericke's 4th Company captured the Aalborg airfields and the causeway linking the islands of Falster and Seeland without a fight. Lt Freiherr von Brandis' 3rd Company overran Stavanger's Sola airport after a short firefight. (Brandis himself was later killed in Holland.) The HQ and 2nd Companies under Walther himself were supposed to have parachuted on to Oslo's Fornebu airport but were prevented from jumping because of fog over the target. However, elements of the 163rd Infantry Division succeeded in landing in their Ju 52s and securing the objective. Lt Herbert Schmidt's 1st Company was dropped further north in the Gudbrandsalen valley near Dombas to block British troops landed at Andalsnes. Isolated in the snow-covered rocky waste-land, they held out for four days before surrendering when all their ammunition was exhausted. Lt Schmidt, who had carried on in command despite two serious wounds, was subsequently awarded the Knights Cross. I/FJR 1 was later dropped at Narvik at the end of May to reinforce the German mountain troops fighting for the port, but by the time they arrived the British had evacuated their forces by sea.

Returning to 1939, in November Kurt Student had begun organizing a small élite unit for the assault on Eben Emael and the three attendant bridges. It was known as *Sturmabteilung* ('Assault Battalion') *Koch* after its commander, Hpt Walter Koch, and comprised the 1st Company from I/FJR 1 plus Oblt Witzig's engineer platoon from II/FJR 1, a total of 11 officers and 427 men. (This unit would later be expanded into the *Luftlande-Sturm* Regiment for the assault on Crete.) The force was subdivided into four Assault Sections: *Granit*, under Witzig, whose pio-neers were entrusted with the attack on Eben Emael itself; *Stahl* ('Steel'), under Oblt Gustav Altmann, whose task was the capture of the Veldwezelt bridge; *Beton* ('Concrete'), under Lt Gerhard Schacht, target Vroenhoven; and *Eisen* ('Iron'), commanded by Lt Martin Schächter, whose mission was the third bridge at Kanne. Their instructions were to take their objectives and hold them against counter-attack until relieved by the Panzers which, they were assured, would 'not hang about'. Meticulous planning and training for the operation, including the study of maps, photos and relief models and practice in the use of shaped hollow-charge explosive devices, took place in great secrecy at Hildesheim.

The battalion lifted off in 42 gliders at 04:30, dropping their tow lines at 7,000ft (2,160m) while still over Germany so that their silent flight across the darkened Dutch countryside to the Belgian border would be undetect-ed. Unfortunately, the tow ropes of two of the gliders had snapped shortly after take-off from Cologne, one of them being Witzig's. The furious officer managed, however, to call up a replacement Ju 52 after hacking a crude airstrip through the hedge on the edge of the field in which he had landed, and staggered into the air to arrive, to his men's surprise and relief, three hours later. Meanwhile, all hell had broken loose.

The remaining gliders of Assault Section *Granit*, temporarily com-manded by Obfw (Sgt-Maj) Helmut Wenzel, had landed without serious mishap on top of the fort, which was studded with the heavy steel cupolas of dozens of gun emplacements. Racing from their gliders, the sappers slapped their hollow charge devices against the gun cupolas. Even when they were unable to penetrate the thick metal, they severely concussed the occupants, allowing the Germans to place smaller charges inside the protruding gun barrels and render them useless. One stubborn ma-chine-gun position had to be taken out by a flamethrower. Additional charges were placed against steel doors leading in to the gun positions and in several places the paras managed to get into the fortress, erecting barricades against counter-attack and hurling grenades down the access tunnels. Within 20 minutes the damage had been done and apart from a couple of gun positions on the northern edge of the fort which continued to fire at Assault Section *Eisen* at Kanne, the fortress was virtually rendered impotent. The Belgians never gave themselves a chance to seize the initiative, and although they launched several half-hearted counter-attacks, supported by fire from field artillery outside the fort, they were unable to dislodge the determined paras.

As the day drew on, the Belgians attempted to send infantry from outside to scale the steep fortress walls and drive the paras out, but their efforts were ineffectual and soon dispersed when Witzig called up a succession of Stuka strikes (which also did further damage to the gun emplacements). It was a similar story elsewhere. The bridges at Veldwezelt and Vroenhoven were captured intact, the paras having achieved total surprise, but Lt Schächter's section was unlucky at Kanne, where demolition charges destroyed the bridge and the men, trapped on the west bank of the canal, came under heavy fire both from Belgian infantry and the surviving gun cupolas on the northern edge of Eben Emael. Schächter himself was killed and command of the depleted section was taken over by Lt Joachim Meissner. But as night fell Koch's four sections were all still holding on. Even at this point a determined counter-attack could have dislodged the paras, who spent a hot, thirsty, anxious and sleepless night waiting for an assault which never came. The Belgians seemed paralysed by indecision. Then, at 07:00 on the 11th, the first troops from Sixth Army — a battalion of engineers — arrived to relieve the paras, who by this time were running very low on ammunition. The operation fully vindicated Student's ideas and rewarded his energy, hard work and enthusiasm. Hitler personally travelled to Eben Emael to congratulate Koch and each of his section leaders, all of whom were awarded the Knights Cross. (The highest German award for valour, the Knights Cross of the Iron Cross to give it its full title, was ultimately awarded to 190 German paras, of whom 25 went on to win the Oak Leaves, six the Swords and one — Bernhard Ramcke — the Diamonds, each successive award being the equivalent of a Bar to an English medal.)

Further vindication of the paratroop concept came in Holland, where both the 7th *Flieger* and 22nd *Luftlande* Divisions were crucially involved in capturing key objectives ahead of the ground forces. Their targets were the Dordrecht and Moerdijk bridges on the approach to Rotterdam and the airfields at Ockenburg, Valkenburg, Waalhaven and Ypenburg. Hpt Erich Walther's I/FJR 1 parachuted in at Dordrecht, where Martin Pöppel landed safely, assembled his men and took cover in a house whose inhabitants had abandoned it so quickly they had left tea and buttered toast still hot on the table! After this temporary reprieve, it was a hard fight to capture the bridge, but it was in the battalion's hands by noon even though German casualties were heavy, for the Dutch army put up a far fiercer defence than the Belgians. Hpt Fritz Prager's II/FJR 1 had a similar success at Moerdijk and refused to be dislodged from their positions north and south of the bridge, despite furious counter-attacks, until relieved on the 13th by the 9th Panzer Division and the SS Regiment *Leibstandarte 'Adolf Hitler'* (whose route, incidentally, took them through Arnhem and Nijmegen, although no-one at the time could have foreseen how those two place names would later resound in the annals of airborne warfare).

Hpt Karl-Lothar Schulz's II/FJR 1 had a rather harder fight on their hands at Waalhaven. Even though, like all the other targets, the airfield had been heavily bombed just prior to the airborne assault, they came under heavy machine-gun fire as they landed. Regardless, they stormed the airport terminal — where the Dutch commander had been celebrating his 40th year of service! — and, reinforced by II/FJR 2, soon secured the field to enable the Ju 52s carrying men from the 22nd *Luftlande* Division to land. One courageous Dutch anti-aircraft gun crew continued to fire until they were overrun and the paras were constantly pounded by artillery fire and attacks by RAF bombers which destroyed a large number of aircraft on the ground, but the gateway to Rotterdam was open. The Dutch even sent a patrol boat up the Nieuwe Waterweg to bombard the airfield, but it was sunk by Stukas.

Casualties were also heavy at the other airfields, seized by the remaining two battalions of FJR 2. At Ockenburg resistance was so strong that the pilots and navigators from the Ju 52s had to grab rifles and join in the fight, and the airfield soon became so congested with wrecked aircraft that reinforcements had to be diverted to Waalhaven. At Ypenburg 11 out of 13 Ju 52s were shot down, the surviving paras being scattered in the surrounding countryside, helpless to take their objective. Only at Valkenburg did the Germans have a relatively easy time, but even here the 22nd Division ran into problems because the grass airstrip was water-logged and the transport aircraft bogged down, preventing further rein-forcements landing.

Fortunately for the men of the airborne divisions the campaign was soon over, the Dutch government surrendering on 14 May after a massive air raid devastated the heart of Rotterdam. (There is still controversy about this. The raid was supposed to have been aborted while negotiations took place, but fewer than half the bombers received the recall signal. Some Dutch sources claim that Göring himself ordered the raid to proceed as arranged regardless of the altered circumstances, but this seems unlikely for this early in the war drug abuse and megalomania had not completely taken over the Reichsmarschall's personality.) Kurt Student personally flew in to Waalhaven to congratulate his men, but in a bizarre footnote was wounded by a stray shot fired by a man from the *Leibstandarte* and had to spend several weeks in a Berlin hospital. Temporary command of the 7th *Flieger* Division was assumed by Maj-Gen Richard Putziger, who oversaw the raising of a third regiment in time for the invasion of Crete the following year. The commander of the 22nd *Luftlande* Division, Gen Graf von Sponeck, was also wounded during the final mopping up.

'Take your time,' Flt Sgt Bill Brereton told Capt Dawes. 'Watch my hand and when you see it fall, pull the handle upward and outward.'

'OK,' the officer said. 'You mean like this?'

'Not now, you bloody fool . . .'

But it was too late. The Captain had gone, whisked away as his parachute was pulled open. Three hours later a search party found him six miles (9½km) away from the dropping zone, dangling helplessly from the top of a tree! Neither the first nor the last training incident to bring hilarity to the Mess.

The German invasion of western Europe and the enforced evacuation of the British Expeditionary Force from Dunkirk had thrown the British nation into a state of shock. Three elements of Blitzkrieg had made particular impact. One was the paralysing speed at which the Panzer divisions had broken through, totally confusing and disorientating the defences. Another was the devastating use of Ju 87 Stukas as airborne artillery right up with the leading edge of the advance. And the third was the remarkably effective use of parachute, glider-borne and air-landed troops. For several months, until the threat of invasion receded, Britain was seized by a parachute 'scare': strangers were regarded with grave suspicion as potential German saboteurs; the police were called out on innumerable occasions to investigate 'mysterious' goings-on; and inevitably, any shot-down flier was menaced by brandished pitchforks. The poor Poles, exiles from their own land who had enlisted in the RAF, suffered the worst, speaking broken English with atrocious accents. In other quarters the German use of airborne forces had provoked a rather different reaction.

On 22 June 1940 the Prime Minister, Winston Churchill, issued a memo calling for the creation of 'a corps of at least 5,000 parachute troops . . . I hear something is being done already to form such a corps,' he wrote, 'but only, I believe, on a very small scale. Advantage must be taken of the summer to train these forces, who can nonetheless play their part meanwhile in home defence'.

Reaction to the memo was prompt even though many people privately doubted the value of training up a force whose primary role was obviously offensive rather than defensive, for after the fall of France the prospect of attacking the Germans on land seemed light years away. But no-one dared cross Churchill and the first steps towards creating a British parachute force were taken in less than a month. Training was entrusted to the Royal Air Force (despite the apocryphal remark from one senior officer that it was the duty of the RAF 'to remain in the air, not to fall out of it') but the first personnel were chosen from volunteers from 'C' and 'D' Troops of the recently formed No 2 (Parachute) (Army) Commando under Lt-Col C.I.A. Jackson, a Royal Tank Regiment officer. They first mustered at Cambrai Barracks, Perham Down, Wiltshire, but a new base was selected at Manchester's Ringway airport, relatively safe from marauding German aircraft, with the volunteers housed at Benchill and a landing ground for practice jumps at nearby Tatton Park. Parachutes were obtained from the Parachute Flight at Henlow. In overall command were Maj John Rock, Royal Engineers, and Sqn Ldr Louis Strange, RAF, while other personalities who were to play an important role in the development of the British airborne force included Sir Nigel Norman, Bt. and Wg Cdr Maurice Newnham.

Initial progress was slow, because no-one had been given a clear brief as to what the new parachute force was to be trained for, and as examples all they had was confused reports of German operations in Holland and Belgium plus a few items of captured German paratroop kit. (The first British jump smock was actually a direct copy of the German model.) Moreover, the only aircraft available were four (later increased to six) Whitley Mk III bombers, obsolescent even before they entered service, with their rear gun turrets removed to provide a jumping platform. Each trainee parachutist, accompanied usually by the senior instructor, Bill Brereton, stood on this, pulled the ripcord and allowed the slipstream to open his 'chute and pull him clear of the aircraft. This was hardly ideal because the parachutist's initial fall was virtually horizontal, resulting in wild oscillation as he descended, and soon exit holes were cut in the aircraft floors by removing the ventral 'dustbin' machine-gun turret. Even this was only a marginal improvement for unless you jumped exactly right, you stood a good chance of cracking your head against the rear edge of the hole. Moreover, the then-standard RAF training parachute, which deployed canopy-first like the German RZ models, proved unsuitable for static line jumping and had to be modified after a number of mishaps resulting in two fatalities and several serious injuries (*see Appendix 1*). The original half-inch silk static line was also replaced by a three-inch webbing strap, to the great relief of the budding paras.

Gradually, and mostly by means of trial and error in the early days, the staff of the Central Landing Establishment (CLE) evolved techniques to take volunteers for the paras through the basics. (CLE was originally known as the Central Landing School, a cover name to disguise its real function, but the last word was changed to 'Establishment' after a letter arrived addressed to the Central *Sunday* School!). The interiors of Ringway's hangars became filled with sections of different aircraft from which the men practised exiting. The first jump tower used a sandbag as a counterweight to simulate the speed of an actual descent, but this was soon abandoned because it took too long to weigh each man and reload the bag to match, and a cable drum was substituted with wind vanes to control the pay-out speed.

After the essential technique of falling correctly had been mastered — a sort of boneless roll with completely relaxed leg and back muscles — the next hurdle was a jump from a basket beneath a tethered barrage balloon. This was, and is, a real test of courage. When jumping from an aircraft, there is a sense of unreality because the machine and the ground are totally divorced. From a balloon, though, there is an acute knowledge of height above the ground which, coupled with the nausea that the basket's movement inevitably causes, creates a horrifying sense of vertigo even among those who are sure they have a good head for heights. Many men baulked at this hurdle, and were sympathetically returned to their parent units with no stigma. The same remains true today, for a man can be a perfectly good soldier while his feet are firmly on the ground but still unable to go through with a jump no matter how much his conscious mind wants him to or how rigorous his prior training.

By the end of September — the month in which the Air Ministry placed its first order for 400 Hotspur gliders (*see Appendix 2*) from the General Aircraft company of Hanworth, Middlesex — over 300 officers and men had completed the course at Ringway, and in November they were awarded their own unit name: No 11 Special Air Service Battalion. Their first proper exercise took place on 3 December, the whole battalion dropping to seize a simulated enemy target. By this time, too, the men were chafing for action and Winston Churchill was demanding to know why his memo calling for 5,000 men had resulted in fewer than 500. Unfortunately, their first venture could not have been less auspicious.

The target was an aqueduct at Tragino, near Monte Vulture in Italy, which carried the main fresh water supply for the naval ports of Taranto and Brindisi as well as several other towns. There was never any hope of putting the ports out of action, but a successful raid would, it was believed, cause at least a degree of inconvenience and at the same time give the fledgeling parachute corps a taste of real action in enemy territory, even though the target was undefended. It would also show the Americans in particular that Britain was beginning to fight back.

Although every man in the battalion volunteered, the task only required a small force and eventually a team of seven officers and 31 other ranks was selected under the overall command of Maj Trevor 'Tag' Pritchard. It included a section of Royal Engineer sappers. On 24 January 1941, while the rest of the strike force was rehearsing using a bridge constructed at Tatton Park, Lt Tony Deane-Drummond flew to Malta — from where the raid would be launched — to supervise preparations, including the assembly of explosives and detonators which would be dropped in supply containers. The rest of the force, designated 'X' Troop, flew out on 7 February.

(Containers were the principal means of supplying paratroops of all nations with heavy items such as machine-guns, mortars and extra ammunition, as well as food, water and medical supplies, since there was a limit to what a man could carry strapped to his person during a jump. Later in the war, the British devised a technique still used in which a kitbag is attached to each man's leg by a length of rope up to 70ft (22m) long. After jumping from the aircraft, the kitbag is released to dangle below the man, accelerating his descent. When it touches the ground, the weight comes off and the parachutist slows down to hit the ground himself at normal speed. This expedient was arrived at after numerous instances of supply containers being blown off course and behind enemy lines for, of course, before the advent of miniaturized laser or radar guidance, there was no way of controlling where the containers would land.)

Operation 'Colossus', as the Monte Vulture raid was codenamed, started at dusk on 10 February. Eight Whitleys were used, six carrying the paras and two loaded with bombs for a diversionary attack on Foggia. The Italians would, it was hoped, believe the other aircraft had simply lost their way. The target was approximately 50 miles (80km) from the coast, and the plan was that after blowing up the aqueduct, 'X' Troop would make its way overland to the mouth of the river Sele where the submarine HMS *Triumph* would pick them up. As it happened, one of the two bombers was forced to ditch, quite coincidentally, right at the pick-up point. The water was soon full of Italian patrol boats and the submarine was recalled, being too valuable at that stage of the war to risk. The paras would have to fend for themselves, although of course they had no way of knowing this.

The drop was successful although, by another stroke of misfortune, the party of sappers landed in the wrong valley. However, Pritchard still had 800lb (363kg) of explosives and placed them on the aqueduct and a small wooden bridge nearby. The bridge was totally demolished and a large section knocked out of the aqueduct so, mission accomplished, the men abandoned all their heavy kit and started making their way towards the coast, lying up in hiding during the day and moving on the next night. As day broke on the morning of the 12th, local villagers spotted their footprints in the snow and sounded the alarm. A horde of children surged up the slope to where the paras lay hidden, followed by their anxious mothers and irate fathers. It was impossible to fire at them so Pritchard ordered his men to lay down their arms and surrender to the *carabinieri* who came puffing up behind the villagers. The team of sappers fared little better. Attempting to commandeer a car to get them to the coast, they were arrested because they had no papers. Several were later to escape from prisoner-of-war camps and make their way back to England where some, including Tony Deane-Drummond, would later win undying fame at Arnhem in 1944.

Although an obvious disappointment which cast doubts on the future value of airborne troops, the raid did alarm the Italian authorities, particularly coming as it did right on the heels of the trouncing their army had just suffered at the hands of Generals Wavell and O'Connor in North Africa. However, all doubts about the value of airborne troops were dispelled in May with the German invasion and capture of Crete, and Churchill reiterated his demand for the creation of a parachute and glider-borne force of at least 5,000 men.

In September the 1st Parachute Brigade officially came into existence, commanded by Lt-Col (later Brig) Richard 'Windy' Gale. The 11th Special Air Service Battalion was rechristened 1st Parachute Battalion, commanded by Lt-Col E.E. 'Dracula' Down — although this was far from the end of the SAS, of course. The 2nd Battalion was led by Lt-Col E.W.C.

Flavell and subsequently by a Scotsman whose name has become synonymous with wartime parachute exploits, Maj (later Col) John Dutton Frost. The 3rd Battalion was commanded by Lt-Col F.W. Lathbury. The brigade's first headquarters and later depot were at Hardwick Hall in Derbyshire, where a new selection procedure was soon established to make sure that only the best soldiers from each intake were accepted for the paras, since when the call for volunteers had gone out the commanding officers of many regiments had used it as an excuse to get rid of troublemakers and persistent offenders!

Returning temporarily to the Special Air Service, in the spring of 1941 Nos 7, 8 and 11 (Army) Commandos had been sent to Egypt to help counter the German forces which Hitler had despatched under Gen Erwin Rommel to aid the hapless Italians. They are generally known as 'Layforce' after their commander, Maj-Gen Robert Laycock, but were soon split up, No 11 being posted to Cyprus and No 7 to Crete, where it helped in the rearguard covering the evacuation after the German capture of Máleme and Caneá. This just left No 8 in Egypt. Amongst its officers was Lt (later Sir) David Stirling, who died in 1990 at the age of 74.

Kicking his heels wondering what to do after the fall of Crete, Stirling decided, together with three friends, to try his own hand at parachuting. Unfortunately, his parachute failed to deploy properly on his very first jump and Stirling had to spend several weeks in hospital. While languishing there he evolved the concept of tiny raiding parties of no more than four or five men which would be much more elusive than a regular commando company of 50 or so, and who could be dropped by parachute or infiltrated by Jeep or small boat deep behind enemy lines on reconnaissance or sabotage missions. After recovering from his injuries, Stirling managed to sell his idea to the then C-in-C in the Western Desert, Gen Sir Claude Auchinleck. The result was 'L' Detachment, Special Air Service Brigade, the latter being a pure cover name to fool Rommel into thinking a strong British airborne contingent had arrived in Africa. However, the name stuck and within months there were two full SAS regiments, the first commanded by David Stirling until his capture in January 1943 and the second by his brother Bill.

Although not specifically airborne troops, whereas all members of the modern Special Air Service Regiments are fully trained in both static line and freefall parachuting, the wartime SAS shared many daring exploits alongside the Long Range Desert Group under Maj Ralph Bagnold and 'Popski's Private Army', the latter being a force of Libyan Arabs commanded by the Belgian-born Maj Vladimir Peniakoff. The SAS took part in a large number of raids in the desert and later in Italy before returning to the UK to be brigaded with a Belgian squadron and two Free French parachute battalions as the 1st Special Air Service Brigade. Working closely with the Strategic Operations Executive (SOE) and resistance groups in occupied Europe, they carried out dozens of operations in support of the D-Day landings, but the brigade was disbanded in October

41

1945. The subsequent history of the reincarnated SAS regiments is recounted later.

Returning to 1941, expansion was rapid following the creation of 1 Para Brigade. On 10 October the 31st Independent Brigade Group, recently returned from India, became the 1st Air-Landing Brigade Group and began to train with Hotspur gliders. In the same month, in India itself a third brigade was also formed, the 50th, comprising the 151st (British), 152nd (Indian) and 153rd (Gurkha) Parachute Battalions. (A difference between parachute and air-landing troops should be noted here. While all paras and a majority of air-landing troops have always been volunteers, many of the latter during the years of conscription were 'volunteered', for there seemed no difference between transporting a man to a battlefield by air than by ship, truck or on foot, so long as he could fight when delivered to the right spot.)

Then, on 29 October Maj-Gen F.A.M. 'Boy' Browning was appointed officer commanding para and airborne troops and given a separate headquarters in London. Britain's equivalent of Kurt Student, he was an experienced, capable and enthusiastic officer, although a strict disciplinarian, who had fought in the Grenadier Guards during the First World War and had later become Adjutant at the Royal Military Academy, Sandhurst. Creation of the Glider Pilot Regiment as part of the Army Air Corps under Maj (later Lt-Col) George Chatterton followed in December: this would provide the pilots and aircrew for the air-landing forces. Thus, by the end of 1941, the nucleus of what would become the 1st Airborne Division was well established. Then, in January 1942, No 38 Wing, RAF Army Co-operation Command, was formed under Gp Capt Sir Nigel Norman specifically to carry the paras into battle. A second parachute brigade started forming in April under Lt-Col M.R.J. Hope-Thompson and together the men of the two brigades of the 1st Airborne Division became members of The Parachute Regiment on 1 August 1942, adopting the famous red (actually maroon) beret as their distinctive trademark and the figure of Bellerophon riding Pegasus as their badge.

By this time British paras had carried out their second operation, a much more rewarding one than the Monte Vulture raid. It was an intelligence-gathering mission. The Germans had developed a new radar, codenamed '*Würzburg*', which they used to vector fighters on to British bombers. In order to devise effective counter-measures, the boffins needed to examine one, and the head of Combined Operations, Lord Louis Mountbatten, suggested that a team of paras could be landed to seize a *Würzburg* installation, dismantle it and bring the equipment back to Britain. The problem was to find an installation at a relatively isolated point close to the coast so that the raiders could be evacuated by the Royal Navy. Eventually, RAF photo reconnaissance revealed a site near the village of Bruneval in northern France. It was close to a suitable cove and believed to be garrisoned by about 100 men billeted in the village, a nearby farmhouse and an isolated house beside the dug-in radar post. The force chosen for the raid, which would be accompanied by an RAF technician to supervise dismantling the apparatus, was 'C' Company of the 2nd Battalion, 1st Parachute Brigade, commanded by Maj John Frost, who had only just completed his parachute training and won his 'wings'; it was popularly known as 'Jock Company' because its personnel were all Scots.

The operation was rehearsed in great secrecy using similar stretches of British coast and countryside and a scale model of the installation and its actual surrounds. One incident caused the paras a certain degree of amusement at the Royal Navy's expense. The landing craft in which they were to practise embarking grounded about 60yds (55m) offshore because someone had misread the tide tables, and could not be refloated until the tide turned! Frost's men were assured that the same mistake would not be made on the night of the actual operation.

Eventually, 27 February 1942 was chosen as D-Day for Operation 'Biting', as it was codenamed, and Frost, together with five other officers and 113 men plus the RAF technician assembled at Thruxton. They were carried into action in 12 Whitleys of No 51 Squadron, part of the newly created No 38 Wing. Moonlight reflected off the snow-covered ground giving nearly perfect visibility and the paras landed without incident, although two 'stray' sticks inadvertently dropped southeast instead of northeast of Bruneval. They fought their way back through the village towards the radar post, arriving as it turned out in the nick of time. There, the remainder of the company had seized the installation and begun dismantling it, photographing parts that were too large to move. The adjoining house had also been captured and a party despatched to secure the beach where the landing craft would come to take them off.

Then the Germans counter-attacked from the farmhouse and it was only the timely arrival of the 'strays' on their flank which enabled the men to reach the beach safely, where a machine-gun position in a pillbox had already been taken out. Now began an anxious period of waiting for the Navy. None of the paras' radios worked and Frost had to fire off Very lights to signal their presence. The landing craft were delayed by having to evade marauding E-boats and there was a brisk exchange of fire between the paras sheltering in the lee of the cliffs and an increasing number of irate Germans. At last, shortly before 03:00 on the 28th, the landing craft arrived and the paras scrambled aboard while supporting MTBs laid down covering fire. Mission accomplished. One man had been killed and seven wounded while another seven failed to make the beach and were captured. A small price to pay for the number of lives which would be saved in RAF Bomber Command once the boffins had fathomed out the secrets of the *Würzburg*.

Meanwhile, events elsewhere meant that Britain was no longer alone in the fight against Nazi Germany. On 22 June 1941 the Panzer divisions had swept into Russia and on 7 December the Japanese attacked Pearl Harbor, bringing the world's two most powerful nations into the battle. Even though the war would drag on for nearly four more weary years, Hitler's defeat was now inevitable.

German paras themselves enjoyed only a minor role in the invasion of the Soviet Union, although parachute-trained members of the army's '*Brandenburg*' commando regiment were dropped to seize bridges in advance of the main onslaught, wearing Russian uniforms to help sow confusion. The 22nd *Luftlande* Division was employed in an ordinary infantry role as part of Army Group South but later played a crucial part in the siege of Sevastopol where it was landed by boat behind Russian lines. Ironically, after this in July 1942 the division was assigned to Crete where it idled away its days as a garrison force until the end of 1943 when it was sent to recapture the Dodecanese islands of Kos and Leros *(qv)*, and was then despatched to Yugoslavia in 1944 to help in the fight against partisans. After the fall of Holland in 1940, therefore, this first-rate fighting formation was never again used in the air-landing role, its abilities almost totally wasted. Meanwhile, after recuperating from Crete, the 7th *Flieger* Division was assigned to Army Group North in December and deployed defensively north of Moscow. Here, it helped contain the first massive Russian winter counter-offensive, its men better equipped by the air force against the bitter sub-zero temperatures than their army counterparts. For the rest of the war, while Britain and America developed their airborne units into strong strike forces which would be used with great effectiveness in the reconquest of Europe, the Germans relegated their paratroops to an élite infantry role as a 'fire brigade' alongside the premier *Waffen-SS* divisions, only using their airborne expertise in a few small-scale exploits which will be described later.

Nor did the Italians or Russians, first in the airborne field, make much use of their paratroops during the Second World War. In 1940 the Italians had two parachute battalions, one army and one *carabinieri*. During April 1941 the 2nd Battalion was dropped on the Greek island of Cephalonia as an adjunct to the German invasion of the Balkans, and captured it. By the end of the year the Italian paras had been expanded to the size of a division, given the honour title '*Folgore*' and shipped to North Africa, where practical command was left in the capable hands of Bernhard Ramcke *(qv)*. Slated for the airborne invasion of Malta which never happened, the division fought as infantry in Libya and Egypt until the second battle of El Alamein in November 1942, when it was practically annihilated. A second division, '*Nembo*', was sent to Sicily at the time of the Allied invasion in 1943 and its survivors later fought alongside the Germans in Yugoslavia against Tito's partisans. Three other battalions were also formed; one army (the '*Arditi*'), one air force (merely given the number '1'), and one from the Marines, given the name '*San Marco*'. The history of the last-named unit, which still exists as one of the world's foremost counter-terrorist forces, is also recounted later.

Soviet airborne forces suffered a severe blow right at the beginning of the 'Great Patriotic War' because the *Luftwaffe* succeeded in days in destroying a large part of the Red Air Force on the ground, only 25 of the 200 prewar TB-3 (ANT-6) bombers used in parachute exercises surviving, whereas to carry a single one of the six parachute brigades into action required 120. The Russian aircraft industry subsequently had to concentrate on building fighters and ground attack aircraft, there being little surplus money, skill or materials for transports. A number of Lisunov Li-2s — copies of the American DC-3 Dakota built originally for Aeroflot — became available later, but never in sufficient quantity to permit large-scale airborne operations. For the most part, Soviet parachutists were therefore dropped in small groups deep behind German lines to bring their expertise in ambush and sabotage techniques, plus supplies of weapons, ammunition and explosives, to the aid of the partisan brigades which tied down so much of the German war effort.

Generally speaking, like their German opposite numbers, the Russian paras were used as élite infantry, with the following known exceptions. The 201st Brigade of IV Corps was dropped at Medzyn during the night of 2/3 January 1942 but a severe blizzard forced it to cancel the planned operation and fight its way back to friendly lines. On the 18th of the same month two battalions of the same brigade, plus the 250th Regiment, were dropped near Vyazma, but failed to drive the Germans out even when reinforced by a further 2,000 men over the period 27 January–2 February. Because of the acute aircraft shortage, the paras had to be dropped a few at a time and losses were heavy. Then, in the middle of February a battalion of the 204th Brigade was dropped near Rzhev to reinforce an encircled army group and help them fight their way out of a German pocket. This was successful but an attempt to drop the remainder of IV Corps to support a ground offensive near Yukhnov between 17 and 23 February was a disaster, high winds and poor visibility scattering the paras across the landscape; most of the survivors joined partisan groups.

After these fiascos the brigades lost their 'Airborne' titles until February 1943 but continued to fight as ordinary infantry until September when, in the wake of the counter-offensive following the battle of Kursk, three brigades (1st, 3rd and 5th) were dropped at Kanev to try to break the strong German defences on the west bank of the river Dniepr. The operation was a disaster, the best part of 10,000 men dying or entering captivity. After this, the paras were only used in small-scale operations to support partisans in Czechoslovakia and Bulgaria.

Meanwhile, across the other side of the Atlantic, the United States of America had actually started creating an airborne arm even before the British, in April 1940, although development was slow until after the German occupation of France and did not really begin to gain momentum until the Japanese attack on Pearl Harbor 18 months later. Thereafter, however, progress was swift and sure. In September 1939 Army Chief of Staff Gen George Marshall had commissioned a study into the paratroop infantry concept and the resultant report was passed to the head of the Army Air Corps, Gen 'Hap' Arnold, for evaluation. It was then decided to set up an experimental unit to test the feasibility of the airborne role, responsibility being assigned to Maj William C. 'Bill' Lee, and volunteers were selected from the Infantry School demonstration regiment at Fort Benning, Georgia (29th Infantry Regiment).

By the end of April the Parachute Test Platoon of 48 men commanded by Lt William T. Ryder had been formed but progress was still slow because of lack of equipment. For example, learning how to fall was taught by rolling off the back of a moving truck (a trick David Stirling would also employ training the SAS in the desert). Then Lee discovered the existence of two 150ft (46.4m) parachute towers in New Jersey, which had been built for the 1939 New York World's Fair. These controlled descent devices, built to give fairground visitors a thrill and not properly constructed for parachute training, were nevertheless a beginning, and the army ordered four from the Safe Parachute Company which, modified to permit free descents, were erected at Fort Benning. (Three still survive at the time of writing!) Then came the German invasions of Holland and Belgium and the American army really started taking paratroops seriously, even though many people still hoped to remain uninvolved in another European war.

Members of the Test Platoon made their first 'live' jump on 16 August and 13 days later the whole platoon made a demonstration drop in front of a number of senior officers, including Gen Marshall. Old Douglas B-18 bombers were used during these early jumps but these were replaced operationally just over a year later by the Douglas C-47, military version of the DC-3 (*see Appendix 2*). The first paratroopers wore normal Irvin-type T-3 parachutes which were redesigned T-4 when experimentally rigged for static-line jumping, and finally T-7, the last-named version being purpose-built for airborne troops with the static line folded under the outer flap after the German style (*Appendix 1*).

The success of the Test Platoon's demonstration was rewarded on 16 September, when the 1st Parachute Battalion began forming around a cadre from the platoon; this was renamed the 501st in November, at the same time that a further three battalions were authorized, although activation of the 502nd would not occur until July 1941 in the wake of the German invasion of Crete. (This operation provided the greatest stimulation of all to exponents of airborne forces in Britain and America, at the time quite understandably even though subsequent analysis shows that the island's fall was caused more by Allied mistakes than by *Fallschirmjäger* prowess, no matter how high the undisputed quality of the latter.) By this juncture the Test Platoon had become the training school with the title Parachute Group (renamed Parachute School in August), still for the time being at Fort Benning, and Bill Lee had been promoted to Lt-Col. The 503rd followed, also in August, and other battalions in rapid numerical succession over the next year. Moreover, the first American parachute tradition had been established, the jump word 'Geronimo!' on the point of exiting the aircraft first used by Pte Aubrey Eberhardt of the Test Platoon and subsequently by all. On top of this, the United States had started looking seriously into gliders and the creation of airborne divisions alon the lines the British were exploring.

The Japanese attack on Pearl Harbor spurred the War Department into a flurry of activity. Further rapid expansion of the airborne forces was ordered on 30 January 1942, the immediate requirement being for four full regiments of 1,958 men, each organized in three battalions. The Marine Corps had also got into the act and started forming its own parachute battalions, but these were not used in the airborne role during the Second World War. The glider programme was also accelerated. This had begun in March 1941 with four firms being asked to tender designs out of which the Waco CG-4A was selected at the beginning of 1942, entering full production in April (*Appendix 2*). The earlier requirement for 100 trained glider pilots was instantly raised to 1,000 and once the CG-4A was in full production to 6,000. This placed an enormous strain on resources and not only were civilian gliders used for training, but civilian flying schools and instructors as well. To administer the huge build-up of gliders and towing aircraft, Air Transport Command (later renamed 1st Troop Carrier Command) was also established in April.

The first American airborne unit to set sail for war was the 2nd Battalion of the 503rd Regiment commanded by Maj Edson D. Raff. On 6 June 1942 it set off for England to train alongside the British 1st Airborne Division (1st and 2nd Airborne Brigades). Bill Lee, by now promoted to Brig-Gen, accompanied it to talk over tactics and techniques with Browning and other officers. The rest of the battalion went out to Australia to form the nucleus of what would eventually become the 11th Airborne Division, and the 503rd Battalion in England was renumbered 509th to avoid confusion. Before then, though, Lee had returned to America where he was ordered to form the first complete airborne division. The 82nd Infantry Division was chosen for the honour.

Disbanded after the First World War, during which it had acquired the title 'All American' because it recruited from every State instead of just one region, this had been reactivated in February 1942 and was training up as a motorized infantry division under Brig-Gen Omar N. Bradley before being assigned its new role. Almost immediately it was decided that two divisions were needed and on 15 August the 82nd was split in two, the 'All Americans' under the command of Bradley's deputy, Brig-Gen Matthew B. Ridgway, and the new 101st, which adopted the title 'Screaming Eagles', under Bill Lee until overwork and ill health forced him reluctantly to surrender command to Brig-Gen Maxwell D. Taylor in February 1944. Because there was insufficient room at Fort Benning for this sudden growth (each division would initially number some 8,000 men, each of two parachute and one glider regiments although the original proposal was for the reverse ratio, each regiment in either case being three battalions strong, and further expansion would follow by the time of D-Day and operation 'Market Garden'), the two divisions moved to Fort Bragg, on the west side of the Hudson north of New York. Fort Benning remained Airborne Command headquarters and all actual parachute training was conducted there.

With two American airborne divisions well on their way to completion and a British one in existence, we must return again to the Mediterranean where Field Marshal Erwin Rommel's *Panzer Armee Afrika* had at long last succeeded in taking the important port of Tobruk and pressing the Eighth Army back on the last natural defensive position before Cairo and the Suez Canal at El Alamein. The Soviet dictator Stalin was also screaming for the Western Allies to open a second front in order to relieve the pressure on the Red Army, which had been driven back to Stalingrad and the Caucasus mountains. This set the scene for the first Anglo-American operation involving airborne forces, and their first meeting with their German counterparts: the stage was Tunisia.

4

The red and the green

Even while the Allies were formulating their plans for a combined amphibious and airborne task force to land in Vichy French North-West Africa, behind Rommel's back so as to trap his forces against the anvil of the Eighth Army, Rommel himself was reinforced by a parachute brigade to help in his assault on the El Alamein position. Known as the *Fallschirmjäger* Brigade *Ramcke* after its commander, Maj-Gen Bernhard Ramcke, it consisted of Maj Hans Kroh's I/FJR 2, Maj Eduard Hübner's II/FJR 5 (the 2nd Battalion of the reconstituted *Luftlande-Sturm* Regiment now commanded by Walter Koch with the rank of Obstlt [Lt-Col]) and two training battalions (*Fallschirmjäger Lehr Bataillon*) under Majs von der Heydte and Burkhardt, plus II *Fallschirmjäger Artillerie Bataillon* (Paratroop Artillery Battalion) under Maj Fenski, a *Panzerjäger* (anti-tank) company under Oblt Hasender, pioneer and signals companies. The brigade entrained for Greece in August, was shipped to Tobruk and taken by truck straight into the front line without any acclimatization period, joining the Italian *'Folgore'* Division on the southern flank of Rommel's line.

The brigade was not involved in the battle of Alam Halfa which lasted from the night of 30/31 August to 3/4 September 1942, being held in reserve to exploit the anticipated breakthrough. As it happened they were not called upon because Rommel's tanks, low on fuel, were unable to exploit early tactical successes and in order to preserve his army more or less intact, Rommel called off the attack, reverting to the defensive. There was now a lull in the desert fighting while Gen Bernard Law Montgomery, newly appointed commander of the Eighth Army, methodically built up his forces for his own counterstrike.

The second battle of El Alamein opened with a tremendous artillery barrage by 1,000 guns at 21:25 on 23 October, followed by infantry attacks to clear paths through the minefields and anti-tank defences for the following armoured divisions. The main blow fell in the north and Ramcke's brigade (the paras' presence, as well as their toughness and the resourcefulness of their commander being known to British intelligence) was largely left alone, only having to repulse probing attacks by the 50th Tyne/Tees Division. The battle dragged on. The Allies' progress was slowed by Rommel's dogged defence despite their enormous superiority in manpower, firepower, tanks, fuel and ammunition, and the Ramcke Brigade continued to hold its position until 2 November when, seeing it was in danger of being outflanked, Rommel ordered it to head back to new positions some 15 miles (24km) west. Within hours this was countermanded: the Allies had finally achieved a decisive breakthrough and the whole of *Panzer Armee Afrika* was on the run back to Fuka, where Rommel hoped optimistically to establish a blocking position.

This left Ramcke's men in a difficult situation to say the very least, for Fuka was well over 100 miles (160km) away across inhospitable sand, rock and scrub, and only the artillery battalion had any trucks. Nevertheless, Ramcke decided to give it a go rather than meekly waiting to surrender. The men trudged off westwards across the desert, harried by air attacks and the odd encounter with a forward patrol, but luck came their way during the night of the 5th/6th when they spotted a convoy of British trucks leaguered down for the night. Attacking just before dawn, they overran the lightly defended convoy, whose vehicles were found to be stuffed with food, fuel and water. To German troops accustomed to eating little else but unpalatable Italian canned sausages, even tins of British 'M&V' (meat and veg) provided a welcome change! Ramcke's surviving 600 men thus drove in well-fed style to rejoin the army at Fuka, where Rommel had given them up for lost — as, indeed, the unfortunate Italian *'Folgore'* Division had been since it, too, lacked transport and had been in a more exposed position than Ramcke's force.

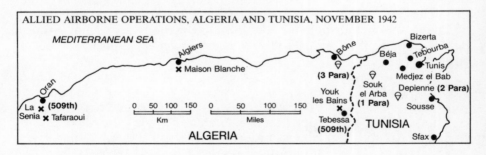

ALLIED AIRBORNE OPERATIONS, ALGERIA AND TUNISIA, NOVEMBER 1942

The joyous news of the Ramcke Brigade's return pre-empted, by barely over 24 hours, much more dire tidings from Morocco and Algeria where, in the early hours of the 8th, a vast Anglo-American armada had begun landing. The operation was politically sensitive because there was considerable French resentment at Great Britain due to the Royal Navy's bombardment of the French fleet at Oran in July 1940, and although many French officers were known to be secret Gaullist sympathisers, nobody was sure how the bulk of the 100,000 French troops in Morocco, Algeria and Tunisia would respond to being invaded. It was therefore decided that the assault force should be predominantly American and that it should be commanded by an American. The relatively unknown Lt-Gen Dwight D. Eisenhower was selected to be commander-in-chief.

The landings were to take place in three waves: one all-American task force would sail direct from the USA to land around Casablanca on the Atlantic coast of Morocco; a second American task force would land around Oran, on the Mediterranean coast of Morocco; and a joint Anglo-American force would land around Algiers. British plans for an assault at Bizerta in Tunisia were vetoed by the Americans, which was a mistake as things turned out because the Germans used the port as the main staging post for reinforcements from Italy.

Gen 'Boy' Browning had persuaded Eisenhower that a parachute force would be invaluable in the invasion, codenamed 'Torch', to capture airfields in advance of the ground forces' approach towards Tunis, and the 1st Airborne Brigade plus the US 509th Para Battalion were therefore assigned to Lt-Gen Sir Kenneth Anderson's First Army in Algeria. The brigade, now commanded by Flavell since Gale had moved to a staff job at the War Office, comprised the 1st Parachute Battalion (1 Para) under Lt-Col S.J.L. Hill ('Dracula' Down having been appointed CO of 2 Para Brigade); 2 Para under John Frost; and 3 Para under Lt-Col R.G. Pine-Coffin, Lathbury also having gone to the War Office. Only two companies of 3 Para actually flew into action, the remainder of the brigade travelling by ship due to the shortage of aircraft. However, the US 509th Airborne was the first to drop.

Edson Raff — known behind his back as 'Little Caesar' and now promoted to Lt-Col — led his men aboard 39 C-47s of the 60th Troop Carrier Command at Predannack and St Eval airfields in Cornwall during the night of 7 November 1942, their targets the airfields of La Senia and Tafaraoui south of Oran. Unfortunately the aircraft became scattered during the long 12-hour flight from England, across Spain and the Mediterranean, while the warship which was supposed to give them a navigational fix as they approached the Algerian coast had been given the wrong radio frequency. As the individual groups of aircraft reached the North African mainland, low on fuel, their crews had to 'eyeball' their approach. The largest group of 21 C-47s found La Senia all right but were disconcerted by anti-aircraft fire — which had not been expected — and turned away to land on the dry salt lake bed of Sebkra d'Oran 30 miles (48km) from Tafaraoui for a council of war. Some local tribesmen started taking pot-shots at them and a couple of squads of men were despatched to deal with them. Then another group of six aircraft appeared, including that in which Raff was flying, and a radio message was sent to tell him the ground force was under attack. Spotting three tanks moving down from the north, Raff thought they were part of the enemy force and decided to parachute down to intercept them. To his surprise, the tanks turned out to be American. Then three more aircraft turned up (the remainder landed at

Gibraltar or in French and Spanish Morocco) and Raff, who had cracked a couple of ribs on landing, decided to proceed overland to Tafaraoui.

After they had gone about 15 miles (24km) Raff received a radio message from ground forces which had already reached Tafaraoui, saying they needed help. He sent the crews of three C-47s in Jeeps to retrieve and fly their aircraft back to where the battalion was now assembled — he could not send more because only three aircraft had enough fuel left, even for this short hop. When they arrived, a company of paras hastily emplaned and the C-47s took off again for Tafaraoui. Moments later they were attacked by French fighters and forced to crash land, three men being killed and 15 wounded before the fighters, having expended all their ammunition, flew off. Leaving the wounded behind with the battalion's doctor, Raff set off again with his depleted force of 300 men, but by the time they reached the airfield they found the ground forces had brought the situation under control. It was an inauspicious beginning for the American airborne troops, even if the failure to capture either of their objectives was not the paras' fault. The main lesson learned, as the British had already discovered at Monte Vulture and Bruneval, was the difficulty of sufficiently accurate night navigation to land the paras all together at the right spot — a problem which has never been completely resolved.

Next to arrive in Africa were the two companies of 3 Para who flew from Cornwall to Gibraltar on the 10th, then staged on to Maison Blanche airfield outside Algiers which was already in friendly hands. Transport was provided by C-47s of the 60th Troop Carrier Command. The battalion's objective was the airfield outside the port of Bône (Annaba), close to the Tunisian border, and therefore strategically important. The Germans thought so too, and unbeknown to Geoffrey Pine-Coffin and his men, at practically the same time they were taking off from Maison Blanche at dawn on the 12th, Obstlt Walter Koch's III/FJR 5 was emplaning in its Ju 52s at El Aouina airfield outside Tunis with the same objective. As the Junkers aircraft approached Bône at 08:30, they saw 3 Para's white silk parachutes already descending on the airfield! The Germans aborted their own landing and returned to Tunisia. As it happened, the British jump was scattered, a number of men also being injured in heavy falls on the rocky ground, so it was lucky that the airfield proved deserted apart from a number of local Arabs who tried to persuade 3 Para's men to part with their parachutes, which could be turned into silk underwear and sold at vast profit! What would have happened if FJR 5 had gone ahead with its own drop is speculative, but 'red devil' would meet 'green devil' in battle soon enough.

While 3 Para, reinforced by No 6 (Army) Commando, secured its grip on the airfield, 1 and 2 Paras were disembarking at Algiers and further *Fallschirmjäger* were similarly arriving in Bizerta. Field Marshal Albrecht Kesselring, German C-in-C for the Mediterranean theatre, had responded with typical energy to this latest threat in North Africa and apart from FJR 5, had assembled an *ad hoc* paratroop regiment from troops of several different units which was given the title 'Barenthin Regiment' after its commander, Obst Walther Barenthin, plus Rudolf Witzig's 21st Pioneer Battalion, two battalions from the 'Herman Göring Regiment and two battalions from the Italian 'San Marco' Regiment. Further reinforcements, including the 10th Panzer Division, would follow later.

The next parachute drop came on the 15th as part of the First Army's general drive across the Tunisian border. Raff's 509th Battalion, which had regrouped with 1 Para Brigade at Maison Blanche after its drop at Oran, was assigned the capture of Youks les Bains and Tebessa airfields, priority being assigned the former. Some 350 men emplaned in 22 C-47s and took off at 07:30, unsure whether they would meet a friendly or hostile reception from the French 3rd Zouave Battalion which was dug in around the airfield. As it happened, the French did not open fire, partly because they had been forewarned of the drop and partly because many men were too busy diving into their trenches and dodging supply containers which were dropping like bricks because their parachutes had failed to deploy properly! The French commander 'surrendered' to Raff, who promptly despatched a company of men to occupy Tebessa, and yet another airfield fell into Allied hands. Even though not a shot had been fired, Raff was promoted to full Colonel for this success.

Lt-Col James Hill's 1 Para had taken off at the same time, intending to drop on comparatively flat ground at Souk el Arba then advance to the important road junction at Béja, only 50 miles (80km) from Tunis, with the intention of persuading the 3,000-strong French garrison to throw in its lot with the Allies. When they arrived over the target, however, it was obscured by low cloud so they had to return to Maison Blanche and try again on the 16th. This time all went well, the battalion's 525 men landing on target with few injuries and only one fatality and heading straight for Béja in captured French trucks. There, they deployed on high ground outside the town and Hill began negotiations with the French commander. Bluffing that his force formed the spearhead of an armoured division, he persuaded the French to allow his men to relieve them. That evening Hill paraded his men through the town, sending them through first wearing their helmets and then a second time wearing their berets so the French would not realise how they had been deceived by such a tiny force! 1 Para then patrolled forward to the Medjez el Bab heights which controlled a key sector of the western approaches to Tunis before being withdrawn when regular infantry arrived. During this skirmishing, Hill was seriously wounded in an encounter with Italian light tanks and his place taken by Maj Alastair Pearson, who would end the war as one of the most decorated officers in the British army.

John Frost's 2 Para had a much more gruelling time. Held in reserve while the 1st and 3rd Battalions were reaping all the glory, his men had had enough of drinking and rough-housing in Algiers by the time a mission was found for them — to capture the three airfields of Pont du Fahs, Depienne and Oudna south of Tunis, then meet up with ground elements of the First Army which would by that time have got through Medjez el Bab to St Cyprien, just outside Tunis. With hindsight, it was not only a perilous mission right in the middle of the German and Italian positions with no guarantee that the ground forces would achieve their objectives, but a total waste of time for neither the *Luftwaffe* nor the *Regia Aeronautica* were using any of the three airstrips. Moreover, the plan was botched right at the beginning for even while the battalion was emplaning in its C-47s at Maison Blanche, Frost received orders to ignore Pont du Fahs and land at Depienne, which had not been studied as a dropping zone (DZ).

After a cold and bumpy flight across the mountains on 29 November, the aircraft approached Depienne and Frost picked on an area of ploughed fields over which to drop. Given the circumstances, he was lucky to lose just one man killed and six injured in the drop itself. Depienne was found to be deserted and Frost decided to move straight on to Oudna that evening, leaving a small rearguard to look after the injured who had been carried into the nearby schoolhouse. What happened next day at Depienne illustrates two sides of war and was recounted to the author by Gavin Cadden, then a L/Cpl in 'C' Company, 2 Para.

The small force in the schoolhouse was discovered and attacked by Italian troops, probably — although this has never been validated — from the 1st Battalion of the 92nd Infantry Regiment and the 557th Self-Propelled Artillery Group. After token resistance during which the senior officer present, Lt Buchanan of the Royal Army Medical Corps, was killed, the survivors surrendered. Shortly afterwards a car drove up and an unidentified German officer, probably from the 19th Reconnaissance Company of the 10th Panzer Division, ordered the prisoners herded outside the schoolhouse while Italian troops set up a heavy machine-gun. The paras brandished 'V' signs, knowing they would soon join their lieutenant in death. Then, out of the blue, an armoured car swept up. From it stepped Oblt Walter Koch and his number two, Hpt Hans Jungwirt (FJR 5 then being involved in the heavy fighting for Medjez el Bab to the west). Koch kicked over the machine-gun and tongue-lashed the German officer who had ordered the execution. He turned to Cadden and the others and said in good English, 'You are paratroopers and you put up a brave fight. You are prisoners of war and will be treated as such.' Koch left some of his own men to look after the prisoners, leaving them medicine, bandages, food and drink. (Gavin Cadden himself later escaped from an Italian PoW camp, joined the partisans, was badly wounded and ended the war in Switzerland. Walter Koch died in October 1943. The official story is that he was driving at high speed at night and crashed into an unlighted tank transporter trailer. Survivors of FJR 5 themselves believe, however, that the 'accident' was arranged by the SS or Gestapo because of Koch's outspoken criticism of Hitler's order that all Allied paratroopers and commandos were to be executed as spies and saboteurs.)

Meanwhile Frost had led off the rest of the battalion in an overnight march, transporting most of the heavy equipment such as mortars in commandeered Arab handcarts. Mid-morning on the 30th they found a well and gratefully refilled their water bottles. Local villagers told them Oudna was deserted, and when they reached the airfield at 16:00 all they found was one abandoned German aircraft. However, their presence was soon detected by the enemy and elements of I/FJR 5, supported by five tanks from the 10th Panzer Division, launched an attack which was beaten off with difficulty. After dark, 2 Para withdrew to the vicinity of the well they had stopped at earlier and took up defensive positions. The morning of the 31st brought devastating news. Frost was told over the radio that the armoured assault through Medjez towards St Cyprien had failed and that the paras were on their own. All they could do was try to get back to First Army lines at Medjez, moving by night and holing up during the day.

Each day that followed was a nightmare of misery. The paras succeeded in beating off attack after attack mainly because the Germans needed all their strength to hold the First Army, but casualties were inevitably mounting. Each night Frost would blow his hunting horn and the weary men would move out westward again, stumbling over the rocky slopes and vineyards and dodging enemy patrols. At one point a section of men were deceived by a pair of German armoured cars bearing First Army markings and were captured. Still the nightmare dragged on, each roll-call showing more men dead, wounded or missing. Eventually, on 3 December, they encountered a genuine American armoured car and thankfully stumbled into the safety of friendly lines, 266 men weaker than when they had set out.

There was only one more parachute operation in Tunisia. On Boxing Day, 26 December 1942, a small force of 32 men from Raff's 509th under Lt Dan DeLeo were dropped to blow up a railway bridge at El Djem. Faulty navigation put them down in the wrong place and after searching unsuccessfully all night for their target, with German troops closing in from both sides, they blew up a stretch of railway track and dispersed in small groups into the desert. Eight men including DeLeo got back to Allied lines, 16 were captured and the fate of the others is unknown. Like their German counterparts, the men of 1 Para Brigade and the 509th Airborne Battalion were subsequently used as élite infantry to plug gaps in the line, even though Flavell had asked for them to be withdrawn so that casualties could be replaced and the men rested for forthcoming missions, including the still top secret invasion of Sicily. It was not to be. So, after a lull following the failure of the November 1942 offensive caused as much by torrential rain as by enemy action, in March 1943 the paras found themselves in the north of the line at Tamera where they faced their toughest opponents — Barenthin's and Witzig's battalions. Indeed, Rudolf Witzig, commander of Assault Section *Granit* at Eben Emael, acquired something of the same reputation amongst the British paras that Rommel himself had amongst the Allies in general. From 7 to 17 March Witzig, who was in overall command on this sector of the front, threw attack after attack against Alastair Pearson's and John Frost's 1 and 2 Para Battalions (3 Para being held in reserve in case of a breakthrough).

Despite being outnumbered, the British troops fought back doggedly, finding — as the New Zealanders had on Crete during the night battle of 22/23 May 1941 at Máleme — that bayonet charges were the thing the Germans liked least. For example, on 10 March Witzig's men broke through to Pearson's headquarters and were only thrown back when all the battalion's cooks and orderlies grabbed up their rifles and charged, screaming their battle cry 'Whoa Mohammed!' at the tops of their voices. 'Dracula' Down, CO of 2 Para Brigade, was paying a courtesy visit to the battalion at the time, and himself had to seize a rifle. By the 17th though, the weight and determination of the attackers paid off, and the British paras were forced to withdraw, but it was practically the last German victory in Tunisia. 1 Para Brigade remained in the line until the night of 14/15 April, when it was at last relieved by the US 9th Infantry Division and returned to Algiers for a well-earned rest. Despite suffering 1,700 casualties — roughly 80 per cent of their original strength — they were luckier than their German counterparts whose loses were far higher. Although Ramcke and most of his brigade, along with Koch, Witzig and other individuals, succeeded in escaping the final battles at the beginning of May, most of the German forces in Tunisia entered captivity. Those paras who escaped were regrouped in Italy, the next battlefield.

Meanwhile, in March 1943 the 7th *Flieger* Division which had suffered an equal mauling during the Russian winter counter-offensive following the fall of Stalingrad (Volgograd), was withdrawn to southern France and disbanded, to be re-formed as the 1st *Fallschirmjäger* Division (FJR 1, 3 and 4) under Richard Heidrich, now a Major-General. One regiment, FJR 2, was detached to form the nucleus of the 2nd Division alongside survivors from Tunisia which became FJR 6 and 7, the division being commanded by Bernhard Ramcke. The 3rd and 4th Divisions began forming towards the end of 1943, the former in Brittany and the latter in Italy. The 3rd (FJR 5, 8 and 9) was commanded by Maj-Gen Richard Schimpf and the 4th, which uniquely contained Italian survivors from the *'Folgore'* Division in addition to FJR 10, 11 and 12, by Maj-Gen Heinrich Trettner. The 5th Division (FJR 13, 14 and 15) began forming at Reims around a nucleus from the *Lehr* (Demonstration) Battalion of XI *Flieger Korps* in April 1944 under Maj-Gen Gustav Wilke.

A further five successively numbered *Fallschirmjäger* divisions would later be created between June 1944 and March 1945, although they were all understrength and do not deserve the title 'division'; moreover, few of their personnel were actually paratroopers and none of them saw action in the airborne role, although the 6th Division under Lt-Gen Walther Lackner would be involved in an airborne operation in 1944 when it fought at Arnhem *(qv)*. An order for the creation of an 11th Division in March 1945 was a pure pipedream.

On the Allied side, the US 82nd Airborne Division had left Fort Bragg on 20 April and arrived at Casablanca on 10 May to spend the next few weeks training up for the invasion of Sicily and getting acclimatized to the Mediterranean heat. Still commanded by Maj-Gen Matthew B. Ridgway, its main components were the 504th and 505th Parachute Infantry Regiments, the 325th Glider Infantry Regiment, two battalions of artillery, a battalion of engineers and an anti-aircraft battalion. The US 509th Battalion (now commanded by Maj Doyle Yardley, for Raff had been assigned temporarily to a staff posting back in the States) was also incorporated in the division — to its men's inevitable displeasure, for they considered their experience made them a cut above the rest . . .

Meanwhile, the British 1st Airborne Division was assembling at Sousse in Tunisia, commanded by Maj-Gen G.F. 'Hoppy' Hopkinson because Browning had been appointed to Eisenhower's staff. It comprised four brigades: the 1st (1, 2 and 3 Para) now under Brig Gerald Lathbury; the 2nd under Brig 'Dracula' Down (4, 5 and 6 Para); the 1st (Air-Landing) under Brig P.H.W. 'Pip' Hicks (1st and 2nd Battalions, South Staffordshire Regiment and 1st Battalion, The Border Regiment); and the 4th under Brig J.W. 'Shan' Hackett. This comprised Nos 10 and 11 Para which had been formed in Palestine in 1942 plus 151 Para from India which was confusingly renumbered 156; 11 Para remained in Palestine and men from 156 who had served out their time overseas were repatriated to Britain to form a cadre for the new 6th Airborne Division, so 4 Brigade was considerably understrength. (152 [Indian] and 153 [Gurkha] Battalions subsequently became the nucleus of the 1st Indian Parachute Division, although they never made an operational drop as such, being mainly used as line infantry.)

The Allied decision to invade Sicily had not been taken without a great deal of soul-searching. To Churchill and most of the British War Cabinet an assault on the 'soft underbelly' of Europe seemed the most cost-effective way of taking some of the heat off their Russian allies — and, indeed, the invasion did cause Hitler to transfer some of the best German divisions from Russia following the failure of the summer offensive around Kursk, Operation 'Zitadelle' ('Citadel'). For their part, the Americans favoured a rapid build-up of forces in the United Kingdom once the Germans and Italians had been defeated in North Africa, so as to launch a cross-Channel invasion of France and head for Germany by the most direct route. But even the Americans had grudgingly to concede that this would be impossible until the following year, so Operation 'Husky' was born.

Everything possible was done to deceive the Germans and Italians into believing that, after the fall of Tunisia, the next assault would either fall on Sardinia, whence an invasion of northern Italy could be launched across the Tyrrhenian Sea; or on Greece, which was made plausible by Churchill's well-known obsession with the Balkans. In the famous case of 'the man who never was', British intelligence had a man's body deposited off the Spanish coast by submarine; papers identified him as Maj Martin of the Royal Marines and an attaché case strapped to his wrist contained despatches giving details of plans for an attack on Greece and a letter from Mountbatten which made a joking mention of sardines — an obvious reference to Sardinia. The *Abwehr* (German intelligence) was taken in with the result that when the Allies did land on Sicily on 9/10 July, barely two months after the German capitulation in Tunisia, the island was only lightly defended.

In the east, guarding the principal approach routes towards Messina, facing the Italian mainland, were the Italian '*Napoli*' and the German *Fallschirmjäger* Division '*Hermann Göring*'. The '*Livorno*' Division and part of the 15th *Panzergrenadier* Division were in the centre, guarding Sixth Army headquarters in Enna, while the rest of the 15th *Panzergrenadiers* plus the Italian '*Aosta*' and '*Assietta*' Divisions were deployed south of Palermo in the west of the island. The Italians lacked fighting spirit and the two German divisions were understrength, while the Allies would be able to throw the full weight of approximately 10 divisions against them in the first wave of a combined airborne and seaborne assault.

The US 82nd Airborne Division was assigned to Gen Omar N. Bradley's II Corps, part of Gen George S. Patton's Seventh Army, which would land on beaches east and west of Gela. To their right, Gen Sir Oliver Leese's XXX Corps would land around Pozzallo on the southernmost tip of the island, while on their right again the 1st Airborne Division would spearhead Gen Sir Miles Dempsey's XIII Corps' attack in the southeast between Pachino and Syracuse (Siracusa). The British and Canadian troops, under overall command of Montgomery's Eighth Army, would head directly north for Messina while the Americans would hook left via Palermo. 'Monty' was after the glory again and it was ironically appropriate that the Americans should reach the goal first, assisted through prior arrangement by the Mafia who helped sabotage German and Italian communications and suborn members of the Sicilian '*Aosta*' and '*Napoli*' Divisions.

The airborne assault itself — the largest use of parachute and glider-borne troops since Crete — began disastrously. In fact the parallels with Crete are very significant, not just because the operations were both against islands, but in the fact that the lightly armed paras in both cases suffered from wide dispersal in the wrong places during the drop and only succeeded in fulfilling their objectives through luck or because they were reinforced by ground troops. The principal difference is that the Allied landings all took place at night.

First in the air at 19:00 on the moonlit evening of 9 July 1943 was Hicks' 1st Air-Landing Brigade whose 129 CG-4A Hadrians and eight Airspeed Horsas were towed by a mixture of American C-47s and British Halifaxes and Albemarles. Their target was the Ponte Grande bridge just outside Syracuse, a key point on the road north to Catánia and Messina. Unseasonably high winds scattered the aircraft on their approach, while others were shot out of the air by trigger-happy naval gunners on the warships

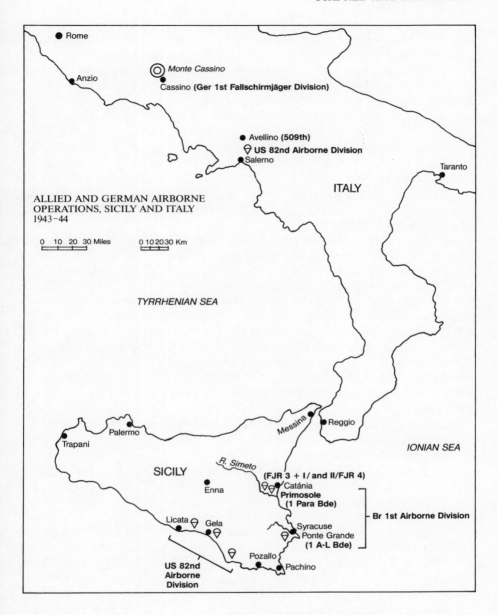

ALLIED AND GERMAN AIRBORNE
OPERATIONS, SICILY AND ITALY
1943–44

0 10 20 30 Miles

0 10 20 30 Km

transporting the bulk of the invasion force by sea. Many pilots slipped their tow lines while miles from the target. Over half the gliders (78) ended up in the sea and 252 men were drowned. The remainder made forced landings anywhere they could find a reasonably flat patch of ground; nearly half of the pilots died or were seriously injured in their attempts.

The gliders were littered across the landscape anything up to 40 miles (64km) from their objective. Brig Hicks and his own pilot, none other than

Chatterton, CO of the Glider Pilot Regiment, were among those who had to swim ashore. Only 12 gliders actually landed anywhere near the correct place but their 83 occupants, led by Lt L. Withers of the South Stafford-shires, miraculously took the bridge and silenced an enemy pillbox with not a single casualty. During the night, other stragglers joined them but at the most there were only 100 or so men defending the bridge at daybreak — this from a brigade of 2,000! By an astonishing feat of arms, they held out against repeated attacks by the '*Napoli*' Division until shortly after 15:00 when, out of ammunition, the 15 or so survivors were finally overrun. One officer and seven men escaped to meet the Royal Scots Fusiliers who arrived considerably behind schedule about an hour after-wards to drive the Italians back. This was not the first and would not be the last time that the late arrival of ground forces would jeopardise or negate an airborne operation.

With the panache which turned Dunkirk into a famous British 'victory', Montgomery transformed this absolute shambles of a battle into a re-sounding success for the glider troops, stating that Syracuse could not have been captured until much later had it not been for their 'skill and gallantry'. Gallantry certainly cannot be denied, but what the operation really showed was inexperience and, again, the hazards of night operations with far from perfect navigation. From an airborne point of view, one of the most significant results of operation 'Husky' was the establishment of pathfinder forces, aircraft piloted and navigated by the most experienced aircrew and small advance parties of paras with radio homing beacons, their transmitters being codenamed 'Eureka' and the aircraft receivers 'Rebecca'.

The Rebecca/Eureka combination had actually been used once prior to the invasion of Sicily, so it is appropriate to digress here back to the first British glider operation of the war, which unfortunately had tragic consequences. British intelligence were concerned about the development of a heavy water plant near Vermork in southern Norway, since heavy water was an essential ingredient in the creation of an atomic bomb. Two teams of volunteers from the Royal Engineers under Lts A.C. Allen and D.A. Methven were assembled at Skitten airfield in Scotland and on 19 November 1942 boarded the two Horsa gliders which would be towed to their objective 400 miles (644km) away by No 38 Wing Halifax bombers equipped with Rebecca. A Eureka transmitter had been smuggled to the Norwegian underground.

However, everything went horrifically wrong. The transmitter failed and one Halifax hit the side of a mountain, all its crew being killed, while most of the sappers in the glider were also killed or injured. The second Halifax, lacking sufficient fuel to get back to Scotland with a glider in tow, released the Horsa even though the 15 men aboard were too few to hope to persevere successfully with the mission. Their glider made a very heavy landing in the rocky terrain, resulting in further casualties. Survivors from both aircraft were captured by the Germans and later executed by the

Gestapo under orders from Hitler — the orders which Walter Koch so vigorously opposed.

If the Rebecca/Eureka system had been used in Sicily it would certainly have helped the US 82nd Airborne, whose principal objectives were the cluster of airstrips and roads around Gela, for they suffered from the same navigational problems as had been encountered earlier despite intensive training and prolonged study of aerial reconnaissance photographs. The forces assigned to the first wave of the assault were Col James M. 'Jumping Jim' Gavin's 505th Parachute Regiment plus the 3rd Battalion of the 504th under Lt-Col Charles Kouns, the 456th Artillery Battalion and a company of engineers from the 307th, a total of 3,405 men. Taking off shortly after the British glider force in 266 C-47s, they too were affected by the strong winds and, despite using Malta as a navigation point during the approach, instead of dropping neatly north of Gela to block the '*Hermann Göring*' Division from interfering with the amphibious landings, were scattered in isolated groups along some 60 miles (96km) of coastline. Once again, the aircraft had been fired upon by 'friendly' troops and there were several casualties, while smoke from fires set by the pre-invasion bombardment obscured landmarks and made accurate jumping impossible.

Given this stage of chaos, achieving their prime objectives was clearly impossible but the 'All Americans' responded well to the situation, clearing targets of opportunity and even at one point repelling an attack by '*Hermann Göring*' Division tanks including Tigers whose armour was so thick that the paras' bazookas were about as useful as slingshots. Nevertheless, they succeeded in disabling one and the others retired, but American casualties were heavy. Ironically, part of the reason for the lack of a determined response to the landings was the fact that reports of paratroopers over such a wide area led the Italian C-in-C, Gen d'Armata Alfredo Guzzoni, to believe that instead of one regimental combat group, the Americans must have dropped four or five divisions around Gela!

Next evening the remainder of the 82nd emplaned under Col Reuben Tucker and headed north across a tranquil sea, the high winds having blown themselves out. Unfortunately, they approached the landing beaches in the wake of a German air raid, and gun crews aboard the warships lying offshore mistook the 144 C-47s for another wave of enemy aircraft. As the hail of flak burst around them, the pilots of many aircraft turned on their lights in an attempt to show they were friendly. This, of course, only served to make them easier targets, and within minutes 23 aircraft had been shot down. Many of the paras survived by throwing themselves out of the doors of their doomed machines, but 88 soldiers and aircrew perished, 162 were wounded and 69 missing. Another 37 aircraft staggered back to Tunisia, riddled with machine-gun and shrapnel holes and laden with badly injured men. What the paras thought of the navy is unprintable! Nevertheless, the survivors joined up with Gavin's original battlegroup and the battered division fought its way through to Trápani on the west coast of the island before being pulled out of the line on 22 July.

The third and last parachute drop on Sicily was a similar shambles but interesting because once again 'red devil' would meet 'green devil'. With Syracuse firmly in his hands, Montgomery's next objective was Catánia, the approach to which had to pass over a steel girder bridge across the river Simeto at Primosole. It was a natural choke point and the Germans and Italians were sure to have mined it with demolition charges, while aerial reconnaissance had revealed the presence of a number of anti-tank guns guarding it. Montgomery therefore decided to use Lathbury's 1 Para Brigade to take the bridge in a surprise attack before it could be blown up and hold it until they could be relieved by tanks heading north from Syracuse. Pearson's 1st Battalion was to seize the bridge itself while 3 Para, now commanded by Lt-Col Yeldham, would land to the north to prevent enemy troops interfering and Frost's 2 Para would similarly protect the southern approaches. Six anti-tank guns would be landed by glider once the objective was in the paras' hands.

The C-47s, followed by Albemarles towing the gliders, began taking off just after 19:00 on 13 July and ran into the same problem the second wave of the 82nd had encountered — warships and troops on the ground opening fire on them. The aircraft took violent evading action, some of them promptly turning back. Pearson himself had to threaten the pilot of his aircraft with his revolver before the man would fly on into the hail of flak. The result was predictable: those aircraft which did arrive over the Catánia plain at about 22:00 were scattered and few men jumped in the right place. Despite this, 50 men led by Capt Rann succeeded in overrunning the bridge, which was in their hands by 02:15 on the 14th. Then Pearson joined up and began rallying stragglers, including some men from 3 Para, into a defensive perimeter.

The bulk of 3 Para had the misfortune to fall into positions held by the *Fallschirmjäger* Machine-Gun Battalion, part of Heidrich's 1st Parachute Division which was in the process of being rushed to Sicily to help in the island's defence. The German paras had been expecting their own Engineer Battalion to land that night, so took the descending parachutists, equipment containers and gliders to be their own. Darkness compounded the confusion, and at one point a German para is said actually to have asked a British soldier if he had found his 'Schmeisser' (MP40 sub-machine-gun)! Around Catánia airfield, British and German paras landed almost simultaneously and a brief but furious fire-fight ensued which the Germans won through sheer weight of numbers.

As day broke the situation began to clarify itself and the Germans — the machine-gunners and engineers now supported by FJR 3 and I/ and II/FJR 4 — launched a vigorous attack on the bridge perimeter, attempting to outflank it across the river to the east. The tinder-dry cornfields and reeds along the river banks were set ablaze by artillery fire and dense smoke covered the German approach. By late afternoon the defenders, pinned down by enfilading fire, were running short of ammunition and Lathbury, who had been wounded by a grenade, decided to pull back under cover of darkness. The German engineers overran the bridge and set up their own perimeter facing south. However, help was at hand for 1 Para Brigade since heavy Churchill tanks of the 4th Armoured Brigade accompanied by men of the Durham Light Infantry began arriving around midnight.

The tanks started rolling forward with daybreak on the 15th but the Germans had brought up one of their dreaded 88mm guns which opened fire at about 900yds (800m) range and rapidly knocked out eight Churchills, forcing the rest to retire. Then British artillery fire put the '88' out of action and the infantry surged forward to recapture the bridge. Not for long, though. The *Fallschsirmjäger*, reinforced by '*Hermann Göring*' Division tanks, counter-attacked and retook it again. However, this victory was shortlived for by this time more and more Eighth Army troops and tanks were arriving up the road from Syracuse and on the 17th the Germans abandoned the bridge for the last time.

Sicily had been something of an all-round disaster for the American and British airborne divisions, and Eisenhower even recommended that they should be broken up and henceforth only used in small units for tactical missions — a reaction almost identical to Hitler's after Crete. Fortunately, although his criticisms were taken seriously, his conclusions were not, and it was decided that what was needed was simply more training, particularly of pathfinder teams and aircraft navigators over unfamiliar terrain at night.

The British 1st Parachute and Air-Landing Brigades were now returned to Tunisia to rest and lick their wounds while the 2nd and 4th Brigades prepared for operations in Italy. They were transported by sea and there were only minor air landings as at Ascola and Pescara in October by 2 and 3 Para to help guide escaped PoWs back to Allied lines; men of the 1st and 2nd Special Air Service Regiments undertook several similar small-scale raids to help the partisans behind German lines. 11 Para from 4 Brigade took part in a minor operation to capture the Dodecanese island of Kos *(qv)* on 14 September and rejoined its parent formation when 1 and 4 Para Brigades and the Air-Landing Brigade returned to the UK in December. 2 Brigade remained in Italy, making one jump in June 1944 when 60 men from 6 Para were dropped behind German lines at Torricella, near Rimini, similarly to help partisans in disrupting enemy lines of communication. This tiny force tied down an entire German brigade for several days. By this time 2 Brigade had been renamed 2nd Independent Parachute Brigade Group, commanded by Lt-Col C.V.H. Pritchard because 'Hoppy' Hopkinson had been killed by a stray shell and 'Dracula' Down had been appointed new CO of the division.

On the other side, Heidrich's paras helped cover the retreat of German and Italian forces to Messina, whence they were shipped back to the mainland, their last rearguard leaving Sicily during the night of 16/17 August. The 1st *Fallschirmjäger* Division would henceforth also fight as ordinary infantry in Italy, winning undying glory in the defence of the town and monastery of Monte Cassino in 1944. It had been joined by Ramcke's 2nd Division in August 1943, which was tasked with taking control of Rome; then Trettner's 4th Division complete with its '*Folgore*' component, was thrown into the battle for the Anzio beachhead alongside the '*Hermann Göring*' Division. But there is no space here to examine the ground campaign whose battles are well covered in other histories.

When the Allies invaded mainland Italy on 3 September, there were no initial plans for airborne operations in support of the amphibious landings, a scheme to drop Ridgway's 82nd to capture Rome being wisely abandoned as suicidal. However, the 'All Americans' soon found themselves in the thick of things in a completely unforeseen operation caused by the strength and determination of the German defence at Salerno. Here, Gen Mark Clark's Fifth Army had stormed ashore on the 9th but its inland dash had been halted in its tracks by Maj-Gen Heinrich von Vietinghoff's Tenth Army and by the 12th of the month the 16th Panzer Division had driven a wedge between the American VI and British X Corps. The situation was so desperate that rapid contingency plans were being drawn up to evacuate the troops by sea. Montgomery, whose Eighth Army had landed on the other side of the 'toe' of Italy, was too far away to help. The only reserve force available was the 82nd on Sicily.

On the 13th Clark wrote a letter which he had urgently flown to Ridgway, couching his request for help in the form of an order demanding an air drop that very night. Ridgway, remembering the bitter lessons of the Sicilian drops, sensibly asked for precautions. The dropping zone was to be clearly marked with a beacon and all anti-aircraft gunners must be ordered not to fire at *any* aircraft. Thanks to these measures, the drop was a complete success, the 1,300 men of Reuben Tucker's 504th Regimental Combat Team landing almost without incident within an area of a single square mile — indeed, most of them within 200yds (180m) of the flaming T-shaped beacon. By dawn they had dug in, ready for anything, and after repulsing a German attack, that evening advanced against fierce opposition to take and hold the heights around Altavilla. That same night Gavin's 505th Regimental Combat Team was dropped in to reinforce them; the crisis on the beachhead was over and the naval evacuation plans were scrapped.

Meanwhile, the 509th had also been in action. Their target was the important road junction at Avellino, 16 miles (24km) behind German lines. Unfortunately, the drop on the night of the 13th was yet another shambles. The surrounding mountains meant the men had to drop from 4,000ft (1,220m), resulting in bad dispersal. Moreover, there was a concentration of German armoured troops in and around the town and many men were promptly captured, including Yardley who had been wounded. It was impossible to capture Avellino with the 500-odd survivors from the 640 who had jumped, so they hid out in the mountains, attacking supply convoys and staff cars and ambushing the German patrols sent out to look for them until they eventually managed in small groups to link up with elements of X Corps advancing inland from the beachhead. After this, like their British counterparts, the men of the 82nd operated as ordinary infantry.

Before leaving the Mediterranean for Normandy, though, three last, audacious and successful airborne operations must be mentioned — all German: Gran Sasso, Monte Rotondo and Leros. On 25 July, while the battle for Sicily was still raging, the Italian King Victor Emmanuel summoned Mussolini, explained that his services were no longer required, and dismissed him into exile with a 'protective escort' of *carabinieri*. Marshal Pietro Badoglio was asked to form a new government and began immediate secret negotiations with the Allies, leading to an armistice on 3 September. (Not all Italian troops laid down their arms, however, and many of the Fascist-motivated formations continued to fight against the Allies and the Communist-inspired partisans until the end of the war.) Meanwhile Mussolini, who had been shuffled from one hiding place to another — for the King had guaranteed his safety from those who wanted to see him executed — had arrived at the end of August at the Albergo-Rifugio Hotel, perched on the Gran Sasso plateau of Monte Corno 6,500ft (2,011m) up in the Apennine mountains.

The day after Mussolini's arrest, Hitler had summoned one of his most trusted veterans, the scar-faced giant Otto Skorzeny who had joined the Waffen-SS because he was simply too tall for aircrew (he had originally volunteered for the *Luftwaffe*). Hauptsturmführer (Capt) Skorzeny was an expert in small-scale commando-style operations and Hitler entrusted him with the task of finding out where *Il Duce* was being held and to effect his rescue. In his postwar writing Skorzeny claimed all the credit for the subsequent operation, but in truth it was carried out by men of the *Fallschirmjäger* who, under Kurt Student's orders, had been monitoring Italian radio traffic and tracing Mussolini's movements even before King Victor Emmanuel surreptitiously passed his location on to Field Marshal Albrecht Kesselring. Mussolini was an embarrassment and the sooner he was out of the way the better. Skorzeny actually went along almost as a passenger in the raid, although it was his task to escort the deposed dictator back to Germany once he had been rescued.

An assault on Gran Sasso posed enormous problems. The mountain could be climbed, or the cable car used, but both approaches were fraught with risk for it was believed that the *carabinieri* had been ordered to kill Mussolini if anyone tried to save him. The altitude and the restricted space on the plateau would have made parachuting at best hazardous and at worst suicidal, so gliders were the only answer. Student selected a volunteer section of the *Fallschirmjäger Lehr Bataillon* under Maj Mors for the attempt. Accompanied by Skorzeny and 16 SS men plus an Italian officer who was supposed to reassure the *carabinieri*, the 90 paras boarded 12 DFS 230 gliders at Practica di Mare airfield north of Rome at 13:00 on 12 September. Two gliders struck bomb craters on the runway and failed to take off but the other 10 slowly gained height. They would have to be released from 10,000ft (3,094m) in order to make a safe descent on the steeply sloping football pitch-sized landing area in front of the hotel.

Using retro-rockets to bring them to a swift halt, eight of the gliders touched down miraculously without mishap although one cracked up badly with several men injured and one flew slap into the steep mountainside, spilling its occupants down the rocky slopes. The surviving paras raced out, preceded by the Italian officer who shouted at the *carabinieri* not to shoot. They didn't and Skorzeny broke dramatically into the room where Mussolini had been contemplating suicide to announce that the Führer had personally ordered his rescue. It had been planned to take the Italian dictator down the mountain by cable car, a second group of paras having seized the station, and fly him off in a Fieseler Storch light utility aircraft. Unfortunately, this damaged its undercarriage in landing. A second Storch flown by Kurt Student's personal pilot, Hpt Gerlach, therefore touched down on the plateau, rolling uphill into the wind, and Skorzeny bustled Mussolini aboard. Then came a terrifying take-off, downhill with a following wind over the precipitous slopes. Skorzeny's famous luck was with him, and they made it back to the airfield where Mussolini was emplaned aboard a Heinkel He 111 bomber and flown back to Germany — in fact, back into imprisonment again.

Three days before this, German paras had again been in action. Following the Italian capitulation, German troops had moved rapidly to disarm units disloyal to the Axis cause and to seize key installations. The Italian General Staff were holed up in a miniature fortress on Monte Rotondo, 525ft (160m) above the countryside northeast of Rome. Maj Walter Gericke's II/FJR 6 was ordered to neutralize this strongpoint. On 9 September Gericke's 800 men successfully stormed the headquarters, capturing 2,500 officers and other ranks and only just missing the Italian Chief-of-Staff, Gen Roatta, who was in Pescara at the time.

The third German drop took place on the island of Leros in the Dodecanese. This group of islands, which includes Rhodes and Kos, lies off the Turkish coast and had been occupied by the Italians since the fall of Greece in 1941. There was also a German garrison on Rhodes. Churchill saw the islands as a stepping stone towards providing further aid to the Greek and Yugoslav partisans and as bases from which the RAF could bomb the Ploesti oilfields, so after secret negotiations conducted by officers of the Special Boat Squadron, British troops from Middle East Command moved in to occupy the smaller islands, 11 Para jumping on Kos in support of the amphibious task force in October. Rhodes, however, was left alone for the moment as too tough a nut to crack. The Germans, fearing that British occupation of the islands could bring neutral Turkey into the war on the Allied side, responded by landing a brigade of Lt-Gen Friedrich Wilhelm Müller's 22nd *Luftlande* Division from the sea on Kos at the beginning of October and retaking the island within a matter of days. Then, on 12 November, an amphibious task force landed on Leros supported by a parachute drop by the 470 men of Hpt Martin Kühne's

I/FJR 2 and the '*Brandenburg*' Regiment's para company. The paras landed practically in the centre of the island and despite casualties caused by the rocky terrain, within 24 hours had cut the defending British forces in two. Although the British counter-attacked vigorously, the Germans poured reinforcements ashore, rapidly gaining numerical superiority while the paras held the high ground, and three days later the island's garrison laid down its arms.

There would be two more airborne operations in the Mediterranean in August and October 1944 when Allied troops invaded southern France and Greece, and we shall return to these after examining the parachute and glider landings on D-Day.

5

From Normandy to the Rhine

As the Allies slowly slogged their way up the 'boot' of Italy during the summer of 1944, finally evicting Heidrich's 1st *Fallschirmjäger* Division from Monte Cassino on 17 May and capturing Rome on 4 June, tension was becoming almost unbearable in the United Kingdom as the hours ticked down to D-Day. The most formidable assembly of men, tanks, guns, ships and aircraft ever seen was poised for action around the southern and south-eastern coasts of Britain, communications in and out of a 10-mile (16km) 'exclusion zone' running from Cornwall to The Wash being strictly controlled. Civilian life had all but ceased to exist and no mail or telephone calls into or out of the zone were permitted, while the strategists of operation 'Overlord' prayed daily that their elaborate deception plans were still working and that the 'phantom army' of dummy tanks, aircraft and ships in East Anglia would continue to persuade the Germans that the assault would fall on the Pas de Calais, not in Normandy.

Amongst this great armada, three airborne divisions would be included, some 17,000 men — the battle-tested US 82nd and the so-far untried US 101st and British 6th; the battered British 1st Airborne would be held in reserve for later operations. In addition, there was the 1st Special Air Service Brigade, its original two regiments swollen by a Belgian para-commando squadron and two Free French parachute battalions. But, while the SAS's role in behind-the-lines sabotage operations, working closely with the French Resistance, the Strategic Operations Executive (SOE) and the American Office of Strategic Studies (OSS), was clearly understood by all, there was considerable dispute over the correct use of the airborne divisions.

Gen George Marshall wanted to use them as the spearhead of the assault, dropping them deep inland to block the Germans from moving reinforcements up to the beachhead. Others favoured using them in small, dispersed battlegroups to sow confusion. Eisenhower was not convinced by either argument, and neither were the airborne commanders themselves, pointing out that, in the first case, lacking heavy weapons, they would be powerless to withstand German Panzer divisions equipped with Tiger and Panther tanks; and in the second, that they would be even further dispersed than normal since accurate navigation at night was still a major problem. There were also squabbles over command. Browning advocated a combined corps structure, but the Americans refused to relinquish their independence and in the end it was decided to use the two American divisions on the right flank of the beachhead in support of Omar Bradley's First and George Patton's Third US Armies, and the 6th Airborne on the left in support of Sir Miles Dempsey's British Second and Henry Crerar's First Canadian Armies. A total of 23 divisions was committed to the assault, 50,000 men in the first wave building up to 200,000 by D+3. Eventually there would be over 39 divisions, some two million men, landed on the Continent.

Bill Lee's 101st 'Screaming Eagles' Division had arrived in Liverpool between August 1943 and January 1944 and begun intensive training. It now comprised the 501st, 502nd and 506th Parachute Infantry Regiments and the 328th and 401st Glider Infantry Regiments plus the 907th Glider Artillery and 326th Airborne Engineer Battalions. Unfortunately, Lee suffered a heart attack shortly after the division's arrival in the UK and Brig-Gen Maxwell D.Taylor was appointed as his replacement. He inherited a keen, fit, trained and disciplined division whose men were determined to prove themselves every bit as good as the 'All Americans'. Many of them affected Mohican-style haircuts and prior to jumping on D-Day would also put warpaint on their faces!

The 82nd, meanwhile, was shipped back from Italy to Northern Ireland in December 1943 and then moved to Leicestershire. Reuben Tucker's 504th Regiment had been left behind and took part in the battle of Anzio before itself being shipped back to the UK in April; by this time it was too weakened by losses and fatigue to participate in 'Overlord' so, like the British 1st Airborne Division, was held in reserve while recuperating. The 509th also remained in Italy to take part in the invasion of southern France in August; since Yardley's capture at Avellino, it had been commanded by Lt- Col William Yarborough, designer both of the US Airborne 'Wings' and their jump boots. To replace these two formations, Ridgway received the inexperienced 507th and 508th Parachute Infantry Regiments to join Gavin's veteran 505th and the 325th Glider Infantry Regiment, 376th Artillery Battalion and 307th Engineer Battalion. Gavin, now a Brig-Gen, was Ridgway's second in command while command of the 505th had passed to Col William Ekman.

The British 6th Airborne Division which had been formed during 1943 under Maj-Gen 'Windy' Gale consisted, after a great deal of shuffling units around, of the 3rd Parachute Brigade (8 and 9 Para plus the 1st Canadian Parachute Battalion) under Brig James Hill (the former CO of 1 Para who had been wounded in Tunisia); the 5th Parachute Brigade (7, 12 and 13 Paras) under Brig J.H.N. Poett; and the 6th Air-Landing Brigade

(1st Battalion, Royal Ulster Rifles, 2nd Battalion, Oxfordshire and Buckinghamshire Light Infantry, and 12th Battalion, the Devonshire Regiment) under Brig the Hon Hugh Kindersley. In addition there was the 'Pathfinder' 22nd Independent Parachute Company, five airborne artillery batteries, an engineer battalion, signals and headquarters troops plus the 6th Airborne Armoured Reconnaissance Regiment and Light Squadron, Royal Armoured Corps.

On 24 April the 6th Airborne had a full-scale dress rehearsal for D-Day, the whole division being air-dropped in the heart of southern England in a three-day exercise, 1st Airborne taking the part of the enemy. A couple of weeks later, on 9 May, the 101st conducted a similar exercise. There was no time for any more, for Eisenhower had set 5 June as the date for D-Day. As it happened, bad weather caused a nail-biting 24-hr delay but at last, just before midnight on the 5th, the first pathfinder aircraft took off into the blustery wet darkness.

Six Albermarles carrying 60 men of the 22nd Independent Parachute Company preceded the 3rd and 5th Brigades of 6th Airborne Division, who were to clear the ground for the following gliders. The division's objectives all lay in a rough triangle of ground bounded at its corners by Ouistreham, Cabourg and Caen, forming a 'shoulder' for 'Sword' Beach where the British 3rd Infantry and 22nd Armoured Divisions preceded by Brig the Lord Lovat's 1st Special Service (Commando) Brigade were to land from the sea. The paras had to seize the bridges over the Caen Canal and the rivers Orne and Dives, and to knock out the heavily fortified battery of four 150mm coastal guns (they actually turned out to be 75mm) at Merville which would otherwise have been in an ideal position to fire into the flank of the amphibious task force.

The pathfinders landed between 00:20 and 00:30 on 6 June, one group near Ranville, DZ for 5 Brigade's 7, 12 and 13 Para, one near Varaville, DZ for the 1st Canadian Battalion and 9 Para, the latter's task being the assault on the Merville battery, and the third near Toufreville, DZ for 8 Para. The winds from the storm which had delayed D-Day were still high and many men were blown off course, on top of which most of the Eureka beacons failed to work and one of those which did was set up in the wrong place, sending out the signal for 8 Para instead of 5 Para Brigade. Despite these mishaps, the second stage of the operation worked extremely well. This consisted of a small task force of six Horsas commanded by Maj John Howard, three assigned to the swing bridge over the Caen Canal at Bénouville and three to the corresponding bridge over the Orne east of Ranville. The gliders landed with near perfection scant yards from the bridges and men of the 2nd Ox and Bucks Light Infantry seized both objectives after a brief firefight. Neither bridge, amazingly, had been rigged for demolition. Shortly afterwards the paras captured a German officer in a staff car, who begged to be allowed to commit suicide for having let 'his' bridges fall so easily. Then the assault teams were attacked by three old French tanks — the Germans normally used these just for training and security tasks — and set one alight, which provided a marvellous rallying point for the rest of 5 Brigade whose men began dropping about half an hour later.

First on the ground was a young man called Richard Todd whose postwar career as an actor included portraying Maj Howard in Darryl F. Zanuck's famous film *The Longest Day*. Todd, then deputy adjutant of 7 Para, recalls the events of that night:

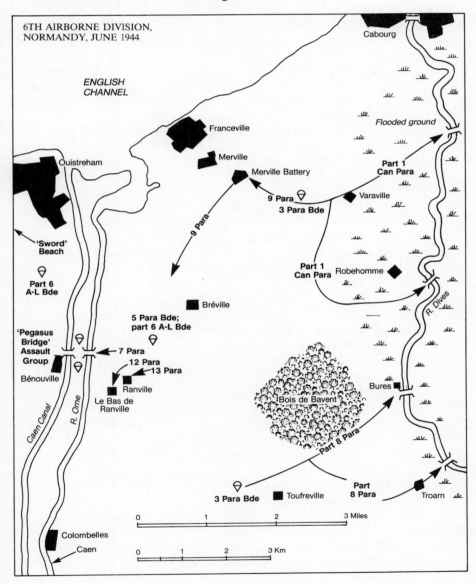

6TH AIRBORNE DIVISION, NORMANDY, JUNE 1944

'At about 23:00 on the night of 5 June we drove around the airfield perimeter, each stick of paratroopers in a three-ton truck, and each truck stopped by its numbered aircraft. Mine stopped at aircraft number 33, as that was the one I was to be in.

'The pilot and crew were lined up beside the aircraft — they shook hands and wished us luck and all the rest of it. The pilot was a very senior officer, an Air Commodore or something. He said to me quite blithely, "As I'm the senior officer going in tonight, I'm going in first, because we've got the gem crew". I thought, "Oh Christ — I'm going to be the first out of the first aircraft," but I couldn't argue because he was senior to me.

'So I got in — and that actually saved my life. I'll tell you why in a minute. I think people thought I was very cool because I fell asleep on the way — but that's a thing of mine. If I'm very worried or really down about something, my tendency is to be like an old ostrich and put my head in the sand and go to sleep.

'I was wakened up — we lined up and hooked up. The old green light came on and out we went, with me in the lead. Incidentally, it was a very big hole in the bottom of the Stirling [Short Stirling four-engined bomber], with enough room for two men to straddle it, and on the word "go" pull their legs together and drop out through the hole. The man behind me had to hang on to me because the aircraft was jinking a bit. I could easily have fallen out — in fact a few people did fall out over the sea — because I hadn't a hand to hold on with as I had kitbags on each of my legs. One kitbag was full of a rubber dinghy and the other had picks and shovels for digging in. I was having to hold these things to my legs. Out I went.

'We dropped from 400ft [122m], which didn't give you much time in the air — about seven seconds. In the flurry of all this, I let the bloody kitbag on my right side slip instead of letting it out hand over hand. That gave me a very nasty burn all down my right hand. Then I thumped down. We had got in with the element of surprise. A certain amount of light flak came up and we could see tracer floating by us — the big stuff hadn't really started, and as I was getting out of my 'chute on the ground, looking up at the other aircraft, they started getting shot down. By that time the ground defences had wakened up to what was happening and the ack-ack guns had gone into action. The aircraft round about the number 30 were the ones that all got shot down, and it was just my luck that I went in first.'

On the ground the men of Lt-Col Geoffrey Pine-Coffin's 7 Para raced to relieve Howard's advance party at the Caen Canal and Orne bridges, but losses during the drop plus the fact that the wind had scattered the battalion meant that to begin with there were a scant 200 men to defend the position, although stragglers continued to turn up throughout the night. 'A' Company occupied the village of Bénouville on the west bank of the canal, fortified against the strenuous German counter-attacks which would last 17 hours by the seemingly endless supply of bottles of champagne which the local café proprietor, Georges Gondrée, had hidden from the Germans in anticipation of the day of liberation.

The other two battalions of 5 Brigade dropped east of the Orne to seize the town of Ranville and adjacent high ground. By daylight 12 Para was well entrenched around Le Bas de Ranville and it was here that Maj J. Sim won the Military Cross. He and 12 other men had dug in behind a hedgerow when, at about 11:00, they were attacked by a strong force of *Panzergrenadiers* supported by two self-propelled guns. The Paras' 6pdr anti-tank gun had been damaged in landing and was unable to fire, so Sim let the armour pass then opened fire on the infantry. After losing about 20 men, the Germans beat a hasty retreat and Sim, his own command reduced to three men, decided to retire. There were many similar acts of courage on that fateful day, and the bridge over the Caen Canal has subsequently been christened 'Pegasus Bridge' in recognition of the paras' achievement.

No 13 Para had Ranville as its objective, its DZ just outside the town. Unfortunately, a number of men were blown off course to land within the town itself, where most were promptly killed or captured. The remainder of the battalion assembled and took the town, but for the rest of the day until reinforcements arrived from 'Sword' Beach were hard pressed by the 125th Panzergrenadier Regiment of the 21st Panzer Division, whose tough veterans at one point almost succeeded in recapturing the town. Then 6th Air-Landing Brigade's first 47 Horsas and two Hamilcars landed, each of the latter carrying a Tetrarch light tank, and the glider troops fanned out to reinforce the threatened sectors of 5 Brigade's positions. Further gliders arrived during the afternoon and early evening until 248 had made successful landings. By this time, too, Lord Lovat's commandos, preceded in legend and film by a solitary piper (although Todd told the author that this was actually 'bloody nonsense'), had reached the Caen bridge. After conferring briefly with Poett, Lord Lovat left part of his brigade to reinforce the canal and Orne bridge detachments and marched the bulk of his men west to help 12 and 13 Paras in and around Ranville. Further infantry and Sherman tanks of the 13/18th Hussars arrived shortly afterwards and occupied hull-down positions on the reverse slopes of the hills west of Ranville, looking out towards the river Dives where 8 Para and the 1st Canadian Battalion from 3 Brigade had been struggling in the flooded river plain to destroy the bridges at Varaville, Robehomme, Bures and Troarn.

These missions were accomplished with speed and panache before daybreak even though the men had been widely scattered on landing, a number of them landing in the river and flooded ground and subsequently having to rely on French guides to get them to their objectives because their maps were too waterlogged to be much help. But it was 9 Para which had the hardest task of all — the guns of Merville. This operation was directly comparable to the German seizure of Eben Emael in 1940, for the battery was deeply dug in under concrete and earth fortifications with steel doors, and lavishly protected by a strip of minefield between 40 and 100yds wide

(36–91m), extensive barbed wire, numerous machine-guns and a dual-purpose anti-aircraft/anti-personnel quick-firing 20mm cannon. Moreover, the surrounding countryside was flat and featureless, offering no cover to an assault party apart from one small orchard, while the German garrison was thought to consist of nearly 200 men (it was actually 130).

The CO of 9 Para, Lt-Col Terence Otway, realized immediately he was entrusted with this target on 2 April that the only hope of success lay in immaculate planning and training. He persuaded the powers-that-be to have a stretch of farmland near Newbury, Berkshire, transformed into an exact 1:1 scale model of the battery, local farmers being compensated by numerous drinks in the Mess. The battalion, plus supporting sappers from 591 Squadron, Royal Engineers, rehearsed the operation nine times in all, four times at night, constantly refining the plan. Secrecy had to be so absolute that military intelligence actually infiltrated a number of their best-looking and most highly trained female operatives into the area to try and get the paras to let slip what they were doing. To their credit, none succumbed to what must have been extreme temptation!

The best military plans are simple, but in this case the problems necessitated complexities which nearly proved the scheme's downfall. The main body of men would drop by parachute south of Merville, out of sight so as not to alert the defenders, while the RAF sent 86 Lancaster and 13 Halifax bombers to pound the battery. The strength of the concrete casemates can be appreciated when you understand that all this was expected to achieve was to give the Germans headaches and destroy some of the mines and barbed wire. Then, once the paras were on the ground, a force of 11 gliders would land the sappers and their heavy equipment, while another party of engineers with mine detectors would parachute in to clear and mark paths through the minefield. The main assault team would then charge the guns, supported by snipers and a diversionary attack on the main gate, while a 'kamikaze' team of 58 volunteers would crash-land three Horsas right on top of the battery itself.

The weather and problems of accurate night navigation, as usual, compounded an already complicated situation and almost caused the operation's undoing, despite the meticulous rehearsals. The flak did not help either, many of the paras being thrown willy-nilly out of the Dakota doors into the sea or the flooded banks of the Dives as their aircraft jinked on the approach. Others were blown wildly off course, and when Otway tried to assemble his 600 men on the DZ shortly before 03:00, he found he only had about 150. Otway had had a narrow escape on landing, too — right alongside a house used as a German headquarters. Numerous pistol shots missed him as he disentangled himself from his 'chute, then one quick-thinking para who landed alongside him heaved a brick through a window. The firing stopped as the Germans dived for cover from what they thought was a grenade, and the CO and his unknown companion made good a hasty exit, accompanied by Otway's batman who had landed straight through a greenhouse roof!

The situation was nasty. The RAF bombers had missed their target so the minefield and barbed wire were more or less intact. Moreover, Otway found he had none of his Jeeps, anti-tank guns or mortars, only a quarter of his snipers, none of his mine detectors, only one machine-gun and no sappers, because the gliders had all landed miles away and these troops would only begin to join up at daybreak. But Otway's own CO, Brig James Hill, had warned each man of the battalion not to 'be daunted if chaos reigns. It undoubtedly will'. Far from being daunted, Otway ordered an immediate advance. Fortunately, when he reached the outer wire perimeter of the battery, he found that a small party of sappers had managed to get there first and, lacking mine detectors or the white tapes usually used to mark paths through minefields, had gone ahead and started clearing paths using the time-honoured method of digging the mines up with their bayonets.

By this time the German machine-guns had opened up but accurate return fire quite remarkably succeeded in silencing six of the 10 within minutes and the two assault parties plus a six-man (!) diversionary team raced forward through the gaps in the wire at 04:30. Now, dead on time, two of the three gliders which were intended to land on top of the battery arrived overhead; the tow rope of one had parted on take-off and its irate crew was stranded in England. Almost inevitably, the Eureka beacon which was supposed to guide them in had been destroyed in the paras' landing, there was not a single mortar to fire a guiding flare, and the glider pilots could not see their objective through the clouds of smoke and dust raised by the RAF bombers. One landed about half a mile away, just skimming over the minefield on its approach, and the other crashed into the orchard where its surviving occupants were immediately engaged by a platoon of German infantry rushing to help in the defence of the gun battery. A four-hour firefight ensued, but the paras kept the Germans at bay while Otway and the rest of his men accomplished their task.

To their surprise, there were no steel doors, just concrete walls to deflect blast, and the assault parties charged into the battery, engaging the enemy with Sten guns, grenades and fists. It was a short, bloody encounter with no holds barred on either side, but within minutes the paras were in command of the four guns while the surviving Germans barricaded themselves into rooms further underground. Otway, having rendered the guns useless with plastic explosive and having lost 70 officers and men in the battle, beat a prudent retreat to the south with his remaining 80 and dug in to wait for stragglers to join them. Next day they were at last reinforced late in the afternoon by the arrival of some of Lord Lovat's Commandos.

Gale's 6th Airborne Division remained in the line until 26 August, repulsing fierce German counter-attacks, especially around Bréville where the 1st Canadian Battalion in particular distinguished itself, before joining in the general advance towards Le Havre and the river Seine. The division was then withdrawn into reserve and the next act would go to the revitalized 1st Airborne, now commanded by Maj-Gen Roy Urquhart following 'Dracula' Down's posting to India to take over the 44th Indian Airborne Division *(qv)*. But first, we must return to 6 June and the operations of the American 82nd and 101st Airborne Divisions in the Cotentin Peninsula.

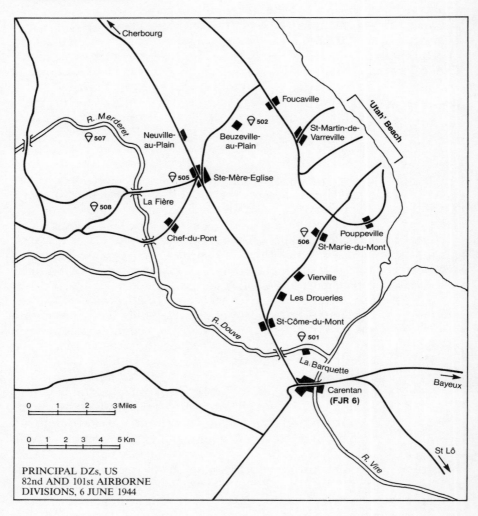

PRINCIPAL DZs, US
82nd AND 101st AIRBORNE
DIVISIONS, 6 JUNE 1944

If 6th Airborne had encountered problems with the high winds and flak scattering many of its troops miles from their objectives, the two American divisions fared even worse. Inexperienced pilots panicked and dropped the men from too great a height or at too high a speed, compounding the problem of having to dogleg around the Cotentin Peninsula to approach their DZs from the south-east instead of directly from the north-west. Few of the beacons landed with the pathfinders worked properly, and as a result an unknown number of men fell into the flooded areas along the rivers Merderet and Douve where they drowned helplessly. Others landed in trees and were unable to cut themselves free without risking a broken leg at best.

The task of the two divisions was to land in a broad triangle inland from 'Utah' Beach where the US 4th Infantry Division would come ashore at daybreak, secure the four vital causeways leading up from the beach and seize and hold road junctions and river bridges north and west of Carentan to prevent German reinforcements interfering with the amphibious assault. That they succeeded is due more to individual acts of guts, determination and initiative than to anything else although, as in the case of the British landings, indecision and confusion among the defenders helped enormously. Only one part of the whole operation actually went off as planned: the 3rd Battalion of Ekman's veteran 505th Regiment (III/505th), commanded by Lt-Col Ed Krause, landed on its correct DZ just outside Ste-Mère-Eglise. Assembling as many of his men as possible, Krause led an immediate attack on the sleepy little town whose garrison had already been alerted because about a dozen paras had landed right in the market square. They were mown down, watched with horror by Pte John Steele whose parachute had caught in the church spire. He hung there, helpless and expecting a bullet any second, until Krause's men captured the town and cut him down.

The 505th's 2nd Battalion under Lt-Col Ben Vandervoort landed close to its DZ and began advancing on Neuville-au-Plain but was then recalled by Ekman to help in the defence of Ste-Mère-Eglise, where Ridgway had established his headquarters. However, Vandervoort (who had broken a bone in his foot on landing) had the foresight to send a small party of 48 men on to Neuville, which they captured and subsequently defended for a critical four hours during which elements of the German 91st *Luftlande* Division (an air-landing division in name only) tried to break through to Ste-Mère-Eglise from the north. Only 16 'All Americans' survived when they were finally pulled back, leaving the town temporarily in German hands.

Meanwhile, Lt-Col Fred Kellam's I/505th had moved up to the bridge over the Merderet at la Fière, which they found heavily defended and were unable to take after three assaults, during one of which their CO lost his life. However, Gavin had managed to assemble an *ad hoc* formation of some 500 men from a mixture of battalions and sent them to la Fière where they finally succeeded in breaking across to the west bank of the river. Unfortunately, instead of establishing a defensive perimeter they continued to advance, hoping to link up with the 507th and 508th Regiments, most of whose personnel had landed in scattered groups west of the Merderet. The Germans brought up tanks and retook the western end of the bridge but the 505th's 1st Battalion continued to hold the east until reinforced by glider-borne troops later in the day. Even then, two attempts by the 1st and 3rd Battalions of the 325th Glider Infantry Regiment failed to retake the western bank and it was not until tanks driven up from the beaches arrived during the night of 8/9 June that the bridge finally fell. They were led by none other than Edson Raff who had now been appointed CO of the special strike force of men from the 325th with supporting tanks and artillery which landed from the sea on 6 June to advance and reinforce the 82nd as quickly as possible.

The battle for la Fière was the toughest the 82nd Airborne had to fight from D-Day to D+3, but there were many other acts of valour, the paras often fighting in small isolated groups with no idea where the rest of their battalions were. The men found each other in the darkness by clicking the toy 'crickets' they had been issued before take-off, then gradually co-alesced into larger groups by the time-honoured method of 'marching on the guns' — ie, heading towards the sounds of firefights. Col George Millet's 507th Regiment was particularly badly scattered during the drop, most of its men landing in the marshy ground west of the Merderet and losing much of their heavy kit, so few of them were able to join in the battle for la Fière (their original objective) but fought in small detachments, ambushing and harassing German patrols sent out to locate them. Millet himself was captured shortly after the drop.

Col Roy Lindquist's 508th was marginally luckier and a couple of hundred men from a mixture of battalions managed to secure the approaches to Chef-du-Pont, denying the Germans access to Ste-Mère-Eglise along the sole remaining road, until themselves relieved by infantry and armour moving up from the beachhead. It was also a patrol from the 508th which by chance ambushed a staff car during the early morning hours of D-Day and killed the commander of the 91st Division, Wilhelm Falley, the first German general to fall in France during the invasion. He had been racing back to his headquarters to try to find out exactly what was going on and his loss contributed to the lack of a positive German response during the critical first hours of the battle.

Maxwell Taylor's 'Screaming Eagles', who dropped south of the 82nd, closer to Carentan, with principal objectives the bridges and causeways over the river Douve, had an equally tough task on their hands — not least because they were opposed by Freiherr von der Heydte's FJR 6 based in Carentan. The rest of Ramcke's 2nd *Fallschirmjäger* Division was still refitting at Cologne after being withdrawn from Italy but was rushed to Brittany with all speed to defend the vital port of Brest. Meanwhile, von der Heydte's three battalions were out on a limb. 'On the first day', he recalls, 'I was on my own. I was my own boss . . . because the French Resistance had prepared well for the invasion, sabotaging the 'phone lines.

'I first saw what was happening when I arrived in St-Côme-du-Mont [a village north of Carentan in the lower bend of the river Douve]. I had come across an old church tower, had got hold of the key, and went up there to take a look out over the coast. I felt that my troops were very vulnerable with no artillery assistance. We had our heavy company with 12cm mortars. I gave the order for them to get forward quickly and fire.'

Von der Heydte noticed from his vantage point that only one of the coastal bunkers was actually firing at the Americans streaming ashore on 'Utah' Beach — one of the reasons for the light casualties here compared with at 'Omaha' where the defence was ferocious. On his way back to his command post he also spotted a bunker in the inland second line of defence which had been abandoned by its panic-stricken detachment. His paras were made of sterner stuff. He despatched II/FJR 6 to probe towards Ste-Mère-Eglise and I/FJR 6 towards Ste-Marie-du-Mont, leaving III/FJR 6 in reserve in Carentan itself. Stupidly, engineers were ordered to destroy the Douve bridges north of Carentan and when von der Heydte's two battalions in the river bend were finally forced to retire, they had to wade across the river, two men being drowned. One was a Jew, and it still comes as a surprise to many people to learn that, despite the Nazi regime's hideous excesses against them, many Jews considered themselves Germans first and fought in the armed forces under assumed identities. Von der Heydte recalls, 'I had two Jews in my regiment. Both used false names. One was the nephew of Albert Schweitzer and the other was the son of a German aristocrat whose mother was Jewish.' (Himself a scion of an aristocratic Prussian family, von der Heydte was an anti-Nazi who had already taken part in one conspiracy to get rid of Hitler, although he was not a party to the 20 July bomb plot which failed so tragically.)

Like the 82nd, the men of the 101st were widely dispersed on landing between the coast and the flooded Douve. Col George Van Horn Mosely's 502nd Regiment was entrusted with clearing the German defences around St-Martin-de-Varreville and securing causeways leading up from the beaches for the 4th Infantry Division. The were luckier than many and soon assembled in reasonable strength, the 2nd Battalion entering the town without difficulty and finding to their surprise that the coastal gun battery overlooking the beach was deserted. The 1st Battalion headed inland to the tiny village of le Mézieres where the German gun crews had their barracks. A small party of 15 men led by S/Sgt Harrison Summers flushed the Germans house to house, killing 15 of them as they sat down to breakfast and others as they tried to flee from buildings set alight by bazooka rounds and grenades. Over 100 Germans died in the carnage, which Summers later said so sickened him that he hoped he would never have to do anything like it again. Then, at about 04:00, they were relieved by men of the 4th Infantry pressing inland, and were able to take a break for a cigarette. The 3rd Battalion, meanwhile, had dropped way off course in the 82nd sector near Ste-Mère-Eglise but its CO, Lt-Col Robert Cole, rallied some 250 men and hurried east through the night to secure two of the causeways, the Americans fighting their way through groups of retreating Germans to find their objectives deserted. They were the first airborne troops to welcome ashore the infantrymen of the 4th Division.

To their south, Gen Taylor had landed in the 501st Regiment's DZ just outside Ste-Marie-du-Mont and, together with his artillery commander, Brig-Gen Anthony McAuliffe, and regimental CO Col Howard Johnson, assembled as may men as possible and began advancing towards Vierville, where it was not long before they bumped into their opposite numbers from FJR 6. Lt-Col Julian Ewell's 3rd Battalion was sent east to clear the path off the beach at Pouppeville, and met up with Cole's troops there. The 2nd Battalion was too dispersed to play any significant part in operations although a small group under its CO, Lt-Col Robert Strayer, also moved on Pouppeville to join up with the 3rd Battalion. The I/501st, commanded personally by Howard Johnson as its own commander, Lt-Col Robert Carrol, had been killed within moments of landing, pushed south to the 'knee' of the Douve where they were to capture a lock at La Barquette, on the right flank of III/506th. This was heavily defended by infantry supported by 88mm guns because von der Heydte had pinpointed the plain east of St-Côme-du-Mont as a likely DZ for paratroopers and had prepared accordingly. The lock was only taken after Johnson called down naval gunfire support from the cruiser USS *Quincy*.

However, it was Col Robert Sink's 506th Regiment which had the worst of it on D-Day, despite having had a personal visit from Gen Eisenhower just before they took off. The 1st Battalion had dropped in a scattered pattern near Foucaville and Beuzeville-au-Plain at the northern end of 'Utah' Beach, and found both towns vigorously defended. However, after a short, fierce firefight through the streets they took the first objective but were pinned down in the tiny village of Haut Fournel on the road to the second until relieved by infantry off the beaches. The 2nd Battalion had landed off course near Ste-Mère-Eglise and had to march over 20 miles (32km) to join up with the headquarters company near Ste-Marie-du-Mont, then had to fight its way through the *Fallschirmjäger* in les Droueries in a three-hour gun battle on the way towards St-Côme-du-Mont.

Finally, the III/506th as we have seen had landed north of the Douve and east of St-Côme-du-Mont, its objectives two wooden bridges. They came under immediate heavy machine-gun and artillery fire, the CO, Lt-Col Robert Wolverton, being killed almost immediately. The DZ was illuminated by roaring flames from barns which the Germans had soaked in petrol, the silhouetted paras making ideal targets for the *Fallschirmjäger* machine-gunners as they struggled to extricate themselves from their 'chutes. Only five officers and 29 men reached their objectives, although they were later joined by stragglers and held on until sappers arrived to blow the bridges. Ptes Zahn and Montilio both received field promotions and Distinguished Service Crosses for their courage and leadership under such nearly impossible circumstances.

American glider operations during the course of D-Day were a shambles. The German anti-aircraft defences were fully alerted and many aircraft in the first wave at 04:00 were shot down. The gliders were thrown wildly off course, only 37 finding LZ west in the 82nd sector and 38 LZ east in the 101st's out of over 100 despatched. Of these, the majority crashed either in the marshes, against the thick hedgerows and farm walls or against the stakes (known as 'Rommel's asparagus'!) which the Germans had driven into the open fields against exactly such an airborne invasion. Many of these stakes were capped with mines and linked together with barbed wire to cause further destruction.

Fortunately, casualties were remarkably light although a grievous loss was Brig-Gen Donald Pratt, Maxwell Taylor's second in command, but much of the heavy equipment, particularly Jeeps and artillery pieces, was lost. The second wave of gliders in the evening of D-Day was luckier, partly because by this time the paras and the 4th Infantry Division had more or less complete command of the ground and had cleared the stakes from the LZs, partly because many of them landed away from where fighting was still going on, and partly because fighters accompanying the gliders in the twilight helped suppress anti-aircraft fire. This was particularly fierce around Neuville-au-Plain but, although 62 out of 100 Haigs and Horsas were write-offs and over 200 men were killed, this time most of the guns and vehicles were saved. And next morning, D+1, a third wave of gliders brought in the remaining 2,000 men of the Glider Infantry Regiments almost without incident.

This ended the airborne part of D-Day, but the 82nd and 101st remained in the line until 8 July, their principal opponents being Ramcke's 2nd *Fallschirmjäger* Division who eventually inflicted some 4,000 casualties on them. Carentan was determinedly defended by von der Heydte until late in the evening of 10 June, when he was forced to evacuate to the south-west, joining up with the 17th Waffen-SS Panzergrenadier Division *'Götz von Berlichingen'*. By the time FJR 6 was pulled out of the line in August, von der Heydte had only 40 men unwounded. The remainder of Ramcke's division was gradually forced back into Brest, where it held out against Patton's Third Army until 19/20 September. For this achievement Ramcke was awarded Germany's highest decoration — the Knights Cross with Oakleaves, Swords and Diamonds. He was the only member of the *Fallschirmjäger* to receive this distinction and, appropriately, Hitler personally ordered the medal to be dropped into the fortress for him — by parachute, of course. By this time another airborne battle was raging in Holland, but before looking at operation 'Market Garden' we must return momentarily to the shores of the Mediterranean.

Operation 'Dragoon', as the Allied landing in southern France in August 1944 was codenamed, is an operation which caused controversy at the time and continues to do so among historians today. Whether one takes the British view that it was a total waste of time and that an invasion of Greece would have served a more useful purpose, or the American view that it both distracted Hitler and tied down German troops which could otherwise have been used in north-west Europe, is really immaterial. Eisenhower wanted a major port through which to funnel troops from the States and since the early capture of a large Channel port seemed unlikely,

President Franklin D. Roosevelt pressed Churchill to accept the importance of seizing Toulon and Marseilles as speedily as possible after D-Day. The operation, originally codenamed 'Anvil', was at one point scheduled for April, but the slow rate of progress in Italy made this impossible. Then it was proposed that the invasion of the French Rivera should take place at the same time as that of Normandy, but this was equally impossible because there were insufficient troopships and landing craft to go around. But once Rome fell and the Allies were ashore in northern France, the operation did at last become practical and planning started in earnest. For the airborne forces, it would be the most successful drop yet.

To support Lt-Gen Alexander Patch's Seventh Army (US VI Corps and French II Corps), a combined Anglo-American parachute and glider force was formed from airborne units in Italy. Commanded by US Maj-Gen Robert T. Frederick, the 1st Airborne Task Force, as it was called, incorporated Brig C.H.V. Pritchard's British 2nd Independent Parachute Brigade (originally, it will be remembered, a component of the 1st Airborne Division), Yarborough's 509th Parachute Infantry Battalion, the 1st Battalion of the 551st, the 517th Combat Team, 463rd Parachute Artillery Battalion and the 550th Glider Infantry Battalion; the 442nd Combat Team of American-born Japanese troops which had established a formidable reputation in Italy was attached to the glider force and began rigorous training at an airfield outside Rome. 2 Para Brigade was the sole and rather begrudged British contribution to the land forces although the RAF and Navy were actively involved and, indeed, Mr Churchill himself watched the landings from a warship (although he soon became bored with the lack of action and retired to his cabin).

German defences in the area were weak because the principal Panzer and Panzergrenadier divisions which had been stationed in the south of France had been sent to Normandy, leaving just seven second-rate infantry divisions and the understrength 11th Panzer Division which was recuperating from its ghastly experiences on the Russian Front. Moreover, the Ninth Army commander, Gen Friedrich Weise, was not expecting an attack because the Germans had failed to detect the troop build-up in North Africa while the assembly of ships in Italian ports was regarded as a prelude to an invasion in the Balkans, Churchill's predilection in this part of the world being well known. Thus, when the Allies stormed ashore around St Tropez on 15 August, the Free French spilling left to take Toulon and Marseilles and the Americans inland up Route 6 and the Route Napoleon towards Dijon and the Swiss border, they met hardly any resistance.

Before the naval force arrived by a deliberately misleading route though, the 1st Airborne Task Force had taken off from 10 airfields in Italy at daybreak and arrived over the beaches at 07:00. As a diversion, slightly earlier a formation of six aircraft, scattering 'chaff' (then known as 'window') to confuse the German radar operators and persuade them the force was far larger, had dropped 600 dummy parachutists on a DZ some miles away — the first time such a trick had been used. Unfortunately, although pathfinders (led by Dan DeLeo, who had headed the team dropped to capture the El Djem bridge in Tunisia) had set up a Eureka beacon successfully in the pre-dawn darkness, this time it was the Rebecca receiver in the lead aircraft which failed, and early morning haze obscured any landmarks. The division's task was to drop some 15 miles (24km) inland near Le Muy to block Route 6 against German intervention on the beachhead, and despite the navigation problem over half the men hit the DZ, Gen Frederick himself landing by pure chance within 15yds (14m) of the beacon.

Other men were scattered in the unusually high 1,400ft (433m) drop necessitated by the height of the hills inland from the beaches, some landing in the middle of St Tropez itself where they quickly linked up with French Resistance *maquis* fighters and overwhelmed the startled German garrison at 07:00, two hours before the US 3rd Division stormed ashore and secured the town. Other groups landed up to 20 miles (32km) from Le Muy and had to walk back in the scorching heat; fortunately, many paras managed to take German prisoners from farmhouses used as billets and men who had been soldiers in the *Wehrmacht* minutes earlier suddenly found themselves acting as involuntary unpaid porters for the US Army! The paras dug themselves in around Le Muy, reinforced by the follow-up gliders carrying Jeeps and anti-tank guns, and waited for a counter-attack which never came because Weise, realizing the futility of even attempting to stop the Allies coming ashore, had withdrawn his divisions away from the coast. When they were relieved by the US 36th Infantry Division on the 17th, Frederick's men had hardly fired a shot. But they had served their purpose.

After this, the British 2nd Independent Parachute Brigade returned to Italy while the Americans liberated Cannes and then fought on as line infantry advancing right up to the Italian frontier in the Maritime Alps. The Task Force was disbanded shortly before Christmas 1944 and its components distributed among other divisions.

This was not quite the end of operations in the Mediterranean, however. From August 1944, quite apart from the problems they had in France, the Germans were facing a significant defeat in the Balkans where their half-hearted allies Romania, quickly followed by Bulgaria, collapsed in the face of the Russian onslaught and promptly changed sides. The bulk of the German forces which had been in Romania and had not either been killed or captured, retired into Hungary, leaving Field Marshal Maximilian Freiherr von Weich's and Col-Gen Alexander Löhr's Army Groups E and F in Yugoslavia and Greece in a difficult situation to say the least. By early October, with Russian and 'converted' Bulgarian troops moving into Yugoslavia to link up with Tito's partisans, the last German troops were evacuating mainland Greece (leaving garrisons totalling about 20,000 men on various islands, including Crete). Churchill was anxious to prevent Greece falling into the Russian sphere of influence so, on 12 October — just a week before Weichs evacuated the Yugoslav capital of Belgrade — leading elements of Pritchard's 2nd Independent Parachute Brigade (pathfinders from 4 Para) dropped on Megara airfield west of Athens as the spearhead of a new British expeditionary force. Luckily, there was no opposition because the rest of the brigade was prevented by bad weather from following until two days later, but 4, 5 and 6 Para marched into Athens on the 15th and took over all the best hotels which had so recently been evacuated by the Germans!

For the next month, reinforced by the line infantry and armoured units landed from the sea, the brigade fulfilled a dual role, harassing the last retreating Germans into Yugoslavia and trying to maintain peace between the various factions who wanted to take control of the postwar Greek government. The strongest of these was the communist-inspired Greek National Liberation Army (ELAS) partisans who had been largely ineffectual against the Germans but whose 40,000 members had now armed themselves with German weapons in an exchange deal whereby they had agreed not to molest the retreating *Wehrmacht* forces. At the beginning of December ELAS troops moved in on Athens with the objective of overthrowing George Papandreou's democratic coalition government, but British forces including the 2nd Independent Parachute Brigade held the city centre. Fierce house-to-house fighting continued until the middle of January, by which time ELAS had been destroyed as an effective fighting force and the Varkiza Agreement had imposed an uneasy truce. Even though the Greek Civil War would drag on until 1949, the communist powerbase had been broken and Pritchard's brigade was withdrawn to Italy again in February 1945 where it remained for the duration of the European war before being sent out to Palestine in October after a brief respite back in 'Blighty'. In the postwar world, peacekeeping would become a major and greatly unloved task for the airborne forces of many nations.

When the Allies finally broke out of the Normandy beachhead, the Americans around Avranches and St Lô (operation 'Cobra') and the British and Canadians, after several abortive attempts, at Caen (operation 'Spring'), they encircled tens of thousands of German troops in a pocket around Falaise in which the cream of the Army and SS Panzer divisions were annihilated by rocket-firing Typhoon and Thunderbolt fighter-bombers. Even while Patch's Seventh Army was streaming ashore on the Riviera the last act of this battle was being played out and suddenly, by late August, the German collapse in north-west France was virtually complete, although reinforced garrisons in the vital Channel ports like Brest would continue to hold out for several weeks. The unexpected speed of the final victory in Normandy took the Allies off balance and they lurched forward into a virtual vacuum which shortly began to create its own unexpected problems because the alacrity of the advance — the

Americans fanning out generally east towards the German border and British and Canadians north towards Holland — soon meant that supply lines were outstripped. This slowed and eventually halted the advance until ports could be captured (particularly Antwerp and the river Scheldt estuaries) so that supplies — and, indeed, sufficient trucks to transport them — could once again be got moving. It was in this atmosphere that operation 'Market Garden' was conceived: the most audacious and at the same time the most ill-fated of all Allied airborne operations.

By this time too there had been substantial reorganization of the American and British airborne forces, for on 20 June Eisenhower had authorized the formation of the First Allied Airborne Army. Overall commander was US Lt-Gen Lewis H. Brereton, a former friend of 'Billy' Mitchell and dedicated advocate of airborne forces since the First World War. The new Army was divided into two corps; I (Br) Airborne Corps under 'Boy' Browning and XVIII (US) Airborne Corps under Matthew Ridgway. The British corps consisted of Roy Urquhart's 1st and Richard Gale's 6th Airborne Divisions, the 1st Polish Independent Parachute Brigade under Maj-Gen Stanislaw Sosabowski and Brig Roderick McLeod's 1st Special Air Service Brigade. To these was attached the 52nd (Lowland) Division which was training in the air-landing role.

With Ridgway's promotion to corps commander, James Gavin assumed command of the US 82nd Airborne Division while Maxwell Taylor remained in charge of the 101st. XVIII Corps also included the new US 17th Airborne Division which had arrived in England during July/August. Originally created around the 513th Parachute and 193rd and 194th Glider Infantry Regiments at Fort Mackall in North Carolina, it now included the veteran 507th Parachute Infantry Regiment (commanded since George Millet's capture by Edson Raff) because Tucker's 504th had rejoined the 82nd after the D-Day operations. The 17th 'Thunder from heaven' or 'Golden Talon' Division was commanded by Maj-Gen William M. Miley. (Fort Mackall, incidentally, was originally known as Camp Hoffman but had been renamed in honour of Pte John 'Tommy' Mackall, fatally wounded during the 509th Battalion's first operation in Tunisia.) XVIII Corps would later incorporate a fourth American division, the 13th Airborne. However, only three of the original divisions would take part in operation 'Market Garden': Gavin's, Taylor's and Urquhart's, plus Sosabowski's valiant Poles.

The basic plan was Montgomery's which still causes surprise because he is better remembered for his meticulous planning and caution than for taking risks, and even though Eisenhower himself was being quietly admonished at the time for not prosecuting the war vigorously enough, he did not accept the bold scheme without misgivings. He had deliberately operated a 'broad front' policy, driving towards the German frontier at all points rather than accepting Monty's earlier suggestion that the whole weight of his own and Bradley's Army Groups should be thrown in a left hook through Holland, crossing the Rhine while the defenders were still disorganized, bypassing the Siegfried Line (known to the Germans as the West Wall) and heading straight into the Ruhr, Germany's industrial heartland. Moreover, Patton's Third Army was making good progress and this would have to be halted if his transport aircraft were withdrawn for an airborne operation.

Eisenhower at this point was juggling eggs. He and Omar Bradley placed more reliance on Patton's success in the Saar (even though this was being held up early in September by stiffening German resistance as well as by supply problems) than on Montgomery's 'pencil-like thrust' which would, if successful, open a narrow salient through Holland and across the Neder Rijn (Lower Rhine) into the Ruhr. But re-opening Antwerp was also a major priority, while 'Ike' was under extra pressure from Churchill to clear the German V2 rocket sites out of Holland (the first of these ballistic missiles had hit Chiswick in London on 8 September). Reluctantly, therefore, on 10 September the Allied supreme commander agreed to give 'limited priority' to Montgomery's scheme. If he had given it greater priority the plan *might* have worked, but he could not completely denude Patton of support with the result that there were insufficient transport aircraft to carry three full airborne divisions in a single wave. Moreover, priority in their assignment was given to the two American divisions, leaving Roy Urquhart, whose men had the most difficult task, no option other than to fly in his division and Sosabowski's Poles in three consecutive waves, diminishing their impact. This decision should not, however, be misunderstood as it sometimes is, as American favouritism at British expense, since it was essential that the two US divisions should seize their objectives with the utmost speed so that ground forces could get through to Arnhem before the British and Poles were overwhelmed and the whole operation negated.

The basic plan was simple: to use the three airborne divisions to seize key bridges along the most direct route from the Belgian border to the other side of the Rhine and lay a 'carpet' along which Gen Brian Horrocks' XXX Corps, spearheaded by the Guards Armoured Division, could race into Germany. Southernmost of the objectives were two bridges over the Wilhelmina Canal just north of Eindhoven at Son and one over the Zuid Willemsvaart Canal some 10 miles (16km) further up the road at Veghel. Beyond these were three bridges over the river Maas at Grave and the Maas-Waal Canal and River Waal either side of Nijmegen. Finally, some 64 miles (102km) behind German lines, was the metal girder road bridge over the Neder Rijn at Arnhem. The first objective was assigned to Maxwell Taylor's 101st, the second to Jim Gavin's 82nd and the third to Roy Urquhart's 1st Airborne plus Sosabowski's Poles.

It seems almost presumptuous to retail the Arnhem epic since I imagine that just about every reader of this book will at least have seen Joseph E. Levine's film based upon Cornelius Ryan's book *A Bridge Too Far,* even if they have not read the book itself. The film does, however, contain a number of errors of interpretation, bias and fact — partly due undoubtedly to the constraints of having to tell a complicated story in a reasonable length of time with the emphasis on 'action', but still with unnecessary alterations to history. This has resulted in particular in both Lt-Gen 'Boy' Browning and German Field Marshal Walther Model being portrayed very unfairly in the public imagination — flaws which I hope the following will correct.

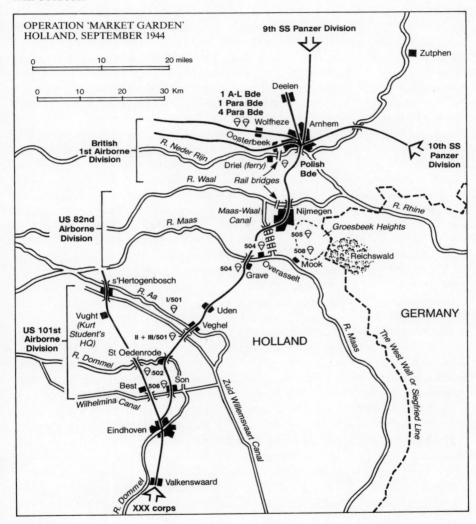

Lewis Brereton, overall commander of the First Airborne Army (who does not even figure in the film), was a flier, a First World War combat veteran who since Pearl Harbor had seen all his action in the Far East as a B-17 Flying Fortress bomber leader, and who had no real experience of warfare on the ground. This is why Browning, the Grenadier Guards officer, was made his deputy and given overall responsibility for planning the operation. The fact that Browning disliked Brereton or that Gavin disliked Browning are personality clashes which have been exaggerated and in no way diminish the effort that all involved put into the operation, despite the misgivings they shared. One of these was the fact that it was to be a daylight operation, like the invasions of Crete and the south of France (a point about which the film is deliberately misleading), because the lessons of Sicily and Normandy had revealed the hazards of night-time drops and American transport pilots still lacked experience in this type of operation — a critical factor especially since there would be no moon. However, it was intended that aerial supremacy in terms of fighters and tactical strike aircraft would, as on Crete or in Normandy, prevent the enemy launching an effective counterstrike. Unfortunately the RAF and USAAF were by this stage of the war too firmly committed to providing escort fighters for the strategic bombing offensive over Germany to spare more than token support for the airborne forces, with the result that Field Marshal Model was able to move his own forces in daylight without interference — something unheard of since D-Day.

In the film Model is depicted as believing the airborne assault was specifically designed to kill or capture him, the credit for the rapid German response being given to Obergruppenführer (Waffen-SS General) Wilhelm 'Willi' Bittrich. In fact it was Model, C-in-C of Army Group B, who, having his headquarters at Oosterbeek only a couple of miles outside Arnhem, was more than any other individual responsible for the speed of the German response to the threat. No slouch at the best of times (although the failure of operation *'Zitadelle'* in July 1943 is often rather unjustifiably laid at his door), Model was a tough, decisive leader who had earned himself the nickname 'the Führer's fireman' on the Eastern Front. Indeed, following Günther von Kluge's suicide in August after the disaster at Falaise, Model had temporarily been given overall command of all German troops in the west before Field Marshal Gerd von Rundstedt was persuaded to come out of retirement to take over this onerous duty. Moreover, one does not use an entire division to capture or kill a single man, no matter how skilled and dangerous an adversary! And, in point of fact, Allied intelligence was unaware of his presence in the vicinity — it was *not* detected by a 14-year-old member of the Dutch Resistance on a bicycle . . .

On one point the film is correct. Browning did choose to ignore the warning of his chief intelligence officer, Maj Brian Urquhart (who is mysteriously given the name 'Fuller' in the film, presumably to prevent the confusion which might arise from two characters sharing the same surname even if they were not directly related), that the crack 9th and 10th Waffen-SS Panzer Divisions *'Hohenstaufen'* and *'Frundsberg'* were refitting at Zutphen and Ruurlo, a mere 20-odd miles (32km) from Arnhem. Although greatly understrength after the mauling they had taken in Normandy, these two formations contained some of the toughest, most skilled and best-equipped troops in the German armed forces and the speed with which they were able to react was a major contributory factor in the ultimate failure of the plan.

Consideration *was* briefly given to employing a fourth airborne division — either the British 6th or the US 17th — to help counteract this threat. But by the time it was acknowledged 48 hours before the operation — planned with breakneck speed for 17 September — it was too late to activate a new formation even if sufficient aircraft had been available. Urquhart's 1st Airborne was therefore deliberately left out on a limb with the glib assurance that 'Jorrocks' XXX Corps would be in Arnhem within two to four days. However, the canny Scotsman, although new to airborne warfare, had seen the problems ground forces had encountered linking up with the paras in earlier operations and planned to hold out for six. In the event, even this was not enough.

One other old chestnut must be laid to rest. Browning is generally reported as having told Montgomery that he feared 'we may be going one bridge too far'. In fact it was Gen Sir Miles Dempsey, not Montgomery, who briefed Browning, so if the remark was made at all it would have been to him. Moreover, although the phrase appears prophetic, it would have been a strange thing for Browning to have said because if the bridge over the Rhine at Arnhem was not captured, the whole exercise would have been pointless. History is full of such pitfalls for the unwary, things which are believed simply because they have been repeated so often.

The operation began with a final short briefing to go over any last queries at Browning's First Allied Airborne Army headquarters at 19:00 on Saturday, 16 September. By this time an enormous armada of 1,545 transport aircraft and 478 gliders under the auspices of the 9th Troop Carrier Command, USAAF, and No 38 Group, RAF, had been assembled at 24 airfields stretching from the West Country to East Anglia — a larger force than had been assembled for D-Day. No 38 Group had expressed its willingness to transport the two British parachute brigades (Lathbury's 1st and Hackett's 4th) plus Hicks' air-landing brigade on day one, taking off in darkness, making the first drop at dawn, then returning to pick up the remainder of the division, leaving just the Polish brigade to go in on day two. This plan was vetoed, partly because of American fears of navigational problems on a moonless night and partly because of the logistical problems of servicing, refuelling and in some cases repairing aircraft for a return trip in such a short span of time.

The result was that only Lathbury's and Hicks' men would land on Sunday, the intention being to reinforce with Hackett's on Monday and Sosabowski's on Tuesday, after which the 52nd (Lowland) Division would be landed at Deelen airfield north of Arnhem to clinch the operation. Spreading the Anglo–Polish effort over this extended schedule had the same effect as sending reserves in to a conventional land battle in dribs and drabs: instead of a decisive *coup de main* the effort was dissipated, giving Model time to throw overwhelming force into the bridgehead. By this stage of the war it should have been realized that an airborne assault can only succeed given the advantages of shock and speed, but at Arnhem these were thrown away.

On top of this, the nature of the terrain around Arnhem plus fears of heavy flak restricted the choice of principal dropping and landing zones to areas well west of the town, meaning that the first troops on the ground would have to cover some eight miles (13km) in order to reach the bridge. This was completely against Jim Gavin's oft-quoted maxim that it is better for airborne troops to take casualties landing on the right objective than to have to fight their way to the target area. It also gave Model — who was drinking a pre-prandial aperitif as the waves of C-47s passed overhead — time to organize an effective defence. He knew his strongest forces were the two armoured divisions of Bittrich's II SS Panzer Korps and, unable to reach their headquarters on the telephone, immediately set out to drive there. He was not in the panic usually portrayed, merely in a hurry because he knew the bulk of the Waffen-SS tanks and assault guns had already been loaded on to railway flatcars to be sent east to help contain Patton, and it would take time to offload them. Bittrich, having received confused radio messages about airborne landings at Arnhem and Nijmegen and unable to get through to Model or Student, had already ordered his two divisions to get ready for immediate action.

The British situation, meanwhile, was further complicated by the fact that Tony Deane-Drummond (of Monte Vulture fame, and now Urquhart's second in command, signals, after his escape from PoW camp) rightfully questioned the reliability of the radios with which the troops, advancing by three separate routes into Arnhem, would keep in touch with each other. As it happened only one battalion, John Frost's 2 Para, would actually reach the bridge.

To avoid aerial congestion on the approach, two air lanes were selected: a southerly one for Taylor's 101st leaving England over North Foreland, passing over Belgium to the Dutch border and then following the road which Horrocks' XXX Corps would take to Eindhoven; and a northerly one exiting the coast at Aldeburgh and heading directly for the Dutch shoreline at Schouwen then on to s'Hertogenbosch, at which point the 1st and 82nd would diverge to their respective targets at Arnhem, Grave and Nijmegen.

The first aircraft carrying the Pathfinder teams which would mark out the DZs and LZs began taking off at 09:45 on Sunday 17 September, followed half an hour later by the C-47s, Stirlings and Halifaxes towing the gliders of Hicks' 1st Air-Landing Brigade. (At least this time, Hicks mused, remembering Sicily, he would not have to swim ashore!) They were themselves followed by Lathbury's 1st Para Brigade then, once all the British 'planes were off the ground, the 82nd and 101st quickly took off. All over southern and eastern England, where special services were being conducted to commemorate victory in the Battle of Britain four years earlier, churchgoers rushed outside to watch as the mighty streams of aircraft rumbled overhead.

Another interested witness was Gen Kurt Student, now commander of the First Parachute Army through which Horrocks' men would have to fight. From his headquarters only seven miles from Eindhoven, he watched the incredible sight as thousands of 'Screaming Eagles' descended around the town. His 'Army' was an army in name only, its only veteran component being von der Heydte's 6th *Fallschirmjäger* Regiment; the remainder consisted of five understrength regiments and a few smaller units whose men had little or no combat experience, and Student understandably remarked rather bitterly to his chief of staff 'Oh what I might have accomplished if only I had such a force at my disposal' ('Wenn ich jemals so mächtige Mittel zur Verfügung gehobt Lätte . . .'). But he spent little time in idle recrimination and immediately sped to see where he could best deploy what troops he had.

The 101st Airborne had encountered heavy flak on its approach but, mercifully, casualties were light. Col Howard Johnson's 501st Parachute Infantry Regiment dropped either side of Veghel and rapidly seized their two assigned bridges over the Zuid Wilhelmsvaart Canal and the river Aa before throwing out a defensive perimeter against counter-attack. Further south, Col John Michaelis' 502nd landed between St Oedenrode and Best. The 1st Battalion promptly seized the bridge over the river Dommel at the former village, killing 20 Germans and capturing 58, while a single company of the regiment was ordered to head for the secondary target of the bridge over the Wilhelmina Canal south of Best. However, here they were held up by determined German resistance and were not able to fight their way through to the bridge until reinforced the following morning, at which point German sappers blew it up.

This was a serious blow because Col Robert Sink's 506th, entrusted with the second and more important bridge over the same canal at Son, had also been delayed by the unexpected fierceness of the German response and sappers had blown that bridge too. However, he managed to collect a small fleet of local boats and ferried some of his men south across the canal to create a bridgehead while sappers hurriedly built a footbridge over which the remainder could follow. Because of the delays he was unfortunately unable to enter Eindhoven before darkness fell so had to dig in for the night. At this stage the whole operation seemed in jeopardy, for unless the four bridges over the Dommel in Eindhoven were captured quickly, XXX Corps would be stopped in its tracks.

As it was, Horrocks, who had ordered his advance to start at 14:15, had failed in his objective of reaching Eindhoven by Sunday evening. His Guards Armoured Division, spearheaded by Lt-Col Joe Vandeleur's Irish Guards Group, had been badly battered by accurate *Fallschirmjäger* anti-tank gunnery and was held up some six miles (10km) south of the town. XXX Corps consisted of some 20,000 vehicles which took up 30 miles (48km) of road — just one road, and not a very wide one either, with the ground to each side too soft for armoured vehicles to manoeuvre on. This was the weakest link in the whole plan and, again, one would have thought the earlier lessons of ground forces failing to link up with the airborne units on schedule would have been studied harder.

Gavin's 'All Americans' had a much more difficult task than Taylor's 'Eagles' for they had to seize and hold more widely dispersed objectives — the enormous nine-span bridge over the Maas near Grave, four road and rail bridges over the Maas-Waal Canal and then the road and rail bridges over the Waal itself on the north side of Nijmegen. In addition they had to capture the Groesbeek Heights, the highest ground in Holland, overlooking the German border and the Reichswald Forest, not only to guard against a counter-attack on their eastern flank but also to secure suitable LZs and DZs for the following aircraft which would bring in their artillery. The 75mm Pack howitzers plus ammunition and crews would arrive first, all dropped by parachute; the rest of the artillery would arrive shortly afterwards by glider. It was on these heights, too, that Browning had decided to establish his field headquarters because radio communications would be enhanced over longer distances. He was flown in a glider piloted once again by the intrepid George Chatterton and landed under fire right at the edge of the Reichswald; both men escaped unscathed.

The 82nd's C-47s flew in through heavy flak, but again without serious losses. The XVIII Corps commander, Matthew Ridgway, rode as an observer in one aircraft to watch 'his' boys perform, and was gratifyingly impressed. The first part of the operation went off to perfection. One company of Reuben Tucker's 504th Parachute Infantry Regiment dropped south-west of the Maas outside Grave, advanced straight on the bridge, took out the German flak tower with two well-aimed bazooka rounds, and shortly afterwards linked up with the rest of the regiment which had dropped on the north bank of the river near Overasselt. That night some of the Americans ventured into Grave, which was still occupied by Germans and, completely unmolested, occupied an inn; the sound of their singing, which lasted until the early hours, could be heard from the bridge! Why the Germans — who were, admittedly, in the process of pulling out — did not interfere remains a mystery.

The rest of the 504th was less lucky. They had four bridges to capture over the Maas-Waal Canal of which the most important, that on the main road from Eindhoven to Nijmegen, was furthest from their DZ. One company from the 1st Battalion headed for the southernmost of the four bridges, which was important because it was known to be strong enough to carry tanks. Here they ran into trouble because a German garrison guarding a powerhouse on an island in the middle of the canal was able to pour heavy fire on the bridge, and only three men succeeded in getting across unwounded before dusk fell. After that the Americans managed to secure both banks and could enfilade the Germans with machine-gun fire and rifle grenades. At 23:00 they surrendered and the bridge, intact, was safely in Allied hands. This was particularly fortunate because the Germans blew up the two intermediate bridges over the canal and put up such a fierce fight for the main road bridge that, although this was captured, it was too badly damaged to support armour.

Meanwhile, William Ekman's 505th — Gavin's original command — had landed on the Groesbeek Heights, many of the men deliberately steering their 'chutes towards German flak positions which they promptly attacked, and secured the village of the same name before setting up defensive positions facing the Reichswald. Robert Lindquist's 508th had also landed on the heights and he promptly despatched part of his 1st Battalion to help the 504th in the capture of the canal bridges, one of which was blown up just as they reached it. His regiment's main task, though, was to take the main road bridge over the Waal on the other side of Nijmegen and as dusk fell Lindquist despatched the remainder of Lt-Col Shield Warren's 1st Battalion on a reconnaissance mission to assess how strongly the bridge was defended.

Guided by Dutch Resistance fighters, they destroyed the electrical detonators linked to the demolition charges on the bridge, little knowing that Model had ordered the bridge held in preparation for a counter-attack, not destroyed, and that its far end was already held by Hauptsturmführer (Captain) Paul Gräbner's reconnaissance battalion from the 10th SS Panzer Division *'Frundsberg'*. Bittrich had urgently sent this on ahead of the rest of the division while waiting for the return of its commander, Brigadeführer (equivalent to Lt-Gen in the British Army or Maj-Gen in the American) Heinz Harmel, who was driving furiously back from Berlin after receiving news of the Allied landings.

Model knew that the Nijmegen bridge was the crucial one. Dutch defenders had held up the German advance here for the best part of three days in 1940 and he was certain — rightly as it turned out — that the 10th SS Panzer Division could better this. Thus, even when Lindquist reinforced Warren's battalion with Lt-Col Louis Mendez's 3rd, they were unable to make any headway, while Gavin on D+1 was more concerned with defending his glider landing zones on the Groesbeek Heights than with making a concerted effort to take the bridge. This, as it turned out, was a mistake.

Meanwhile, at Arnhem itself men of the 21st Independent Parachute Company had landed at 12:40 on the 17th to mark out the landing zones for Hicks' gliders, which began arriving north of the railway line 20 minutes later. There was little opposition and Lathbury's 1 Para Brigade also made a successful drop south of the line an hour afterwards. So far, so good, and the battalions formed up rapidly in good order. Urquhart entrusted the main assault to Lathbury's brigade, leaving the bulk of Hicks' with the secondary but still important task of defending the dropping zone on which 'Shan' Hackett's 4 Para Brigade would land next day. The men set off in good spirits in three columns. John Frost's 2 Para had the most direct, southerly route, codenamed 'Lion', skirting Oosterbeek into Arnhem along the northern bank of the Neder Rijn. On his left Lt-Col F.A. Fitch's 3 Para's 'Tiger' route took them through the centre of Oosterbeek while Lt-Col David Dobie's 1 Para had the northern-most approach, 'Leopard' route, skirting Oosterbeek along the high ground to the north to secure the planned supply dropping zone just outside Arnhem and block approach roads down which, unfortunately, leading elements of the 9th SS Panzer Division *'Hohenstaufen'* were already streaming. 1 Para was preceded by Jeeps of 1st Air-Landing Brigade's reconnaissance battalion.

The idea of advancing on three axes was to establish which was the least defended route, whereupon the full brigade would converge on that which seemed most promising. Unhappily, insufficient account had been taken of the speed and quality of the German response, for it was believed the troops in the area were battered and demoralized survivors from Normandy who would be incapable of putting up an effective resistance. No-one had reckoned on Model and Bittrich, nor on the totally unknown Sturmbannführer (Major) Sepp Kraft.

Kraft commanded an SS *Ersatz* (training and replacement) battalion of young, inexperienced recruits, only three companies strong — 306 men. From his headquarters in the village of Wolfheze he subdued the inevitable panic as he watched Hicks' gliders landing on the heath barely a mile away. One of his companies was stationed in Arnhem and he promptly recalled it, realizing that the surest way to neutralize an airborne landing was to counterstrike immediately. The result was catastrophic for 1 Para, who ran into such withering fire as they approached Wolfheze and the northern heights that it was soon apparent to Dobie that he could not achieve his objectives without reinforcements. Then, hearing over the radio that 2 Para had seized the northern end of the bridge, he decided to change the direction of his advance and go straight to Frost's aid. However, Lathbury, fatally, allowed his men a night's rest before resuming the attack in the morning. Kraft's tiny force of teenagers, who were rapidly reinforced themselves by armoured cars and then tanks of the 9th SS Panzer Division, had unwittingly bought the vital time the Germans needed to defeat the 1st Airborne Division.

In the centre, Fitch's 3 Para had also run into trouble at a crossroads on the outskirts of Oosterbeek, although they had the good fortune to ambush a staff car carrying Maj-Gen Kussin, the town commander of Arnhem, and killed him. Kraft had warned Kussin to use side roads, but had been ignored. Now, however, Fitch's men came under heavy mortar and self-propelled artillery fire and momentarily tried to dig in instead of charging forward.

Lathbury caught up with them at this point and ordered them forward but by nightfall they had only succeeded in reaching the outskirts of Oosterbeek, now heavily defended by the 9th SS Panzer Division. Roy Urquhart, who had moved up from the LZ to confer first with Dobie, had now joined his brigade commander but neither man at this stage was aware that 2 Para had actually reached the bridge. Nor had Urquhart succeeded in making contact with Browning in Groesbeek. Tony

Deane-Drummond's misgivings about the reliability of the radios were coming home to roost. Accordingly, like 1 Para, 3 Para was now allowed to rest for the night apart from 'C' Company which volunteered to try to slip through German lines to reconnoitre the situation at the bridge. They got through in the darkness after two brief encounters with German patrols to find that Frost's battalion had control of the northern end of the bridge but had been unable to cross it.

Taking the southerly 'Lion' route that afternoon, 2 Para's initial advance had resembled a triumphal procession rather than a military operation, with cheering Dutch townspeople flocking out waving flags, throwing flowers and offering drinks — and, from the girls, kisses and embraces. There was isolated resistance which caused the civilians to dive for cover, but the southern parts of Oosterbeek and Arnhem were remarkably free of Germans, most of them being concentrated in the north and west. By a lucky coincidence, too, Gräbner's armoured column from the 10th SS Panzer Division crossed the bridge on its way to Nijmegen scant minutes before the arrival of the first of Frost's men.

On the approach, Frost had detached his own 'C' Company to try to get across the rail bridge, west of the road bridge, and assault the southern end of the latter while the rest of the battalion took the northern. This plan failed because the Germans blew a span of the rail bridge. Returning into the town, 'C' Company caught a party of SS men forming up after getting out of their trucks and scattered them with a hail of fire, but they then got embroiled in another firefight in the centre of the town and never did rejoin the battalion. Meanwhile, 'A', 'B' and HQ companies had reached the northern end of the road bridge at dusk, forced the occupants of the pillbox there to surrender after a murderous barrage of fire, and taken up blocking positions in surrounding buildings.

A pontoon bridge that aerial reconnaissance had shown was now no longer present, so, with the railway bridge down, the main road bridge could only be seized by frontal assault. Two attempts to take the southern end in this way were costly failures since it was defended both by another pillbox and by an armoured car which Gräbner had left behind as a precaution, against which the paras had no effective weapons with sufficient range to reach. However, as a trickle of reinforcements reached him during the night, including 'C' Company from 3 Para and part of the air-landing brigade's reconnaissance battalion, Frost was not yet too worried. What concerned him most was that he had been unable to make contact with Urquhart, who had been forced to hole up for the night in a house which was practically surrounded by Germans. Nor did anyone know whether the 101st and 82nd had succeeded in taking their own objectives, or what progress XXX Corps was making.

As day broke on Monday, 18 September, Gen Maxwell Taylor ordered Robert Sink's 506th Parachute Infantry Regiment into Eindhoven to capture the four bridges over the river Dommel. They encountered stiff opposition, particularly from a pair of German 88mm guns, but a platoon succeeded in outflanking these and killing their crews from the rear. By midday the paras had cleared the town and miraculously taken all four bridges intact. During the afternoon they were substantially reinforced when 428 gliders landed carrying Lt-Col Joseph Harper's 327th Glider Infantry Regiment with howitzers, anti-tank guns and Jeeps. But where was XXX Corps? Unable to manoeuvre, the Guards Armoured were having to fight for virtually every yard of road, and it was not until dusk that they finally reached Eindhoven. The schedule was falling further and further behind and Royal Engineers laboured mightily through the night to erect a Bailey Bridge over the Wilhelmina Canal at Son. Thus it was not until the early hours of Tuesday, 19 September, that XXX Corps was able to resume its advance towards Nijmegen.

Here, Gavin's 'All Americans' were in trouble. An early morning attack on the Waal road bridge had been stopped with heavy casualties by Gräbner's self-propelled guns; the Captain himself was heading back towards Arnhem with his armoured cars and half-tracks. Then Student, whose First Parachute Army was being reinforced by elements from Gen Gustav von Zangen's Fifteenth Army to the west, launched a heavy attack out of the Reichswald against the Groesbeek Heights with an *ad hoc* formation of *Fallschirmjäger, Luftwaffe* personnel and even some sailors! Sheer weight of numbers initially prevailed and the Germans overran the landing zones for the gliders which were due to arrive at noon. Fortuitously, their take-off from England had been delayed for two hours by fog and, although Gavin was forced to recall the bulk of the 508th from Nijmegen to help in the struggle, after a four-hour battle the LZs were back in American hands.

However, the Germans kept up an intense fire from the edge of the forest and many of the gliders were riddled as they came in to land. Others, distracted by the intense flak, landed up to five miles (8km) away, some of them in Germany itself. Nevertheless, 385 out of 454 gliders landed with remarkably few casualties on the LZs, and the field and anti-tank guns of the 319th and 320th Glider Field Artillery and 456th Parachute Field Artillery Battalions were soon vigorously engaging the enemy. Then, early next morning the first tanks of the Guards Armoured Division at last linked up with the 82nd at Grave. But Harmel's 10th SS Panzer Division still held the vital Waal bridge and would receive further reinforcements during the night, ferried by improvised rafts across the Neder Rijn east of Arnhem, while the situation at Arnhem itself was getting increasingly desperate despite the landing of Hackett's 4th Parachute Brigade on Monday afternoon.

At about 09:30 on Monday morning Frost's men on the Arnhem bridge were cheered to hear the roar of heavy vehicles driving up from the south. 'Good old XXX Corps,' they thought; 'They've made cracking time.' But it was not, of course. It was the returning part of Paul Gräbner's reconnaissance battalion with some 20 armoured cars and personnel carriers. Gräbner had boldly decided to take the bull by its horns and

Parachute training for balloon observers during the First World War. (Crown Copyright.)

Wearing the early style of British parachute helmet, a volunteer throws himself from the tower and will slide to earth down the sloping wire. (Crown Copyright.)

Men of the 501st Parachute Battalion board a C-53 for a practice jump. This photo was taken only days before the Japanese attack on Pearl Harbor. (US Army/MARS.)

Gen Kurt Student, founding father of the German airborne forces, in conference with other officers. (Bundesarchiv.)

Fallschirmjäger race from a DFS 230 glider during an exercise. (Bundesarchiv.)

Fort Eben Emael guarding the junction of the Albert Canal with the River Meuse.

One of the gun emplacements on Eben Emael after the battle. (Bundesarchiv.)

The Führer with members of Sturmabteilung Koch after the mission. Left to right: Lt Egon Delica, Oblt Rudolf Witzig, Hpt Walter Koch, Oblt Otto Zierach, Hitler, Lt Helmuth Ringler, Lt Joachim Meïssner, Oblt Walter Kiess, Oblt Gustav Altmann and Oberarzt Dr Rolf Jäger, the team's doctor. (Bundesarchiv.)

German paratroops descend outside Rotterdam, May 1940. (IWM/MARS.)

German paras guard British prisoners after the jump at the Corinth Canal. Note the leg pocket for the gravity knife.

Fallschirmjäger drop from Ju 52s over Crete.

Men of Julius Ringel's 5th Gebirgsjäger Division await the order to board their Ju 52s before being flown to Crete.

Luftwaffe Gen Alexander Löhr confers with Fallschirmjäger officers after the capture of Máleme.

103

Men of Obst Bruno Bräuer's FJR 1 parade through Stendal on their return from Crete.

During training for the Bruneval raid, British paras practise with the landing craft and gunboats which would bring them home. **(IWM H17392.)**

Above left: *After his capture at Depienne, Cpl Gavin Cadden talks to Walter Koch's second in command, Hpt Hans Jungwirth.*

Above right: *Walter Koch in Tunis, 1943, after receiving a head wound.*

A Junkers Ju 52/3m, workhorse of the German airborne forces, seen here in Russia. (Bundesarchiv.)

A Fallschirmjäger with the 7.92mm FG 42 assault rifle which was specially developed for airborne troops and had a significant effect on the development of postwar infantry weapons. (Bundesarchiv.)

German paras in winter clothing on the Russian front. The foreground figure carries an MP 40 sub-machine gun and a magnetic anti-tank mine. (Bundesarchiv.)

Above: *British parachute kit at the time of the Sicilian landings. This sergeant wears the 'X' Type parachute over a sleeveless green tunic under which a lifejacket does nothing for his figure. He carries the kitbag which would dangle on a rope below him during a jump.* (IWM/MARS.)

Above right: *This lance-corporal shows the side view of the 'X' Type parachute and carries a Bren light machine-gun in its specially designed valise.* (IWM/MARS.)

Right: *An NCO checks a glider trooper's kit. He is carrying a 3.5in anti-tank rocket launcher.*

Left: *A member of the Italian 'Folgore' Parachute Division at Anzio. The Italian jump smock was similar to the German one but had a different camouflage pattern.* (Bundesarchiv.)

Right: *Fallschirmjäger in the ruins of Cassino. Richard Heidrich's 1st Division gave the Allies a hard time with their stubborn defence here.* (Bundesarchiv.)

German paratroops race forward after landing on the Gran Sasso plateau to rescue Mussolini, 12 September 1943.

Mussolini with some of his rescuers. Otto Skorzeny is the tall figure on his right.

The Horsa, principal British glider. Overhead are transport aircraft of the US 101st Airborne, during pre D-Day exercises. (US Air Force/MARS.)

CG-4A Haigs/Hadrians damaged during the D-Day landings. (Bundesarchiv.)

'All Americans' check their weapons and kit before boarding their Horsas on the eve of D-Day. (US Air Force/MARS.)

Proving the accuracy of their landing, three Horsas photographed on the morning after their landing beside Pegasus Bridge. (Public Record Office/MARS.)

Pegagus Bridge itself, securely in Allied hands on 10 June 1944. (IWM/MARS.)

CG-4As litter the ground as a fresh wave of paratroops descend over the Normandy countryside. The photograph was probably taken on 7 June.

On their way to battle: C-47s towing CG-4As across the English Channel. (US Air Force/MARS.)

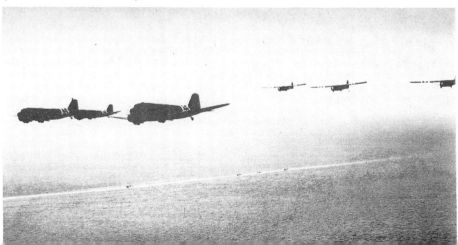

Inside a C-47, men of the 101st Airborne on their way to the Cotentin Peninsula. (US Army/MARS.)

Trying to relax before the drop. The man standing is hanging on to the cable to which the paras' static lines were hooked. (US Air Force/MARS.)

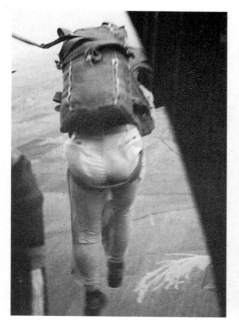

Above: *Go! A US para launches himself over the French countryside.* (US Air Force/ MARS.)

Above right: *C-47s bank away over gliders in a Normandy field.* (US Air Force/ MARS.)

Men of Friedrich-August Freiherr von der Heydte's FJR 6 grab a moment's rest during the fierce fighting near Carentan. (Bundesarchiv.)

Dozens of parachutes blossom over the French riviera at the beginning of Operation Dragoon in August 1944. (US Air Force.)

On the road to 'a bridge too far', American Liberator bombers arrive over the 101st Airborne's landing zone outside Eindhoven to drop supplies. (US Air Force/MARS.)

The main bridge at Nijmegen which gave the 82nd Airborne so much trouble to capture. (US Army/ MARS.)

French members of the SAS, part of a radio link team in Holland during the drive towards Arnhem. (ECP Armées CTT 14303.)

Roy Urquhart just before taking off for Arnhem. (IWM BU1136.)

Men of the 1st Airborne Division emplane for Holland. (IWM K7588.)

On their way — British paras full of confidence before dropping at Arnhem.
(IWM K7586.)

The Arnhem bridge itself, looking north to the area so valiantly held for so long
by 2 Para. (IWM MH2061.)

Men of 2 Para advance with hardly any opposition towards the bridge. (IWM BU1090.)

Tough veterans of the 9th and 10th SS Panzer Divisions march forward to meet them. (Bundesarchiv.)

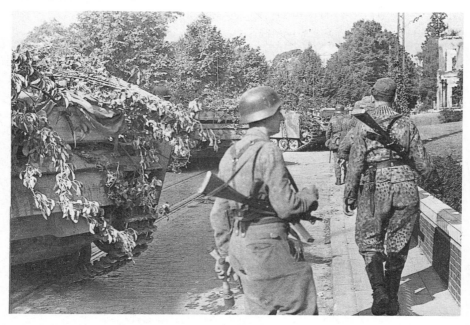

Unloading gliders on the LZ outside Arnhem. (IWM/MARS.)

British paras during the bitter fighting in Oosterbeek. (IWM/MARS.)

The Rhine crossings: American paras tumble from their aircraft.

CG-4As outside Brussels having been reclaimed following the successful airborne assault over the Rhine. (US Air Force/MARS.)

The Korean War: American paras in training prepare for a jump in February 1952. (US Army.)

Come on down! Reinforcements and supplies drift down over Dien Bien Phu. (SIRPA/ ECP Armées France.)

Even though used to fighting in isolation far from immediate support, the paras found little to write home about from Dien Bien Phu. (SIRPA/ECP Armées France.)

The Mitla Pass, scene of a hard-fought Israeli para victory in 1956, seen here strewn with burned-out Egyptian vehicles in the wake of the 1967 Six Days War. (Dartford/MARS.)

The postwar era: US paras receive briefing before a Stateside exercise. The air-craft is a C-130 Hercules. (MARS.)

Victory! A British para armed with a Sterling sub-machine-gun herds Argentine prisoners into captivity in the Falklands. (Express Newspapers/MARS.)

C-141 Starlifter on the still uncompleted runway at Point Salines, Grenada, in 1983. (MARS.)

The Soviet airborne forces are the strongest in the world. Here, initial jump training is conducted in assembly-line fashion. (TASS.)

Soviet paras deploy around an ASU-57 tank destroyer, now obsolete. The square shape of their parachutes is clearly apparent. (TASS.)

Prior to Zimbabwe gaining independence, Rhodesian paras were counted among the best in the world. These are soldiers of the SAS with their captured pet monkey!

A member of the Australian SAS takes a tumble in a high wind. (Australian War Memorial.)

Basic jump posture with a static line 'chute has largely remained unchanged since the war, as demonstrated by men of the New Zealand SAS over Changi, Singapore.

A vital part of NATO's rapid deployment capability, the British Parachute Regiment frequently exercises with its allies, as here in Turkey in 1973. (Crown Copyright/MARS.)

The Parachute Regiment also possesses the world's best freefall skydiving display team in the form of the Red Devils, seen hugely enjoying themselves as they leap from their Hercules. But freefall jumping is not just a carnival stunt; it has serious applications in time of war. (MARS.)

In 1982, one of the largest airborne operations since the Second World War was conducted when the US 82nd Airborne joined Egyptian paras and ground forces in the first Bright Star exercise. Still wearing the same desert camouflage, the 82nd was one of the first units into Saudi Arabia in August 1990 when Iraq invaded Kuwait.

charge straight through 2 Para's positions to retake the northern end of the bridge. And he almost succeeded. His leading five armoured cars raced across the bridge at such speed that they smashed through into the town, but the slower-moving half-track personnel carriers met the full weight of the now fully-alerted paras' 6pdr anti-tank guns, PIATs and Bren guns. Five were immobilized and the sixth abandoned, creating a road block which the following vehicles could not pass, so Gräbner called off the assault. It was only a temporary reprieve for 2 Para, though.

The next attack came from the north, preceded by two tanks. One was knocked out by a 6pdr, the other by a PIAT, but German infantry with mortars succeeded in driving part of the garrison out of houses on their perimeter. Then, while they were preparing a new assault as dusk fell, Frost seized the initiative and dispersed them with a bayonet charge, his men all screaming the battle cry they had learned in Tunisia, 'Whoa Mohammed!'. They were encouraged to learn that 'Shan' Hackett's 4 Para Brigade had now landed, freeing Hicks' 1st Air-Landing Brigade from its task of guarding the LZ, and that the 2nd Battalion, South Staffordshire Regiment, was heading to their relief.

Meanwhile, 1 and 3 Para had failed to achieve any headway, being caught up in vicious house-to-house fighting. 3 Para fought its way to the northern outskirts of Arnhem, taking heavy casualties, but was then stalled by tanks and murderous artillery and machine-gun fire. 1 Para, having disengaged during the night, had set off south towards 'Lion' Route only to get embroiled in the same battle. This was virtually as far as they would get. Meanwhile, command of 1st Airborne Division had devolved on to Hicks, since Lathbury had been badly wounded by machine-gun fire and no-one knew what had happened to Roy Urquhart. In fact he was still holed up in a house with his batman, unable to move because of a German self-propelled gun sitting on the doorstep.

The fog which had luckily delayed the take-off of the US 82nd Air-borne's gliders that morning had also, of course, delayed the take-off of 4 Para Brigade, which did not begin landing until 14:00 instead of at 10:00 as planned. Even so, it is unlikely that the outcome of the battle would have been altered had they been able to keep to schedule. Regardless, after Urquhart's Chief of Staff, Col Charles Mackenzie, had explained the situation to Hackett, Hicks sent the South Staffs off along 'Lion' Route and 11 Para behind them to try to link up with 1 and 3 Para and force a passage through to the bridge. Lt-Col W.D.H. McCardie's South Staffs, having only managed to advance three miles (5km) in 13 hours, so tough was the opposition, eventually reached the survivors of the two para battalions in the early hours of Tuesday morning. Thus reinforced, they tried to move forward but were blocked near the Ste Elizabeth Hospital, German snipers firing from the roofs of buildings, mortars and artillery pounding them and every road blocked by a tank or self-propelled gun. Then, at daybreak, they came under fire from a battery of four-barrelled 20mm cannon on the opposite side of the river. These wrought enormous carnage and Dobie ordered the remnants of his battalion to retire into Oosterbeek. In the process he was wounded and captured but managed to escape later in the confusion. Following suit with his own battalion, Fitch was killed. 1 and 3 Paras had ceased to exist as effective fighting formations and 2 Para was not much better off.

Even on that fateful night of 18/19 September, victory could have been salvaged if Hackett's brigade had been sent west down the northern bank of the Rhine to Driel, where a Dutch ferry was still operating as normal. But Hicks, somewhat intimidated by the fact that Hackett was actually his senior even if Urquhart had specifically nominated him as his successor after Lathbury, chose to ignore this possibility and by the time Urquhart finally managed to escape from the house in which he had been holed up and got back to his HQ shortly after 07:00, 4 Para Brigade was too heavily embroiled in and around Arnhem to be pulled out. Urquhart signalled Browning, requesting that the Polish Parachute Brigade be dropped at Driel, but the weather refused to co-operate, fog clamping down again, and when they were finally dropped two days later — a classical example of too little, too late — Sosabowski's Poles found the overlooking heights in German hands. They were thus able to contribute little of substance to the battle, to their immense chagrin. How different things might have been had two airlifts been made possible on the Monday . . .

With Lt-Col G.H. Lea's 11 Para tied down on Hicks' orders in Arnhem, Hackett had taken his other two battalions (10 and 156 Para) plus the 1st Battalion, the Border Regiment, and the 7th Battalion, King's Own Scottish Borderers, from the Air-Landing Brigade, to try once more to secure the heights behind Wolfheze whose capture was essential as a prelude to seizing Deelen airfield for the 52nd (Lowland) Division. Blocked by tanks, armoured cars and self-propelled guns crewed by the tough, skilled and fanatical men of the 9th SS Panzer Division, and repeatedly strafed by German fighters, they suffered heavy casualties and were only able to make minimal headway. The problem was exacerbated by the fact that designated DZs for supply containers were mostly in German hands, despite the heroism of the aircrews making the drops under intense anti-aircraft fire. (One of the Arnhem's five Victoria Crosses went to Flt Lt David Lord, who continued to fly his blazing Dakota while four Army despatchers hurled the vital canisters from the door until the aircraft exploded). Over three-quarters of the ammunition, food and medical supplies fell into German hands.

For the record, the other four VCs were allocated as follows. One went to Capt Lionel E. Queripel of 10 Para who, although wounded in the face after carrying an injured Sergeant to safety, single-handedly attacked and destroyed an anti-tank gun covered by two machine-guns and, now wounded in both arms as well, then covered the retreat of the rest of his men with grenades before being killed. One went to Lt John Grayburn of 2 Para, who led the two assaults over the bridge on the first night of the battle and who, although also wounded in the face, selflessly supervised his men's withdrawal from German tanks on Wednesday 20 September, before being killed. And two went to men of the South Staffs, one to L/Sgt John Baskeyfield and one to Maj Robert Cain. The former single-handedly took over a second 6pdr anti-tank gun after his own was knocked out and destroyed two German tanks and two self-propelled guns before being killed. The latter was the only survivor of the five. Renowned for being freshly clean-shaven regardless of the circumstances, Cain destroyed at least six tanks and a number of self-propelled guns using his PIAT at suicidally short ranges during the last stages of the fighting in Oosterbeek before shepherding the remainder of his men across to the southern bank of the Rhine during the final withdrawal.

But this is jumping ahead, and we must return to 'Black Tuesday' when the four battalions which had been fighting in Arnhem had pulled back into Oosterbeek, reduced to some 250 men. John Frost was on his own.

Nor was there any encouraging news from Nijmegen where an attempt to get behind 10th Panzer Division by using the rail bridge had been thwarted. However, the arrival of the first British tanks eased the pressure somewhat and Gavin sent the II/505th with the support of the Grenadier Guards to try to push the 10th SS Panzer Division out of its perimeter on the southern side of the Nijmegen bridge. The defenders' fire was so murderous that, as night fell, they were still 300yds (274m) from their objective. The 508th, meanwhile, continued to hold the Groesbeek Heights against repeated attacks. Gavin came to realize that the only way of forcing a passage was to take the bridge from the rear but was unable to find any boats. When Horrocks arrived at 82nd Airborne headquarters, he volunteered the use of the 33 canvas assault boats which XXX Corps sappers had brought along against just such an eventuality. But because of the traffic congestion, it would not be until the following afternoon that the assault, entrusted to Tucker's 504th, could go in.

Meanwhile, Wednesday 20 September brought other problems. The German II *Fallschirmjäger* Korps, commanded by Eugen Meindl and spearheaded by von der Heydte's FJR 6, launched a devastating attack on Gavin's south-eastern perimeter, taking the villages of Mook and Beek and threatening the one intact bridge over the Maas-Waal Canal. Gavin threw I/ and III/505th into the counter-attack, taking personal command, and the threat was staved off. Meanwhile, Tucker's men assembled nervously behind the shelter of the dike on the southern bank of the Waal. They were paratroopers, not marines! Eventually the boats arrived and were quickly assembled by British sappers and, under cover of an artillery barrage which produced a smoke screen, Maj Julian Cook's 3rd Battalion embarked at 15:00. The boats came under a hail of fire but all managed to get across, even though half of them were so badly damaged they could not be re-used for the return trip to ferry more men across. Undeterred, Cook's battalion fought its way yard by yard towards the northern end of the bridge and finally raised the Stars and Stripes there at 19:00. Seeing this, Grenadier Guards' Sherman tanks raced for the bridge and, although two were knocked out by 88mm guns, the others were soon across. They were lucky because, in defiance of Model's orders, Gen Heinz Harmel had mined the bridge; fortunately, the detonator wires had been cut at some point by stray gunfire and they did not go off.

With the final bridge before Arnhem in Allied hands at long last, XXX Corps now had only 11 miles (17.5km) to go, but there were to be further infuriating delays and it was, in fact, too late for the embattled 1st Airborne. Harmel brought up reinforcements at Nijmegen to try to throw the paras and guardsmen back, but they were defeated, principally by one man. Pte John R. Towle of the 504th single-handedly took on two tanks with his bazooka, then with another round killed nine Germans who had dived for shelter in a house. Moments later Towle was killed; he was posthumously awarded the Congressional Medal of Honor. But the Germans backed off. Even then the British tanks were stalled for lack of fuel until petrol tankers could fight their way up the road to the 82nd's positions, and the advance could not resume until the 21st, to the disgust of Tucker's men whose accomplishment — rated as one of the finest of the war — seemed to them to have been for nothing. And by the time leading elements of XXX Corps finally did reach the southern bank of the Neder Rijn on the 22nd, it was indeed 'a bridge too far'.

At 10:00 on the morning of Wednesday the 20th, Frost had finally succeeded in making radio contact with Urquhart. He succinctly described 2 Para's plight and asked for ammunition and medical supplies, neither of which Urquhart was in any position to provide because the remainder of his three brigades were no better off after the failure of the supply drop the previous afternoon. The desperate fighting around the northern end of the bridge continued throughout the day. Most of the paras had abandoned the houses which were proving death traps under the weight of German artillery fire and had dug themselves foxholes. Frost was wounded in both legs early in the afternoon and command was taken over by Maj Freddie Gough of the Air-Landing Brigade's reconnaissance battalion. He was particularly worried about the 200-plus wounded men sheltering in the cellars of a house which was threatened by fire from other burning buildings, and arranged a truce. SS medics and stretcher bearers moved in to evacuate the injured and the paras were impressed with the gentleness with which the Germans treated their erstwhile adversaries, handing round cigarettes and chocolate. The irony was that these had come from captured British supply containers. Then the truce was over and battle recommenced. The paras hoarded their last remaining clips of ammunition — the PIAT and 6pdr shells had all long since gone — and made their last stand underneath the very ramp of the bridge. Reduced to a mere 110 active combatants, they were finally overrun at 09:00 on the 21st.

Urquhart, meanwhile, found the rest of his decimated division surrounded in a steadily shrinking perimeter around Oosterbeek. Both his parachute brigades had virtually ceased to exist, several battalion commanders had either been killed or captured, and Hackett would soon join

Lathbury as the second wounded brigade commander to go in 'the bag'. On the 21st the fog which had prevented Sosabowski's brigade from taking off finally lifted and early that evening they dropped south of the Neder Rijn near Driel, only to find that the ferry had been cast adrift by the Germans. Sosabowski managed to get about 250 men across the river the next night, using inflatable rubber boats, but the fire from the overlooking heights was so intense that any attempt to link up with Urquhart's survivors would have been impossible. However, the Poles' arrival did have the effect of causing Model and Bittrich to move more troops to the southern side of Arnhem bridge to guard against an attack there, especially when leading elements of XXX Corps — men of the 43rd Infantry Division's Dorsetshire Regiment — roared up in their trucks on the 22nd to join the Poles. Pursued, it must be added, by slower-moving tanks of Harmel's 10th SS Panzer Division, whose ranks they had broken through. The Dorsets had some DUKWs (amphibious trucks) but the steep and slippery banks of the dike defeated them and not one was launched.

On Saturday the 23rd the RAF finally gave the airborne forces some fighter-bomber cover using the same rocket-firing Typhoons which had wrought such havoc on German armour in Normandy. If only they had been available earlier, II SS Panzer Korps would not have been able to move about with the impunity it had enjoyed. As it was, this support came too late and on Sunday the 24th the agonizing decision was taken to evacuate the survivors from Oosterbeek. The operation took place next night, under cover of an artillery barrage which temporarily convinced Bittrich that XXX Corps was attempting a major amphibious assault. While volunteers, most of them wounded, continued to fire to persuade the Germans that 1st Airborne was still in the town, the battered remnants were ferried back across the dark, swift-flowing Rhine. Of 10,005 men dropped at Arnhem, a mere 2,163 escaped, the remainder being killed or entering captivity although a few were sheltered by Dutch families and eventually made their way back to the new front line south of the Rhine.

One of these was Tony Deane-Drummond who, earlier in the battle, had become so infuriated with the radio failures that he had gone on a personal and unauthorized recce to see what had befallen 2 Para at the bridge. Trapped in a house, he held out for three days hidden in a lavatory before being able to escape, but was captured making his way back to friendly lines. A couple of days later he escaped and hid in a cupboard! There he remained for an incredible 13 days until he managed to slip out of a window to the ground. Some six weeks later he and Gerald Lathbury, who was also helped by the Dutch Resistance, succeeded in reaching safety.

As the official history of the operation records: 'Now these things befell at Arnhem'. The town itself and its courageous population who had done so much to care for the wounded and provide food and water, would not be liberated until 15 April 1945.

The failure at Arnhem yet again cast doubts on the value of airborne forces, yet by no stretch of the imagination can that failure be laid at the doors of the paras and glider-borne infantry, American, British and Polish, who fought so valiantly and so nearly won. The failure was one of over-optimism, of thinking the enemy was already defeated, of faulty intelligence and deliberate ignorance of genuine intelligence, of faulty equipment, of hasty planning (although in fairness this was not as hasty as it might appear, because a detailed study had already been made for an aborted earlier operation codenamed 'Comet'), of insufficient allowance for adverse weather conditions and, in particular, of allowing insufficient time for the ground forces to link up despite earlier lessons which should have become axiomatic. Lack of aerial close support was a major factor and so, of course, was the speed and quality of the German response. The next airborne operation in Europe would be rather different, but before that took place the paras would have to endure a rather different ordeal.

The full story of the 'Battle of the Bulge' is readily available elsewhere (but again, take no notice of the film!) and the only airborne assault, by the Germans, was a disaster, so we must be brief. By dint of almost superhuman effort, the German High Command managed by mid-December 1944 to assemble three complete armies for a counter-offensive in the west which Hitler intended would sweep all the way to Antwerp, cutting off the American, British, Canadian and French forces in Belgium, Holland and north-western Germany. This, the dictator thought, would cause the Western Allies to agree an armistice on more favourable terms than the unconditional surrender they were demanding, and free the German armed forces to concentrate on holding the Russians. The plan was for two Panzer armies — Gen Hasso von Manteuffel's Fifth and SS Gen 'Sepp' Dietrich's Sixth — to sweep through the Ardennes, where the Germans had won their surprise victory in 1940, while Gen Erich Brandenberger's Seventh Army protected their southern flank from interference by Patton's Third Army to the south. The formations assembled for the assault included eight Panzer divisions and two *Fallschirmjäger* divisions, Lt-Gen Wadehn's 3rd and Maj-Gen Ludwig Heilmann's 5th.

The assault broke in the dark early hours of 16 December and looked in imminent danger of breaking through the line of the river Meuse for the Allied troops in the Ardennes were either battle-fatigued or new arrivals who had in either case been assigned a quiet sector of the front well away from the ferocious battles taking place north and south of them. The only reserves immediately available were the US 82nd, which had been withdrawn from Holland between 11 and 13 November, and the 101st which had similarly been withdrawn between the 25th and 27th. They had been sent to camps outside Reims in France to recuperate alongside the 509th and 551st Parachute Infantry Battalions, the 463rd Parachute Field Artillery Battalion and the 517th Parachute Combat Team, all of which had seen fighting in the south of France since August. Reims was then both Eisenhower's headquarters and the HQ of Ridgway's XVIII Airborne

Corps, but when the storm broke Ridgway was in England, Maxwell Taylor in the States and his deputy, Gen Gerald Higgins, also in England. This left XVIII Corps under the temporary field command of Jim Gavin, recently promoted Maj-Gen, and the 101st Airborne under Brig-Gen Anthony McAuliffe, who was to enter the history books for his utterance of a single word.

As the seriousness of the German assault became apparent on the 17th, Gavin was alerted to have his two divisions ready to move at 24 hours' notice, and at daybreak on the 18th the 'All Americans' boarded their trucks for the tiring journey to the Luxembourg border, followed early in the afternoon by the 'Screaming Eagles'. Their task was to block the crucial two road junctions in the Ardennes at St Vith and Bastogne. Meanwhile, after a 24 hour delay a *Fallschirmjäger* battlegroup commanded by Freiherr von der Heydte had made a night drop to secure a third road junction near Malmédy for Dietrich's Sixth Panzer Army. The aircraft were widely dispersed, several crashing in the mountains, and the 500-odd survivors, deep in enemy-held territory, were helpless to achieve their objective. In the end von der Heydte, in agony from a broken arm, split his command up into small groups to make their way independently back to German lines. Only about 100 succeeded, and their courageous commander was himself captured.

Gavin's 82nd Airborne held out on the heights in front of St Vith until Christmas Eve when they were reluctantly forced to withdraw under heavy pressure from the 2nd and 9th Panzer Divisions, but they had delayed the assault sufficiently long for within a couple of days massive reinforcements were arriving from other sectors of the front. Moreover, the overcast weather which had prevented Allied fighter-bombers from operating finally cleared and by 3 January 1945 the tables had been turned and the Allies had resumed the offensive, punching through the West Wall towards the Rhine.

At Bastogne, however, the 101st Airborne had been completely surrounded while the 2nd Panzer Division went haring on to actually get within a stone's throw of the Meuse at Dinant before being halted. Enclosed in a steadily shrinking ring of small villages and farms around Bastogne by tanks, self-propelled guns and heavily armed Panzergrenadiers, the lightly equipped 'Screaming Eagles' fought tenaciously to hang on until reinforcements from Patton's Third Army to the south could break through to their relief. On 22 December a German emissary delivered a note demanding the Americans' surrender. When he received it, McAuliffe said 'Aw, nuts!', and 'Nuts!' was the reply he sent back. But by Christmas Day the 101st's position was truly critical. They had suffered heavy casualties and were very low on ammunition. Friends shook hands silently, knowing the chances were that they would not see each other again. But still they held out and then, miraculously, on Boxing Day tanks of Patton's 4th Armored Division finally broke through to them. The feisty General had achieved one of the most remarkable feats of the war, disengaging the bulk of his entire army from action and wheeling it through 90 degrees in a mere couple of days. Roy Urquhart — who, better than anybody, knew what the 101st had gone through — telegraphed McAuliffe a message of congratulations expressing the admiration of the British 1st Airborne Division.

The two American divisions remained in the line until the middle of February, reinforced by the unattached battalions which had also been stationed in Reims and by William Miley's fresh 17th Airborne Division, which first went into action on their right flank on 4 January. The British 6th Airborne Division also took part in the counter-offensive before being assigned, with the US 17th, to the last major airborne operation in Europe — the final crossing of the Rhine. (The US 13th Airborne Division [513th and 515th Parachute and 326th Glider Infantry Regiments], commanded by Maj-Gen Eldridge Chapman, also arrived in France at the beginning of March but never saw combat.)

Once Hitler's ill-conceived Ardennes offensive had been contained, the Allies kept up the pressure along the whole line and by the beginning of March 1945 had reached or almost reached the Rhine along a 250-mile (400km) front from Emmerich, east of Nijmegen, in the north to Strasbourg in the south. They were divided into three Army Groups: Montgomery's 21st in the north (Canadian First, British Second and US Ninth Armies); Bradley's 12th in the centre (US First and Third Armies); and Maj-Gen Jacob Devers' 6th in the south (US Seventh and French First Army). They were opposed respectively by Gen Johannes Blaskowitz's Army Group H in the north, which had the vital task of defending the Ruhr; by Model's Army Group B in the centre and by SS Gen Paul Hausser's Army Group G in the south. And, however battered and exhausted they were, the Germans were still skilled and dangerous opponents, made more so as they were pushed back on their last natural frontier, one of great psychological as well as strategic importance. Appropriately, it was men of Lt-Gen Courtney Hodges' US First Army, who had suffered worst in the Ardennes, who got across the Rhine first when, on 7 March, they miraculously captured a bridge intact at Remagen, just north of Koblenz. As it happened, this had little effect on Allied plans because the bridge was in the wrong place and the terrain on the eastern bank unsuitable for rapid exploitation, but nevertheless Eisenhower authorized a build-up in the bridgehead which would at least tend to divert German attention away from the main crossing points which had been selected.

As before, the prize of being first across the Rhine had developed into a race between Montgomery, who wanted the glory to go to Gen Sir Miles Dempsey's Second Army in the north, and Patton who wanted to get his Third Army across first in the south. Monty's troops, with a smaller distance to travel, had actually reached the Rhine earliest, and during February and March the Field Marshal meticulously built up his forces in readiness, constructing new bridges across the Maas to expedite the supplies now flooding in through Antwerp, amassing landing craft and DUKWs in his usual cautious and pedantic manner. This was not Patton's style and on the moonlit night of 22/23 March he stole Montgomery's thunder by launching Gen Leroy Irwin's 5th Infantry Division across the river between Nierstein and Oppenheim, rapidly following up with further infantry and armoured divisions once sappers had constructed pontoon bridges and sending other divisions across north and south at Mainz and Worms on the 26th. Montgomery, who had scheduled his own assault for the night of the 23rd/24th, was piqued to say the very least.

Where the Americans had roared across the river with hardly a check and had scarcely encountered any resistance from Hausser's weak and badly fragmented forces, Blaskowitz had had plenty of time to study Montgomery's elaborate build-up and prepare accordingly, even though his First Parachute Army in particular was sadly depleted from the almost continual fighting in the six months since operation 'Market Garden'. Realizing similarly that the opposition was likely to be tough, Montgomery planned to supplement his amphibious crossing (preceded by a heavy bombing raid and artillery barrage and screened by banks of smoke projectors) by a daylight airborne drop on the 24th in order to reinforce the bridgehead as quickly as possible. Instead of acting as the tip of the cue, so to speak, the airborne units were this time to fulfil the role of the weight in the haft. The divisions entrusted with this task were Miley's US 17th and the British 6th Airborne, now commanded by Maj-Gen Eric Bols since, with Browning's departure to the Far East to become Mountbatten's deputy, Gale in turn had become Brereton's new deputy. XVIII Corps commander Matthew Ridgway was in overall charge of the airborne part of the operation, codenamed 'Varsity'.

To the airborne troops, so accustomed to navigational errors dropping them miles from their objectives, to being fired upon in the air by their own troops, and having to wait too long for ground forces to catch up with them, 'Varsity' was a revelation in what paras and glider-borne infantry could accomplish under correctly evaluated and planned circumstances. As at Arnhem, they would drop in daylight but the difference was that ground forces would already be across the Rhine to effect a link-up on the same day as the airborne assault. Moreover, the paras would all go in in one drop, not staggered as before, and they would be able to call on artillery support from Montgomery's massed gun batteries on the west bank of the river.

The 6th Airborne began taking off from its airfields in England at 07:00 on the 24th, 699 C-47s and 429 Haigs, Horsas and Hamilcars, the latter for the first time carrying a few of the new American M-22 Locust light tanks. Over Brussels they linked up with the 831 C-47s, 72 of the new Curtiss C-46 Commandos and 897 gliders of the 17th Airborne which had taken off from 12 airfields around Paris at 07:20. Between them they carried 21,680 troops, all of whom would be landed decisively in an area of just a few square miles. The LZs and DZs were located around the Diersfordter Wald on the high ground overlooking the town of Wesel which would already be in Allied hands when they landed. The paras and glider-borne troops would then push on to the river Issel to the east in order to prevent Blaskowitz sending reinforcements to interfere with the build-up in the bridgehead. Bols' 6th Airborne had the northern sector of the landing area, Miley's 17th the southern.

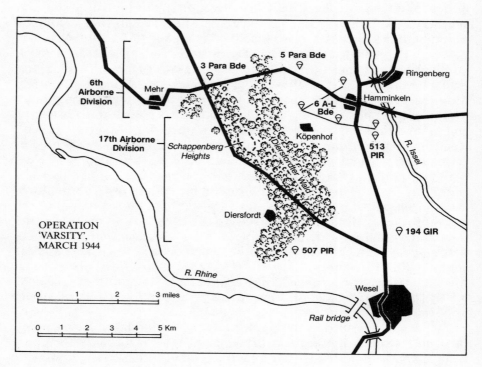

It was singularly appropriate that Edson Raff, who had led the first American airborne battalion to see action in Tunisia, should be the first man out of the leading plane. Now CO of the 507th Parachute Infantry Regiment, Raff had been entrusted with the capture of the Diersfordter Castle and surrounding wooded heights. Although most of the men were dropped off target because of the intense flak, by 11:00 Raff had assembled the majority after knocking out a mortar position and two tanks and capturing an artillery battery. Some of them moved in to assault the castle, knocking out a further three tanks, and by 18:00 the Stars and Stripes flew from one of the castle turrets. The remainder of his men marched to their proper DZ, by which time the gliders carrying the 75mm guns of the 464th Field Artillery Battalion had also landed safely and were in action against targets of opportunity. Early in the evening they linked up with British ground troops advancing from Wesel, one para unfortunately being shot by a jittery sentry. Other than this, the operation had been a total success with minimal casualties and several hundred prisoners taken into 'the bag'.

Col James Coutts' 513th Parachute Infantry Regiment was less fortunate. To begin with, he had been assigned the new C-46s, which were a supposed improvement over the C-47 because they had jump doors in both sides of the fuselage, allowing the men to be dropped faster and in a tighter formation. Unfortunately, their wing-mounted fuel tanks were not self-sealing which made them particularly vulnerable to ground fire, and 22 were shot down in flames while 38 others were badly damaged. Luckily, most of Coutts' men managed to get out of the aircraft before they, and their brave crews, crashed, but their troubles were still not over. (Ridgway refused flatly to use the C-46 for airborne operations after this disaster.) Due to faulty navigation caused by ground haze and drifting smoke, they dropped on the LZ assigned to the gliders of the British 6th Air-Landing Brigade just outside the town of Hamminkeiln on the Issel.

The ground was thick with Germans and several paras were killed by civilians as well as by soldiers as they struggled to extricate themselves from their 'chutes, many of which had hung up on trees. Both the American and British official accounts of the subsequent battle are laudatory about the way in which the 513th charged straight into action against the dozens of German gun positions which ringed the town. Dodging from the descending gliders swooping down on them — and taking fire which otherwise would have resulted in higher British casualties — Coutts' men played a major part in the successful occupation of Hamminkeln and the seizure of the river bridges and surrounding countryside by Brig R.H. Bellamy's 2nd Oxfordshire and Buckinghamshire Light Infantry, 12th Devonshires and 1st Royal Ulster Rifles. PFC Stuart Stryker won a posthumous Congressional Medal of Honor in this battle, leading his platoon in a frontal charge against entrenched machine-gun positions which they overran, taking 200 prisoners. (Most glider losses seem to have been due to flak setting light to the fuel tanks of the Jeeps which many were carrying.) Nor did Col James Pierce's 194th Glider Infantry Regiment have an easy time, landing dead on target but right in the middle of a cluster of flak and field artillery positions. Exiting their gliders under heavy fire, the American paras soon had the situation under control, though. The Germans had simply not expected an airborne invasion *after* an amphibious assault.

Bols' 3rd and 5th Parachute Brigades also had hard but short battles to secure their own objectives along the northern and western sides of the Diersfordter Wald. Brig James Hill's 3 Para Brigade enjoyed an almost perfect drop on the west side of the woods although there were a number of casualties among those who landed in the trees, one of them being Lt-Col J.A. Nicklin, CO of the Canadian Parachute Battalion. The 'Canucks' also won a Victoria Cross: it was awarded to a medical orderly, Cpl F.G. Topham who, although wounded himself, went under fire into a pool of blazing petrol to rescue other injured men. 8 Para had trouble winkling

Fallschirmjäger out of woods near Kopenhok farm but by early afternoon they had linked up with ground forces, all objectives secured. Similarly, 9 Para seized the Schnappenberg Heights after a brief firefight. Brig Nigel Poett's 5 Para Brigade dropped slightly off target due to the same haze and smoke experienced by Coutts' 513th Regiment and his men were forced to regroup under heavy machine-gun and artillery fire, particularly from a battery of '88s' which was finally taken out by a bayonet charge. But again, by mid-afternoon, all principal objectives had been secured and they, too, had linked up with the ground forces.

That night, however, XVIII Corps commander Matthew Ridgway had a narrow escape. After crossing the Rhine by boat, he had made his way by foot to Miley's field HQ. At about 20:00, he and Miley boarded a Jeep to drive to Bols' 6th Airborne headquarters. After settling their plans for the following day with the British CO, the two American Generals started their return journey just after midnight only to run slap into a group of equally startled *Fallschirmjäger* who were trying to find their own front line under cover of darkness. The Germans opened fire and one of them threw a grenade which wrecked the Jeep. They were not looking for a fight, though, and slipped away into the darkness. Ridgway, however, had collected a grenade fragment in his shoulder, a souvenir he retained all his life.

After operation 'Varsity', the airborne troops in Europe operated purely as line infantry, some of them advancing as far as the Baltic for a planned operation against Norway which never materialized because of Hitler's suicide and the German surrender, some to the river Elbe where they met up with victorious Russian troops sweeping west. A plan to use the 82nd to drop on Berlin in order to give the Western Allies greater bargaining power in postwar Europe was abandoned in favour of using them in the invasion of the Japanese mainland — an operation itself rendered unnecessary by the atomic bomb attacks on Hiroshima and Nagasaki. Before looking at the rundown and subsequent reconstruction of airborne forces in the postwar world, however, we must turn back to the Japanese attack on Pearl Harbor in December 1941 and paratroop operations in the Far East and Pacific.

6

Islands, jungles and rivers

Airborne operations in the Far Eastern and Pacific theatres during the Second World War were on a much smaller scale than the major ones in Europe but no less effective in their own way for that. The Japanese started the ball rolling on 11 January 1942, a month after Pearl Harbor and only days after the fall of Hong Kong, when men of the German-trained Yokosuka 1st Naval Special Landing Unit emplaned at Davao on the Philippine island of Mindanao and dropped on Manado airfield on the island of Celebes (Sulawesi) in advance of amphibious forces. They met little opposition and thus early established a forward airfield for themselves at this important crossroads in their campaign through the Dutch East Indies. A month later, on 9 February, 700 paratroopers of Col Kume's Army Parachute Brigade dropped on three zones around the important airfield and oil refinery at Palembang on Sumatra. Despite fierce resistance, this time from Australian, British and Dutch troops, they succeeded in holding their objectives until relieved on the 16th by leading elements of the 38th Infantry Division which had been landed by sea. Thereafter, however, the Japanese only made minor use of paratroops in relatively small commando-style raids although they did use Ku-8 gliders (*Appendix 2*) in the Philippines and in resupply operations to isolated forces when the Americans began their comeback.

The first Allied para unit to see action in the Far East was Maj Robert Williams' 1st (Marine) Parachute Battalion which took part in the assault on Guadalcanal on 7 August 1943, but they were put ashore by boat not parachute and, indeed, the 'leathernecks' never did mount a wartime airborne operation. Honours really go, therefore, to the 503rd Parachute Infantry Regiment. (It will be remembered that the 503rd's 2nd Battalion, sent to England to take part in operation 'Torch', had been renumbered 509th to prevent confusion.) Commanded by Col Kenneth Kinsler, the 'Wildcats' had spent eight months training up in Queensland, Australia, and were chafing at the bit for action. It was soon to come. On 18 August the three battalions (I/ III/ and the new II/503rd) emplaned to Port

141

Moresby on the southern peninsula of New Guinea. Japanese troops were being slowly but steadily pushed off the island and the paras were to be used in support of an attack by the 9th Australian Infantry Division in the Huon Gulf on the north side of the island. They were to attack Nadzab airfield a few miles inland from the coastal town of Lae and hold it so that the 7th Australian Infantry Division could be air-landed in C-47s behind the Japanese positions.

The 9th Division landed virtually unopposed on 4 September some 20 miles (32km) north of the town and began marching towards it. The paras were supposed to drop on the following day but Port Moresby was fogbound so they could not take off until the 6th. The C-47s, flying in three streams and heavily defended by fighters while Gen Douglas MacArthur watched the operation from a high-flying B-17, made a perfect approach. The drop from 400ft (122m) was uneventful until the paras hit the ground. The area was covered with grass so tall the men could not see each other to group up and in the confusion two parties opened fire, each thinking the other was Japanese. Fortunately the mistake was soon discovered. There were no Japanese in occupation of the airfield, which had become heavily overgrown since it was abandoned earlier in the campaign, and the paras made short work of clearing the area with flamethrowers. Shortly afterwards a couple of bulldozers were flown in to complete the task and next morning the 7th Infantry Division began arriving. The paras only saw one brief firefight on the 16th when a party of Japanese fleeing from the Australians accidentally bumped into the 3rd Battalion, which drove them off at the cost of eight men killed. Next day the 503rd returned to Port Moresby and then back to Australia.

The regiment did not see action again until the following year. During his drive through New Guinea, a thorn in Gen MacArthur's side was the island of Biak, off the northern coast. He could not work out how its garrison was managing to hold out so long until, in the middle of June, he discovered they were being regularly reinforced and resupplied by barges sailing at night from the island of Noefmoor some 80 miles (130km) to the west. From 20 June to 1 July the air force pummelled the Japanese positions on Noefmoor in preparation for an amphibious invasion on the 2nd. This duly went in as planned at 08:00 and to begin with seemed to be going well. But then Brig-Gen Edwin Patrick, in charge of the operation, received information from a prisoner that 3,000 Japanese reinforcements had been brought in a few days earlier. Alarmed, he called for help from the 503rd, now commanded by Lt-Col George Jones since Col Kinsler had inexplicably committed suicide shortly after the Nadzab operation.

The regiment by this time was based at Hollandia, on the northern coast of New Guinea, and Jones rapidly completed plans for the 1st Battalion to fly in on the 3rd and the other two on the 4th. I/503rd duly arrived over Kamiri airfield — already in American hands — at 10:00, but some of the aircraft suffered from faulty altimeters resulting in 72 men, 10 per cent of the battalion, being severely injured through jumping from too low an altitude. Next day II/503rd suffered nearly as badly, with 56 casualties, so the 3rd Battalion was brought in by sea. The paras then fought alongside the American and Australian infantry to secure the island, which was finally cleared of opposition on 31st August. The 503rd would see its third and last combat drop on Corregidor in February 1945.

Meanwhile, the 11th Airborne Division had been shaping up and was ready for action. Its existence officially began at Fort Mackall on 25 February 1943 and it consisted of the 511th Parachute and 187th and 188th Glider Infantry Regiments plus the 457th and 674th Artillery Battalions and the 127th Engineer Battalion. The CO was Maj-Gen Joseph Swing, a former artillery commander in the 'All Americans'. It thus preceded Miley's 17th Airborne Division by six weeks. After months of training and working-up, the 11th was first committed to action on Leyte in the Philippines on 28 November 1944, although only in the line infantry role on the ground. Col Orin 'Rock' Haugen's 511th made good progress despite the steep slopes and thick jungle and by 4 December had claimed the Manarawat plateau, but they desperately needed close artillery support if they were to get any further — and all the guns were miles away. Undaunted, the CO of the 457th Artillery Battalion managed to scrounge a single C-47 from the few available and persuaded its pilot to undertake 13 round trips to drop the personnel and six 75mm Pack howitzers of his 'A' Battery to them on 6 December. By sheer coincidence, early the same evening 300 Japanese paras of the Katori Shimpei Force were dropped close to Swing's headquarters at San Pablo airstrip near Burauen. Grossly outnumbered in this kamikaze gesture, the unfortunate sons of the Rising Sun were contained by the 127th and 674th and wiped out next day by the 187th. The 11th Airborne continued fighting in the ground role until the end of the year and was finally taken out of the line on 15 January 1945 — the next target, Luzon, northernmost of the principal islands of the Philippine group.

The division's first mission here was the capture of Tagaytay Ridge, a prominent tactical feature overlooking the main road to the capital, Manila. The terrain was totally unsuited to gliders, so it was decided that Swing's two glider battalions would go in by sea and then be reinforced from the air by the paras of 'Rock' Haugen's 511th. The glider troops landed near Nasugbu on 31 January 1945 and, encountering little opposition, pressed inland to the highway. As they approached Tagaytay Ridge next day, however, they came under heavy fire from Mount Cariliao and Swing decided to delay the 511th's drop until 3 February. Because of aircraft shortages, the men would have to be transported in three waves. The first two drops went awry, most of the paras being dropped five miles (8km) short of the ridge which, fortunately, was devoid of Japanese troops or the few who did land in the right place would have had a hard time. The third drop on the morning of the 4th was spot on target. The 11th Airborne then marched on Manila, which was very heavily defended and did not finally fall until 21 February. During the fierce fighting, 'Rock' Haugen was wounded and command of the 511th passed to Lt-Col Edward Lahti. In total the division lost 900 of its 8,000 men but Japanese losses exceeded 3,000.

Even while the battle for Manila was still raging, the 11th's next mission was being planned in great secrecy. The Japanese were known to have a large prison compound just inland from Los Banos on the shore of Laguna de Bay. There were believed to be some 2,200 American civilians there, men, women and children captured when the Japanese overran the Philippines in 1942, and it was feared that their guards might massacre them as American troops approached. Swing was ordered to lay on a rescue mission. This took careful planning because of the risk to the prisoners if the guards did begin shooting at them, but the mission has entered history as a model for similar operations. First, a platoon of paras accompanied by Filipino guerrillas as guides would land at night on the shores of the lake and proceed secretly through the jungle to take up positions; some of the men were to secure a stretch of beach, some to ring the camp so they could fire straight into the watchtowers, and some to choose and mark a suitable drop zone as close as possible. Then, in the morning, a company of paras would be dropped from nine C-47s, their task together with the men already in place to kill all the guards. Particular stress was laid on the care to be taken to avoid accidentally hitting any of the prisoners. Next, a further three companies would travel across the lake in 59 LVT-2 tracked amphibious personnel carriers ('amtracs') borrowed from the Marines and debark at the selected beach. They would hold this against counter-attack while the LVTs raced to the prison compound to evacuate the prisoners. Finally, a diversionary attack would be launched overland to draw off Japanese troops in the area.

Lt John Ringler's 'A' Company of the I/511th was chosen for the drop itself and the rest of the battalion for the amtrac assault while the reconnaissance platoon would accomplish the initial infiltration. I/188th Glider Infantry Battalion would provide the diversion. Everything went miraculously smoothly. The recce platoon slipped ashore in the early hours of the morning of 22 February and hid out during the day before moving into the chosen positions during the following night. Then, at 07:00 on the 23rd, while the guards were holding the usual roll-call of their prisoners, smoke flares were ignited on the DZ and the nine aircraft carrying Ringler's company roared overhead. As they approached, one of the recce platoon blasted the pillbox guarding the camp entrance with his bazooka and the rest of the men opened fire on the watch towers. Then, within three minutes of an almost perfect touch-down, Ringler's men were racing into the camp. It was all over in 20 minutes with 243 Japanese dead and not a single fatality among either the 2,147 prisoners or their rescuers. Then the amtracs arrived and the deliriously happy prisoners were shepherded to safety.

The 11th Airborne, given the nickname 'Angels' after the Los Banos rescue, remained fighting on Luzon throughout the spring and summer, the I/511th making one more drop on 22 June to help ground forces secure the airstrip at Camalaniuga. The division was then shipped to Okinawa in preparation for the planned assault on the Japanese mainland which was forestalled by the dropping of atomic bombs on Hiroshima and Nagasaki at the obvious saving of thousands of Allied lives. After the Japanese surrender, the division remained on garrison duty in Japan until 1949 when it finally returned to the States to be disbanded in the postwar rundown.

In the meantime, while the 11th was struggling to capture Manila, on 16 February the 503rd had also made its last combat drop. The target was Corregidor island at the entrance to Manila Bay which was not only heavily fortified and garrisoned by nearly 5,000 tough Imperial Japanese Marines but also had several powerful batteries of coastal guns which constantly fired at passing shipping. However, Allied intelligence grossly underestimated the strength of the enemy garrison and a mere four battalions of troops were selected for the combined amphibious/airborne assault: I/, II/ and III/503rd and the 3rd Battalion of the 34th Infantry Regiment. III/503rd plus 'D' Battery of the 462nd Parachute Field Artillery Company and 'C' Company of the 161st Airborne Engineer Battalion would drop in the first wave in the morning, followed by II/503rd and 'B' Battery in the afternoon and I/503rd plus 'A' Battery the next day. Shortage of transport aircraft for the airborne role was a constant problem in the Far East, much more so than in Europe. On Corregidor a further problem was the small size of the DZs — the parade ground of the former US Army Topside barracks and a golf course! This meant that each aircraft could not drop a complete 'stick' but would have to deposit half a dozen men and return for a second pass.

The assault was preceded by an aerial and naval bombardment which did little damage to the well dug-in Japanese positions, and the paras suffered many casualties on landing from shattered rocks, trees and blocks of concrete which, due to the high prevailing wind, they were almost helpless to avoid. The wind also pulled a number of paras over the cliffs to their deaths on the rocks beneath before they could deflate their 'chutes or release their harnesses. Nevertheless, within a couple of hours the paras had succeeded in capturing Topside and killing the Japanese commander, Capt Akira Itagaki. The amphibious side of the assault had also been comparatively successful with few casualties, but the battle for the island would last until 27 February because the Japanese marines either holed themselves up in tunnels and caves from which they had to be winkled one by one, or launched suicidal frontal charges screaming 'banzai!' at the tops of their voices.

Further casualties were caused by two enormous subterranean explosions. Beneath Malinta Hill in the centre of the island lay a tunnel used as a bomb-proof ammunition dump. The naval bombardment had sealed off the entrances, trapping some 2,000 Japanese soldiers. In an attempt to break out, they used explosives to blast a gap but sympathetic detonation caused all the ammunition to explode which created a veritable earth-quake and killed six paras in a rockfall. However, there were only 600 dazed Japanese survivors from the explosion. There was a similar, smaller tunnel beneath Monkey Hill which had been used by American naval intelligence — who had cracked the Japanese 'Purple' cypher in much the same way the British had cracked 'Enigma' — to intercept Japanese radio messages. This too was blown up, killing 150 Japanese and 52 Americans. Nevertheless, Corregidor was finally cleared of all organized resistance by 27 February and on 2 March Gen MacArthur returned to the island he had been forced by order of President Franklin D. Roosevelt to abandon three years earlier. He saluted George Jones' paras underneath the still-standing flagpole on the parade ground and for the remainder of its brief existence the men of the 503rd wore a new sleeve badge showing a white eagle over a red outline of the island. Their last campaign was as amphibious troops on the Philippine island of Negros in April, after which the regiment was disbanded although the 1st and 2nd Battalions later formed the cadre for the 173rd Airborne Brigade in Vietnam.

British paras only undertook one major operation other than as ground forces in the Far East. It will be remembered (Chapter 3) that the 151st Parachute Battalion had been formed in India on 18 October 1941, followed by the 152nd (Indian) and 153rd (Gurkha) Battalions which together formed 50 Airborne Brigade. Then, in 1942 the 151st, renumbered 156th, was sent to North Africa to form part of 4 Para Brigade, being replaced by a new 154th (Gurkha) Battalion. This itself had been part of a new 77 Airborne Brigade and in turn was replaced by the 1st Battalion The Assam Regiment. The two brigades together formed the 44th Indian Airborne Division, commanded from the beginning of 1944 by 'Dracula' Down, now with the rank of Major-General. On his arrival the energetic Down ordered a general re-organisation. The Assam Regiment departed; 152 Para was split in two — the 1st and 2nd (Indian) Para Battalions — while the 153rd became the 2nd (Gurkha) Battalion. These constituted 50 Brigade. The 77th comprised the 154th, now renamed 3rd (Gurkha) Para Battalion, plus two battalions of former Chindits with air-landing experience, the 15th (King's) and 16th (South Staffordshire) Para Battalions. (There was no 1st (Gurkha) Para Battalion.) Finally, Down fleshed out his division with the 14th Air-Landing Brigade composed of the 2nd Battalion The King's Own Regiment, 2nd Battalion The Black Watch and 4th Battalion Rajputana Rifles, the latter also being an erstwhile Chindit unit.

(The Chindits' official title was 77th Independent Brigade. The unofficial but more popular title came from the name of the mythical beast which guards Burmese temples, the Chinthe. The brigade had been brought into existence late in 1942 by the unorthodox and deeply religious Brig Orde Wingate to penetrate in small columns deep into the Burmese jungle, attacking Japanese supply convoys and blowing up railway lines and bridges. In their first operation during February–April 1943 the Chindits blew up railway lines in 75 places and, more importantly, proved that the war could be taken to the enemy on equal terms. Their second major operation was in February the following year. By this time the Chindits were six brigades strong, but only three were used in the first phase, the 16th, 77th and 111th. They would form the point of Lt-Gen William Slim's Fourteenth Army which was to strike into Burma from Assam and link up with Gen Joseph 'Vinegar Joe' Stilwell's joint US–Chinese army pressing down from the north. The 16th Brigade marched overland towards the river Irrawady while the other two were flown in Waco Haig gliders to land in three jungle clearings astride the main railway line, codenamed 'White City', along which supplies were transported to the Japanese fighting in China. Although Wingate was killed in an air crash on 24 March 1944, flying in with the 14th and 3rd West African Brigades, his Chindits succeeded in tying down and crippling the best part of three Japanese divisions for four months, the exhausted survivors finally linking up with Stilwell's forces in June.)

The only airborne operation conducted by 44th Indian Airborne Division occurred on 1 May 1945 and was appropriately codenamed 'Dracula'. An amphibious assault was planned up the estuary of the River Rangoon to the Burmese capital city of the same name but a major obstacle to the success of this was a number of strong Japanese artillery positions on Elephant Point at the mouth of the river. Down put together a brigade-size assault group consisting of the 1st (Indian) and 2nd and 3rd (Gurkha) Para Battalions which dropped at dawn without mishap. Attacking the gun positions unexpectedly from the rear, they had overcome all resistance by late afternoon and next morning were able to sit on the casemates to cheer as the landing craft streamed unopposed up the river. It was a minor classic of an operation and showed clearly how airborne assault methods had improved since the early fumbling. The 44th Indian Division, renamed 2nd Indian Airborne Division, would next see action in Malaya in September.

7

Wars in peace

The end of the long battle against Germany and Japan produced an immediate rundown in the Allied armed forces, although this was nothing like as sudden or complete as in the weeks following the Armistice on 11 November 1918. Quite apart from the need to maintain forces of occupation in the former enemy countries, the colonial powers — principally Britain, France, Belgium and Holland — encountered considerable resistance and resentment at their return to the Far East. The Japanese had encouraged nationalism and allowed a limited degree of self-government in the countries they had overrun, and the inhabitants of Burma, Malaya, the Dutch East Indies and Indo-China had no wish to revert to being ruled from London, Paris, Brussels or The Hague. The same feeling also existed within the frequently communist-inspired resistance groups who had fought against instead of co-operating with their conquerors, collaborating with the Europeans and Americans through expediency rather than desire. The warring factions of different political, religious and racial or tribal groups would provide a large part of the problems with which successive postwar governments would have to deal, with varying degrees of success.

Nor was this 'Third World' wave of nationalism confined to those countries alone. India was chafing for independence and similar demands would gather strength in many other places around the world over the next few years, particularly in Africa. The new global super-power, the Soviet Union, with communist domination of the Earth its goal, would foster these movements and this would exacerbate the problem of finding peaceful solutions in Africa, Indo-China and Latin and Central America for decades. The emerging role of China as a fourth world power would complicate the issue, and in the meanwhile, as if that was not enough, civil war was raging in Greece and there was the tricky question of Palestine.

Over the years since 1945 many other countries have developed airborne forces and a large number of demobbed American and British paras found lucrative jobs as advisors and instructors, while numbers of Germans found their way into the French Foreign Legion and new battles in Algeria or Indo-China. Because of their mobility, such forces have played several key roles over the years either in helping legal governments suppress insurgents or, equally importantly, in the humanitarian roles of rescuing hostages and flying to the aid of earthquake, flood and famine victims. Paras have only been involved in five full-scale wars with battles matching those of 1939-45 — Korea, Vietnam, the Arab-Israeli Wars of 1967 and 1973, and the Gulf War in 1991 against Iraq — but they have seen action in many smaller-scale conflicts although more often as élite infantry than in the true airborne role. Since we are dealing here with the subject of airborne assault, the latter type of campaign — as earlier at Cassino and Bastogne — can only be given cursory attention.

Two other postwar phenomena must be noted: the growth of international terrorism and the establishment in recent years of élite counter-terrorist units, almost all trained in the techniques of parachuting, to deal with them. Most of these, in whichever country, are drawn from the ranks of existing para and marine units (although some are police or border guard paramilitary formations) and have developed high levels of professionalism. Finally we must take note of the arrival of the helicopter which has totally replaced the combat glider and revolutionized all aspects of modern warfare. (The first operational use of military helicopters in a war zone was actually in 1944 when Lt-Col Philip Cochrane's No 1 Air Commando, USAAF, flew 23 missions with Sikorsky R-4 twin-seaters on resupply and casualty evacuation roles in support of the second Chindit mission.)

In September 1945 the British 5th Parachute Brigade, 6th Airborne Division, recently sent to India to take part in the invasion of Japan, joined the 2nd Indian Airborne Division in helping to restore order in Singapore and Malaya, then spent three months in Java assisting the locals rebuild water, sanitation, medical and electrical services. The remainder of the division, minus the 6th Air-Landing Brigade which was re-formed as the 23rd Independent Infantry Brigade, was sent to Palestine as a peacekeeping force where it had many run-ins with the Jewish terrorist groups Haganah and Palmach until Britain withdrew in 1948 to let the Jews and Arabs fight it out among themselves. The 1st Airborne Division had been disbanded in November 1945 and the 6th Airborne was progressively run down too. At the time of its arrival in Palestine it consisted of 1 Para Brigade (1, 2 and 17 Para), 2 Para Brigade (4, 5 and 6 Para), and 3 Para Brigade (3, 8 and 9 Para). 17 Para joined 5 Brigade (alongside 12 and 13 Para) in Java in 1946 and 1 Brigade received 7 Para in return. All this was very shortlived, however, for by the beginning of 1948, 3 and 5 Brigades had ceased to exist. In February 1948 2 Brigade was sent to Germany and next month 1 Brigade began to return to the UK. Almost immediately the 6th Airborne Division was also disbanded because the new cost-conscious Labour government which had replaced Winston Churchill's wartime coalition had decided the army only needed a single brigade.

To commemorate the wartime 1st and 6th Divisions, this was given the title 16th Parachute Brigade. It consisted of a new 1 Para formed from the amalgamated 4th/6th Battalions while 5 Para was renumbered 2 and 7 Para as 3. In addition, as a pathfinder force, the brigade contained the 200-strong 1st (Guards) Independent Parachute Company. All were part of The Parachute Regiment, the CO being Brig-Gen Sir Kenneth Darling. Further troubleshooting followed in Cyprus in 1951, and Egypt in 1951–4 when the brigade was principally used to defend the Suez Canal in the wake of the military coup which deposed King Farouk in February 1952.

Meanwhile, the two wartime Special Air Service Regiments had also been disbanded but in 1947 the War Office (today the Ministry of Defence) decided that the army still had a need for such a specialist raiding force and reactivated a Territorial Army regiment, The Artists' Rifles, as 21 Special Air Service Regiment (Artists) — (Volunteers). Then in 1950 Brig Michael Calvert, wartime CO of 1 SAS Brigade, was sent out to Malaya at the request of Gen Sir John Harding, C-in-C Far East Land Forces. After evaluating the situation, Calvert established a small counter-insurgency force which he called the Malayan Scouts (SAS). This was so successful in its difficult task of beating the insurgents and winning the 'hearts and minds' of the villagers that it rapidly grew to four squadrons, one of them Rhodesian, and was given the official title 22 Special Air Service Regiment in May 1952. Training was in the capable hands of Maj J.M. Woodhouse, whose influence can be seen in all later formations of the same type. Among the rather dangerous airborne assault techniques the SAS pioneered in Malaya was that of parachuting into the densely packed jungle tree-tops carrying a 100ft (30m) length of rope, using which the men could abseil down to the ground. After many broken limbs, this technique was abandoned except for emergency use when there was simply no other way of reaching a target.

In 1956 the Rhodesians returned to their own country and were replaced by a New Zealand squadron; but from these small beginnings both Rhodesia (now Zimbabwe) and New Zealand developed their own Special Air Service Regiments, organized and trained along British lines. Shortly afterwards a party of 80 volunteers from 16 Para Brigade under Maj Dudley Coventry arrived and formed a fifth squadron, the Independent Parachute Squadron. Subsequently a second Territorial regiment was raised and ever since then the establishment of the Special Air Service Regiments has been 22 SAS, the Regulars, based at Bradbury Lines, Hereford; 21 SAS (TA), which recruits in the south of England; and 23 SAS (TA) in the north. Members of each all undergo the same strenuous selection and training procedures although in the Territorial regiments the time scale is stretched to allow the men to fulfil the demands of their normal civilian jobs as well.

This is perhaps an appropriate point at which to examine the training which makes a modern para and the extra effort which has to be put into being accepted for the SAS (which the army calls 'Sass', without the

definite article) or similar élite behind-the-lines reconnaissance and sabotage teams. (It should be noted that, although it receives the most
publicity, the counter-terrorist role for the SAS and most of its equivalents
is really a secondary one as far as the military are concerned.) Since
methods only vary in detail from army to army — a couple still using
balloons but most having dispensed with them — and since drop speeds
and altitudes are fairly standardized regardless of aircraft, a fairly typical
training course for a para can be summarized as follows.

In most armies, including the British, volunteers for parachute training
have to go through an extremely arduous physical toughening-up process
lasting several weeks. In America and some other countries volunteers are
only selected from the ranks of existing regiments and merely have to pass
a medical and a physical fitness test before going straight through to jump
school at Ford Benning. While there, though, they have to do a strenuous
amount of PE each day and infractions of the slightest rule result in a
minimum of 10 press-ups as punishment. Where there is a pre-jump
course, the emphasis is on endurance, toughening the men both physically
and developing a mental posture which allows them to keep on going with
lungs burning raw and every muscle screaming for respite. The paras do
not need Olympic athletes or muscle-bound weightlifters, they do not need
Arnold Schwarzneggers but they do need men who will not give up
because the ability simply to endure is one of the most important a soldier
has to develop. This is particularly so in parachute units because the men,
as we have seen in earlier chapters, may be called on to hold out deep in
enemy-controlled countryside for considerable lengths of time before
being relieved by ground forces.

Aggression is another attribute which has to be developed because,
although man is the most aggressive creature on this planet, civilized
modern societies do not normally encourage it except in symbolic form, as
in sport. A soldier has to overcome the instinctive fear of getting hurt and
to learn that the best way of avoiding pain is to lay the other man out first.
Thus compulsory boxing matches form a part of para training, and those
who flinch will be weeded out. Discipline is also strict, not through sadism
but as a means of developing the self-discipline and sense of pride and
self-reliance which are further hallmarks of the trained paratrooper.

Obstacle courses, including swarming along ropes suspended 50ft (15m)
above the ground to further weed out anyone without a head for heights
and crawling through muddy pools to get rid of the natural aversion to dirt
and wet feature strongly in the training, as do cross-country runs in all
weathers either wearing PE kit or full combat fatigues and rucksack. These
get progressively longer as the physical toughening-up process eliminates
'flab' and begins building muscle tone and stamina. Then, of course, there
is weapons training with the basic infantry weapons of rifle, sub-machine-gun and grenade followed by the gamut of other modern weaponry
including portable anti-tank and anti-aircraft missiles. Map reading and
fieldcraft, cross-country navigation by day and night, camouflage and the

skills of living off the land are all learned, and for those men who later volunteer for the SAS or similar equivalent elsewhere, these are further refined to an unbelievable degree. Recruits are constantly assessed by their instructors at every stage in the initial training period, which will normally last three or four months. Then, for the survivors — since many of the original candidates will have dropped out voluntarily or been told they are unsuitable — comes the moment when they have been waiting for, the jump course. This normally lasts three weeks: ground week, tower week and jump week, to which the British army adds an extra in the form of a jump from a tethered balloon before the men actually get into an aircraft.

During the first week recruits learn how to don the parachute harness, how to hook up their static lines in a mock aircraft fuselage, and the proper posture for exiting an aircraft door. The latter is vital because, even with modern 'chutes, a faulty exit can result in spinning or the rigging lines getting twisted or, worst of all, a thrown line causing partial or complete deflation of the canopy. The recruits also practise the correct techniques for landing, either making controlled descents in harnesses suspended from the roof of an aircraft hangar or from a small training tower usually some 30–40ft (9–11m) high. A fan similar to the wind machine used in making movies simulates the effect of the aircraft slipstream at a typical drop speed of 125kt. During the first week each man will make literally hundreds of mock jumps under the critical eyes of the instructors, for landing is the time when injuries are incurred if you fail to roll properly, keeping your elbows in, feet together, knees bent and using hips and shoulders to cushion the shock.

After ground week, recruits move on to the tower. These vary in height from country to country between 150 and 250ft (46–77m). After either climbing a ladder to the top or being bodily hoisted on a cable, the men are released on controlled descents while instructors on the ground shout advice or curse their parentage. There are also jumps from the exit trainer designed to accustom the men to jumping out of an aircraft door and descending down a sloping cable to the ground. After this, in most armies the trainees go straight on to an actual jump from an aircraft, but in the British army there is an additional ordeal to face — the balloon jump.

Strapped into their parachute harnesses, which the previous week's tower practice will have taught them to adjust correctly to prevent injury to their most sensitive parts, the men enter the balloon cage. Its cable is paid out and the balloon rises slowly to 800ft (247m). Inside the cage, sweating and dry-mouthed, the men watch the ground recede while the instructor cheerfully points out local landmarks as they become visible. This is the most terrifying moment of all. The swaying motion of the basket induces nausea and, whereas in an aircraft there is a sense of psychological detachment from the ground which reduces vertigo, in a balloon cage one is acutely aware of how far away the ground has become. Then, static lines hooked up, the men jump one after another at the instructor's command. The trick is not to look down. Suddenly the swaying of the balloon has gone. 'One thousand and one, one thousand and two . . .' With a jerk the static line pulls the canopy open. Terror is replaced by exhilaration as the recruit realises he has actually done it and is floating gently to earth on a real parachute, not a length of cable. This feeling quickly changes to panic as the ground is suddenly rushing up. Knees bend — thump! Roll and gather in the shrouds, slap the quick-release button and bundle up the canopy. A tremendous sensation of relief and achievement, each man feeling nine feet tall and covered with hair.

Unfortunately, the balloon proves too much for some and they refuse to jump. They are not pushed because the instructors know that if a man cannot pass this test voluntarily, he will not make a para no matter how good he is at everything else. However, his other skills will be put to good use in another regiment. For the men who have managed the balloon jump, the next descent from an aircraft is easy. Different countries demand different numbers of jumps to qualify for the paratroop Wings: in America, for example, it is five, in Britain seven. The first jumps are 'clean' but the last two or three are with full equipment, drop heights varying from 1,000 to 2,000ft (308–616m), and one of them is at night. Then, finally, comes the passing-out parade but even then training never really stops, particularly for those who go on to one of the élite deep penetration units such as the SAS or other special force. Now the men must practise simulated combat drops in varying types of terrain, from the frozen wastes of Canada, Norway or northern Russia to arid deserts and jungles, for the modern para has to be ready to be sent anywhere in the world at only a few hours' notice.

A totally unexpected location for a full scale conflict in 1950 was Korea. On 8 August 1945, immediately following the Potsdam Conference between Churchill, Stalin and the new American President Harry S. Truman, Russia had declared war on Japan and the Red Army swept through Manchuria and on into northern Korea. By prior agreement the Russians halted at the 38th Parallel, leaving the Americans to occupy the southern half of the country. Subsequent elections in 1948 established two rival governments, a communist one in the north and a democracy in the south. Each laid claim to the whole country, however. The Soviet army evacuated the north in December 1948 and the Americans the south in July 1949. Then, just before dawn on 25 June 1950, the Democratic People's Republic of (North) Korea invaded the Republic of (South) Korea. The United Nations Security Council promptly called for a ceasefire and asked member nations to send military aid to the south. The Americans were in first, followed rapidly by Britons, Australians and ultimately contingents from another 13 countries.

The only parachute unit to see action during the war, which would last until 27 July 1953, was the 187th Regimental Combat Team (RCT) from the US 11th Airborne Division. The division itself, having returned from Japan to Fort Campbell in Kentucky in 1949 to be disbanded, was a mere shadow of its former self but within two months of the North Korean invasion of the South the 187th, a former glider unit, had been rebuilt to full strength as a parachute outfit. Commanded by Col Frank Bowen, it comprised 4,400 men in three rifle battalions (I/, II/ and II/187th), an artillery battalion, an anti-aircraft battery, an engineer company and two pathfinder teams, which all sailed for Korea in September 1950. At this time, two months before China unexpectedly entered the war and caused a rapid reversal, the South Korean and UN armed forces had the North Korean People's Army (NKPA) on the run following the amphibious landings at Inchon and were closing on their capital Pyongyang.

The 187th was air-lifted in to Kimpo airfield on 24 September, coming under immediate fire from snipers even though American ground forces had supposedly cleared the area. The regiment then spent the next three weeks assisting forces in clearing the Kimpo peninsula before preparing for the first of the two combat drops it would make. This came on 20 October. There were two railway lines heading north from Pyongyang, along which trainloads of North Korean VIPs and American prisoners of war were being sent, and Gen Douglas MacArthur decided to use the 187th to block these at Suk'chon and Sun'chon some 30 miles (48km) away, to intercept any more trains and at the same time cut off the line of retreat for NKPA troops north of the capital.

Heavy rain delayed the paras' departure until noon but eventually the first of 40 C-47s and 73 of the new C-119 'Flying Boxcars' (*Appendix 2*) lumbered into the air from Kimpo. The 1st and 3rd Battalions, with Col Bowen in the lead, dropped from 600ft (185m) at Suk'chon in the face of light rifle fire which killed one man, and there were 25 injuries on landing. Trucks, Jeeps, 105mm howitzers and 75mm recoilless guns followed, most landing without damage. The two battalions immediately fanned out to establish road and rail blocks north and south of the town but as it happened they had missed the last train out of Pyongyang by about four hours thanks to the weather. The 2nd Battalion dropped without incident at Sun'chon, although again there were 20 casualties from awkward landings, and they quickly moved to link up with the 6th South Korean Division; unfortunately the Koreans failed to recognise them to begin with and opened fire, but the mistake was soon corrected. The 2nd Battalion had just missed a second train, which the North Koreans hid in a railway tunnel. There were 89 American PoWs aboard. With the paras at their heels, the North Korean guards herded the prisoners off the train and machine-gunned them. Only 23 men survived by feigning death and two of those died subsequently from their wounds.

Next day Bowen's III/187th started moving south towards Pyongyang but soon bumped into the 2,500-strong 239th Infantry Regiment which the North Koreans had left behind as a rearguard to cover the retreat of their other forces. They had established a strong line in the hills between Yongyu and Opa-ri straddling both the railway and the main road but the paras' attack in their rear took them completely by surprise. The battle continued throughout the night with the Koreans making four determined but largely unsuccessful attempts to break through the 187th's positions. Then, on the morning of the 22nd, the British Commonwealth 27th Brigade, which included armour as well as infantry and artillery, moved up from the south, trapping the North Koreans in a pocket from which there was no escape. At the end of the day the 681 survivors surrendered. The 187th had only incurred 66 casualties in the battle, a remarkable accomplishment.

On 26 November 1950 Mao Tse-tung's communist government of mainland China openly came to the assistance of North Korea, sending 18 divisions of troops, some 200,000 men, across the border. At this time it must be remembered that the United States regarded Chiang Kai-shek's government in exile on Formosa (Taiwan) as the legitimate rulers of the country. Many people in America were saying that MacArthur should not stop at the river Yalu but should drive on through Manchuria to Peking (Beijing). Others went further and suggested he should press on to the Russian port of Vladivostock. MacArthur himself shared these sentiments and when he went public on them early in 1951, Truman had no alternative but to relieve him of his command in April. His replacement, to the paras' particular delight, was none other than Matthew Ridgway, who had already succeeded to command of XVIII Corps the previous December.

The 187th's second drop came on 23 March 1951. By this time the Chinese offensive had run out of steam and the UN forces had succeeded in stabilising the situation, recapturing Inchon and Seoul after a fierce struggle. The 187th was to drop at Munsan-Ni, co-operating with ground forces in a pincer move to destroy the North Korean bridgehead over the river Imjin. Taking off at 10:00, the heavily-laden 'Rakkasans' — a nickname meaning 'falling down umbrella' which they had acquired in Japan — dropped in hilly farmland north of the town and were immediately involved in a heavy firefight with troops of the North Korean 19th Division. The 1st Battalion landed in the wrong place, practically in the middle of a strong communist position, and had to fight their way out, but the other two battalions occupied their chosen positions on two hills flanking the main road north from Munsan-Ni — ironically, re-occupying foxholes they had abandoned in the earlier retreat. By mid-afternoon a column of British tanks had arrived and the enemy had retreated over 20 miles (32km) to a ridge at Paron-Ni. Dislodging them would take a further two days.

The 187th did not undertake any more drops, but served as ordinary infantry for the remainder of the war which only dragged to a reluctant and uneasy end after the newly-elected American President Dwight D. Eisenhower made a non-specific but obvious threat to use nuclear weapons. This was far from the end of US military involvement in the Far East, however, for the disastrous conflict in Indo-China (Vietnam), Laos and Cambodia (Kampuchea) would follow all too soon. Here, French troops had been involved since 1946 in an ultimately futile attempt to restore colonial rule after the Japanese defeat. They were bitterly opposed to Ho Chi Minh's communist-inspired Viet Minh and French paras saw some of the roughest action, particularly at Dien Bien Phu.

The first French parachute unit was a platoon from the 5th Infantry Regiment which began jump training at the American Kun Ming air base in China in 1945. Rapid expansion followed as French determination to hang on to Indo-China was only equalled by Ho Chi Minh's determination to throw them out, and by 1947 a complete parachute division, numbered the 25th, was in existence. However, French law precluded conscripts from Metropolitan France serving in this theatre, the brunt of the fighting falling on colonial troops, so in the spring of 1948 the Foreign Legion began raising and training its own paratroop units. The first was formed from a company of the 3e Régiment Étranger d'Infanterie (3rd Foreign Infantry Regiment) in Hanoi on 1 April and this was rapidly followed by two full battalions, 1er and 2e Bataillon Étranger de Parachutistes (1st and 2nd Foreign Parachute Battalions, usually abbreviated to 1er and 2e BEP). 1er BEP had its headquarters at Khamisis just outside the Legion's famous depot at Sidi bel Abbeś and 2e BEP at Sétif, both in Algeria. Until 1951 they used ex-Luftwaffe Junkers Ju 52s as their transport aircraft before these were replaced by C-47s, C-119s and, later Nord Noratlas N2501s (*Appendix 2*).

Between them, French paras made 156 drops during the long drawn-out war against the Viet Minh forces commanded by Vo Nguyen Giap, the first being near Haiphong on 18 March 1949 and the last between 9 and 21 November 1954 near Dien Bien Phu. It is impractical to chronicle them all here, but in principle the French used their paras to penetrate areas which could not be reached by ordinary infantry, either reinforcing existing garrisons or attacking arms dumps deep in the jungle. The reasons for the French, and later the American, failure in Indochina, lay principally in the simple fact that the indigenous population did not want them there. The wars were not those simplistically portrayed in many accounts as 'democracy' versus 'communism'. The Vietnamese people wanted and fought and died for the right to self-determination without unasked-for outside interference. And, despite the lives they cost, the wars created a cultural revolution in Western society which is slowly, belatedly and with inevitable wrong turnings on occasion, turning the world into a better place to live. Similarly, Soviet experience in Afghanistan was the real stimulus towards the recent reforms in Eastern Europe which have pushed back the barriers to international relationships and understanding so dramatically and, to a soldier of the 1950s, so incomprehensibly. Polemics aside, airborne forces have, however unwittingly, played a far from inconsiderable part in causing these changes, so I plead the reader's indulgence.

The French, and later the Americans, faced not only a complex problem of logistics with men and supplies having to be ferried in across thousands of miles, but also made the mistake of trying to fight a conventional war against a guerrilla force which could merge into the civilian background and largely refused to be drawn into open battle. The Viet Minh, completely at home in the mountains, jungles and paddy fields, could run rings around motorized troops who by and large were forced to stick to the roads, and the French found themselves engaged in a war of attrition in which no convoy was safe from ambush. From the beginning they only really controlled a wedge-shaped area of the country centred on Hanoi and the Hong (Red) River Delta while the communists controlled the north with its supply lines into China (after Chiang Kai-shek's defeat in 1949 and the establishment of Mao's People's Republic on 1 October), as well as most of the south.

The war in Indo-China falls broadly into five phases. In the first, from March 1946 to February 1950, there was no real war at all because Giap's troops withdrew into the hinterland and there were only sporadic, small-scale brushes. In 1949, for example, the 1er BEP dropped near Loung Phai after an ambush on a French convoy on 13 October but missed the enemy who had evaporated into the jungle, a characteristic of the fighting which was to become typical. Then Giap started the second phase by launching his first major offensive, taking Lao Kai and Dong Khe in rapid succession and cutting off the French garrison in Cao Bang by mid-September. The 1er BEP dropped on That Khe over the 17th/18th to go to their relief but, faced with an estimated 15 battalions of Viet Minh infantry, were forced to give up the attempt until 3 October, when the garrison began a breakout attempt towards Hanoi. Accompanied by three battalions of Moroccan infantry, the paras did their best and after constant ambushes, particularly one in the gorge at Coc Xa, managed to link up with the garrison troops on the evening of the 7th, virtually out of ammunition. By the time they had struggled pack to That Khe, however, there were only 29 survivors from the battalion's original 499. And on the 17th Lang Son, still further south, also had to be abandoned. The 2e BEP was dropped at Sin Ma Kay on the 20th to help the stragglers retreat to Lao Kai through the heavily forested mountains and after a three-day forced march with numerous rearguard clashes they marched into the town in column and singing. There was not, in truth, much to sing about, but para panache is undeniable. The French had actually lost over 6,000 men in total during this short campaign, a signal defeat which encouraged the growing public demand in France to bring the troops home.

Instead, one of France's foremost Generals, Jean de Lattre de Tassigny (who had led the Free French forces which recaptured Toulon and Marseilles in August 1944), was sent to take control of the situation. In the third phase of the war he repelled three major Viet Minh offensives between January and June 1951 and established a line of 'hedgehog' defences — heavily fortified military compounds with barbed wire, minefields, dugouts, bunkers and concealed artillery and machine-gun positions — around the Red River Delta. Behind this line de Lattre began building up a mobile reserve of armoured and motorized as well as parachute battalions to take the war back to the enemy. The decimated 1er

BEP had been re-formed and in March 1951 the paras were reinforced by the arrival of the new 3rd Battalion from Algeria; this was followed by the creation of the first native Indo-Chinese parachute company in May.

De Lattre then had three battalions of paras dropped on the important Viet Minh supply base of Hoa Binh over 10–13 November, which they captured without difficulty. Instead of counter-attacking as de Lattre had hoped, though, Giap employed the best part of three divisions to simply cut them off from their supply lines. By January 1952 their situation was hopeless because the airfield was under constant artillery fire, making airlifts hazardous and costly, and on the 18th the new French commander, Gen Raoul Salan — de Lattre having fallen sick and returned to France where he had died on the 11th — sent a relief force to re-open the road and bring them out. This they achieved on the 29th and after fighting on for a further three weeks, the whole garrison was withdrawn in a running battle between 22 and 24 February.

There was now an eight-month lull in the fighting before Giap returned to the attack in October 1952, taking Nghia Lo ridge between the Red and Black Rivers and prompting Salan into an ill-conceived assault by air-borne and motorized troops deep into Viet Minh territory at Phu Doan. Codenamed operation 'Lorraine', the attack involved the Foreign Legion's 1st and 2nd Para Battalions and the 3rd Colonial Para Battalion. They dropped from 450ft (137m) on 9 November, capturing and destroying several major dumps of Viet Minh guns, mortars, ammunition and trucks, then linked up with ground forces advancing up Route Coloniale 2. However, Giap refused to be drawn into battle and on 16 November the paras withdrew without incident. The ground forces following them next day, however, were ambushed by two Viet Minh regiments in the Chan Muong gorge and lost 1,200 men.

The 1er and 2e BEP were then flown in to Na San near the Laotian border where they helped repel wave after wave of suicidal Viet Minh frontal attacks, leaving hundreds of enemy dead lying on the barbed wire before being withdrawn to Hanoi in January 1953. The paras subsequently operated principally as security forces until 16 July when 2e BEP together with the 6e Bataillon de Parachutistes Coloniale (BPC) and the 8e Groupement Coloniale de Parachutistes (GCP) took part in operation 'Hirondelle' to seize another major Viet Minh arms dump at Lang Son. While the colonial troops took the main objective the Legion paras jumped at Loc Binh to capture, repair and hold the bridge there, covering the withdrawal of the 6e BPC and 8e GCP two days later after a totally successful raid.

The final phase of the war began in April 1953 when Giap's troops invaded Laos. This put an entirely different complexion on the war. The French still held Hanoi and the Red River Delta by the skin of their teeth but the rest of Vietnam beyond the de Lattre Line was almost totally controlled by the Viet Minh. Even at the time it seemed absurd to continue the war, as increasing numbers of Frenchmen at home were saying, and with the 20:20 vision of hindsight it now seems yet more so. However, the newly arrived third French commander in Indo-China, General Henri Navarre, started making plans to counter the latest threat in May, although they would not be complete until November because a number of options — including a virtual replay of operation 'Lorraine' — had to be scrutinised first. Eventually, however, the decision was taken to seize and hold the valley plateau of Dien Bien Phu, high in the T'ai Mountains 170 miles (272km) from Hanoi. This would block Giap's principal supply route into Laos, cutting off the Viet Minh troops already in the country, and provide a secure base from which French troops could also launch offensive operations into the northern Vietnamese heartland. Because of its isolation, Dien Bien Phu could only be reached and kept supplied by air, so the whole operation was to all intents and purposes dropped in the paras' collective lap.

The first wave, comprising the army's 1er and 6e BPC and the 2nd Battalion of the 1er Régiment d'Infanterie Légère, jumped into the valley on 20 November and rapidly secured the area against light opposition. Reinforcements flown in over the next two days included the 1er BEP, 8e GCP and 5e Bataillon Indochinois de Parachutistes Légère Étranger. They took over the two airstrips outside Dien Bien Phu and pushed patrols into the surrounding hills while further regular infantry battalions, including three Algerian, two T'ai (Vietnamese montagnards) and one Moroccan, were air-landed to reinforce them. Giap was slow to react and the French, commanded by Gen Christian de Castries, were allowed time to construct a number of fortified redoubts around the valley floor, all named by the CO after past and present girlfriends! This, however, was merely the lull before the storm. Viet Minh artillery, firing from well-concealed positions in the hills, began a leisurely barrage on 31 December which intensified through January, but the real battle opened on 11 March 1954.

At this time the French garrison consisted of 12 battalions, some 10,800 men, with 24 105mm guns, four 155mm howitzers and 10 American-built M-24 Chaffee light tanks. Against them Giap ranged five full divisions, nearly 50,000 men with over 200 artillery pieces and large numbers of heavy calibre mortars. The first round went to the Viet Minh, the north-eastern redoubt, 'Beatrice', falling in a night attack on 13 March, the northernmost position, 'Gabrielle', having to be abandoned on the 15th, followed by 'Anne Marie' to the north-west during the night of the 17th/18th. This left four redoubts surrounding the immediate vicinity of the principal airstrip with a fifth one further south down the river Nam Oum virtually isolated. The Viet Minh now had control of all the surrounding hills and the artillery bombardment around the airstrip became increasingly effective. The landscape began to resemble the cratered surface of the moon and the last C-47 departed with its cargo of wounded on the 27th. The garrison was now completely cut off and Giap intensified his efforts against the four redoubts still guarding the north, east and west of the airstrip, 'Francoise', 'Huguette', 'Dominique' and

'Elaine'. All except the smallest, 'Francoise', held out and by 4 April, having lost some 2,000 men in kamikaze frontal attacks against the well dug-in defenders, Giap had to pause and rethink.

The Legion's 2e BEP parachuted in to the garrison's assistance in three drops over 9–12 April, coming under heavy fire and almost immediately losing 29 men. It was a brave but forlorn gesture, for the French Air Force, on whom the defenders relied both for supplies and for fighter-bombers to keep the enemy at bay, was losing too many aircraft to accurate fire from Chinese-supplied anti-aircraft guns. The redoubts crumbled one by one, the two Legion para battalions sharing the brunt of the fighting and by 25 April having suffered such heavy casualties that they had to be amalgamated in a single composite unit. The final Viet Minh assault began on 1 May and outpost after outpost was overrun in close-quarter struggles which resembled those of the Western Front during the First World War. Eventually, having lost 7,184 men out of a garrison which at its strongest had numbered 16,000, on 7 May de Castries ordered the white flag raised. Two months later, on 21 July 1954, agreements were signed in Geneva giving Laos and Cambodia independence but, ominously in the light of the Korean experience, dividing Vietnam at the 17th Parallel into Ho Chi Minh's communist Democratic Republic of North Vietnam with Hanoi as its capital and the pro-Western Republic of South Vietnam under Ngho Dinh Diem ruled from Saigon. This set the scene for another war a decade later which would virtually tear America apart.

The French returned to their homes to find themselves almost immediately embroiled in two more conflicts which would similarly create vast rifts in their own society. The first was the battle against the Moslem nationalist ALN, or Army of National Liberation in Algeria, which sought to throw off French rule and which, after de Gaulle's *volte face* in 1959 to which we shall return momentarily, produced a mutiny in the French army in which the paras played a significant part. First, however, we must look at operation 'Musketeer', the joint Anglo–French airborne and amphibious invasion of the Suez Canal zone in 1956.

Following the fall of King Farouk of Egypt in 1952, the anti-British Col Gamal Abdel Nasser (who had been a German sympathiser during the Second World War) became the country's dictator. Worried by this development, the British kept a military presence in the country until the end of March 1956 when the last troops were withdrawn. At this time the UK was still putting financial backing into the Aswan Dam project, but when Nasser promptly began buying Soviet arms and equipment this aid was withdrawn in June. The Egyptian President retaliated on 26 July by nationalising the Anglo-French Suez Canal Company in order to collect its revenue to pay for the dam and, in contravention of international law, forbade passage through the canal to Israeli shipping. When diplomatic negotiations failed the only solution appeared to be a military one, but planning the execution of this took time.

One of the reasons for this was the sad fact that the men of the 16th

Parachute Brigade — whose 1st and 3rd Battalions were then engaged in the battle against EOKA ('National Organization of Cypriot Fighters') terrorists under Col George Grivas on Cyprus — had had virtually no experience or practice in parachuting since 1945. Moreover, unlike the French who had built up their airborne forces from scratch since 1946 and equipped them with modern weapons and aircraft, including folding stock rifles which could be fired while the paras were actually descending, the men of the three British para battalions only had old Lee-Enfield rifles and wartime Sten sub-machine and Bren light machine-guns. On top of this, while waiting for the new Blackburn Beverley transport aircraft (*Appendix 2*) which could carry the equally new Austin Champ ground mobility vehicle, they had to put up with ageing Handley Page Hastings, Vickers Valettas (*Appendix 2*) and Jeeps. Nevertheless, once 2 Para was installed in Cyprus in August, 1 and 3 Paras were returned to Aldershot to get some hasty practice jumps in. They were given 10 days in which to complete four drops, in between which most men managed to get at least 48 hours leave, resulting in a baby boom in The Parachute Regiment nine months later! Then it was back to Cyprus.

The invasion plan was amended several times and the final one adopted was something of a rushed compromise which succeeded against the odds. The airborne side of the operation was to be conducted by the 600-strong British 3 Para under Lt-Col Paul Crook and the 500-man French 2e Régiment de Parachutistes Coloniaux (RPC) under Col Pierre Château-Jobert, with Col Conan's 1er Régiment de Chasseurs Parachutistes following later in the day and 1 and 2 Para plus the Foreign Legion's rebuilt 2e Régiment Étranger de Parachutistes coming in with the amphibious task force over the next two days. Compared with the British, most of whom had never made a combat jump, many of the Frenchmen were veterans of more than one drop in Indo-China. Against them was ranged an Egyptian army with a mixture of old British, French and American plus new Soviet equipment, including MiG-15 jet fighters. To draw the bulk of this off, clandestine arrangements (which have never been fully admitted in public even though they are totally transparent) were made that Israel would precede the Anglo-French invasion by a ground offensive across the Sinai Desert towards the Suez Canal. In this way the European 'intervention' would, it was optimistically hoped, be seen around the world as a peacekeeping move. Sometimes politicians are very naïve . . .

The Israeli offensive opened on 29 October and 24 hours later Britain and France cynically demanded a ceasefire and the right to send in troops to safeguard passage of the canal to all shipping. This was, of course, ignored by both sides so on the 31st British and French air force and naval aircraft began an intensive four-day bombardment of Egyptian air force installations which wiped out most of their aircraft. Then, shortly before midnight on 4 November, the paras began donning their kit and checking their weapons and at 04:15 on the 5th the first aircraft began lifting off from Nicosia, the slower British machines preceding the French. The plan was that 3 Para would drop on Gamil airfield, which lies on the narrow isthmus west of Port Said between the Mediterranean and Lake el Manzala at 07:15, just after first light, followed 15 minutes later by 2e RPC whose objective was to secure the two Raswa bridges south of Port Said on the western side of the Suez Canal which connect the port with the mainland.

As the British aircraft lumbered towards Port Said, an English Electric Canberra bomber dropped a smoke flare on Gamil airfield to both mark the DZ and indicate wind strength and direction, for one of the problems foreseen was that, given such a narrow strip of land on which to drop, there was a very real risk of many men being blown out to sea. The aircraft flew into fierce but fortunately inaccurate flak as the paras hooked up and began throwing themselves out of the doors and there were few casualties. Within 10 minutes the battalion was on the ground and, having retrieved their weapons from their containers, began fanning out, taking casualties from several Egyptian machine-gun positions and pillboxes. 'A' Company quickly cleared the control tower and airport buildings while 'B' Company moved east to take out a troublesome pillbox with a bazooka round and 'C' Company another to the south. HQ and 'D' Companies then established a headquarters for Brig M.A.H. Butler, CO of 16th Parachute Brigade, who had elected to go in with the drop rather than with 1 and 2 Para next day. The airfield was secured within half an hour but by this time the paras were taking casualties from artillery and Russian 'Katyusha' multiple rocket launchers deployed west of Port Said.

Crook now sent 'A' Company west of the airfield to demolish the Gamil bridge and prevent an Egyptian attack from that direction while 'B' Company, which had suffered the heaviest casualties in the airfield battle, moved east towards a sewage farm where another pillbox was causing trouble. During this attack the company CO, Maj Dick Stephens, was badly wounded and his place taken by Capt Karl Beale. The Egyptians had now entrenched themselves in a cemetery still further east and Crook passed 'C' Company through 'B' Company to drive them out. The attack went in at 10:30, preceded by a massive air strike which caused many Egyptian casualties, but their fighting spirit remained high as Maj Ron Norman's men charged forward and there was a fierce close-quarters battle among the gravestones before the paras finally drove them out. They chased the Egyptian troops back towards Port Said, on the outskirts of which four heavily armoured Russian SU-100 self-propelled assault guns had been shelling the airfield. Another air strike so demoralized their crews that they abandoned the vehicles!

However, heavy machine-gun fire was still coming from the ground floor of a block of flats. Spotting an abandoned Egyptian Bren Gun Carrier, the CO of the paras' Machine-Gun Platoon, Lt Mike Newall, jumped into it with Sgt Davidson and drove straight towards the flats, killing the crews of the machine-guns with several well aimed bursts.

Tragedy nearly followed because, as Newall and Davidson raced back towards the cemetery, a trigger-happy gunner with a 106mm recoilless anti-tank gun nearly opened up on them, being prevented in the nick of time by a quick-thinking NCO. The paras then consolidated their positions, having been warned not to try to advance any further or they would be exposed to the naval artillery bombardment which would precede the main amphibious assault in the morning.

Meanwhile, their French counterparts had been equally busy and equally successful. The Noratlas aircraft flew in tight formation because the DZ south of the Raswa bridges was only 150yds (140m) wide so close grouping was essential, and dropped their sticks of paras at 520ft (160m). With no need to open weapons containers, 2e RPC was in action within four minutes of hitting the ground. They had taken several casualties while in the air and more followed as Egyptian infantry, well dug-in in trenches and supported by machine-gun nests and 40mm Bofors anti-aircraft guns, poured a withering hail of fire into them. Dodging from cover to cover, the paras pressed on regardless and several of the advance Egyptian positions were soon overrun. However, as the number of dead and injured mounted, the attack began to falter and Col Château-Jobert, who was in radio communication with a command aircraft circling overhead, called for an air strike: 20mm cannon shells from low-flying air force and naval Thunderstreak and Corsair fighters ripped the Egyptian positions to shreds and the paras surged forward again.

At 08:30 Egyptian sappers blew up the eastern bridge and Château-Jobert was desperately worried that they might do the same with the more important western one which carried the main road down which the invasion force would have to move to secure the western bank of the canal. As it happened, this was defended by fanatical 'Death Commandos' who were determined to hold the bridge at all costs. This meant, though, that it could only be taken by frontal assault for the French could not call in another air strike for fear of seriously damaging or destroying the bridge. The commandos fought back tenaciously, grudgingly yielding ground inch by inch, but as the paras' numbers and superior firepower began to tell, they started falling back towards the golf course on the far side of the bridge. Soon there was only a single man still denying the paras' success but finally he, too, fell. The paras raced across the bridge and dug in on the far side while further air strikes kept the Egyptians' heads down.

Later, at 13:45, the 1er RCP dropped on Port Fuad, on the eastern bank of the canal, and after fierce house-to-house fighting routed the defenders. A temporary truce was arranged and the paras dug in to see out the night. Then, at 04:30 on the 6th the first wave of the amphibious assault force began landing. The Egyptians in Port Said attempted to break out over the remaining Raswa bridge but 2e RPC, helped by further air strikes, managed to hold them and by mid-morning Port Said and Port Fuad were firmly in Anglo-French hands while the newly arrived 2 Para roared across the Raswa bridge and on to El Cap, 19 miles (30km) to the south. Just before midnight President Nasser agreed to a ceasefire. The paras had completed a difficult task with professional skill and courage, but unfortunately their achievement was to be thrown away by the politicians and under pressure from the United Nations General Assembly, led by the United States, British, French and Israeli troops were forced to withdraw and a UN peacekeeping force was sent in their stead.

The British and French were not the only nations to use airborne skills during the 1956 Suez campaign. One of the critical points the Israelis knew they had to capture during their drive across the Sinai Desert towards the Suez Canal was the Mitla Pass, a 20-mile (32km) defile barely over 50yds (45m) wide in many places, edged with steep cliffs. It carries the main road to Suez itself and was thus a natural bottleneck for the Egyptians to wish to seal up once the Israeli invasion became a reality. The only way to prevent this was to seize the pass by means of an airborne assault before the Egyptians could react. This task was entrusted to the 1st Battalion of the newly-formed 202nd Parachute Brigade.

The Israelis had begin experimenting with airborne forces in 1948, during the middle of the War of Independence, when on 26 May the 'Parachute Corps' came into existence. It then consisted of a mere 100 men who had responded to a call for volunteers from Maj Yoel Palgi. Their parachutes were second-hand war surplus ones originally purchased to be made into silk shirts, and their aircraft was a solitary C-46 Commando. The only men who had any airborne experience were the handful who had fought as part of the British Parachute Regiment during the Second World War. Beset with official reluctance to treat his tiny force seriously, Palgi resigned in 1949 and Yehuda Harari took his place, introducing a tough 36-day training course culminating in five qualifying jumps which basically remains unchanged to this day. The corps grew slowly and early in 1956 was amalgamated with the commando Unit 101 to form a 202 Para Brigade under Col Ariel Sharon. Its main shortage was aircraft, although some elderly C-47s had now been acquired, 16 of which would be used in the assault on the Mitla Pass.

The 1st Battalion, 359 men under Lt-Col Rafael Eitan, was the first Israeli unit to cross the Egyptian frontier on 29 October 1956. Taking off at 15:00, they preceded the ground forces by an hour and dropped from 1,500ft (460m) at 16:59. Their planned DZ was the Parker Memorial at the eastern end of the pass but, unfortunately, they dropped three miles (5km) short of the target. Realising the error, Eitan drove his men furiously forward and, after a brief firefight with a few Egyptian sentries, they secured their objective and dug in to await the arrival of the rest of the brigade. Travelling overland in old American M3 half-track armoured personnel carriers accompanied by 13 French AMX-13 light tanks, a battery of 25pdr guns and a number of mortars, the rest of the brigade had to cover 125 miles (200km) of desert from the border at El Kuntilla through the Egyptian positions at El Thamad and Nakhl. It was a situation very reminiscent of XXX Corps' drive through Eindhoven and

Nijmegen towards Arnhem, but only superficially because both the terrain and the quality of the opposition were far different: it would take another two decades of intermittent warfare to produce the fine fighting machine which is the modern Egyptian army.

Sharon fought a short, sharp skirmish at El Kuntilla and raced through the night towards El Thamad, 84 miles (135km) from the Mitla Pass, arriving at dawn with the sun behind his troops (and therefore blinding the Egyptian defenders). Charging straight into the attack behind the extra cover of a smokescreen, the Israelis' sheer aggression forced the Egyptians to flee leaving 50 dead for only four paras. After giving his men only brief pause to rest and grab something to eat and drink while the air force parachuted fuel containers in, Sharon resumed his headlong advance, chased the demoralized Egyptian garrison out of Nakhl without a fight between 16:30 and 17:00 and reached the 1st Battalion's positions at 22:30. By this time, though, the Egyptians had brought up the best part of two battalions of their 2nd Brigade and dug in along two ridges riddled with caves, setting up concealed machine-gun positions.

Defying orders giving him permission to reconnoitre but not to attack, Sharon now made the mistake of sending two companies forward next morning. Their half-tracks were ambushed and their occupants pinned in a shallow saucer of ground. A suicidal relief attempt was repulsed and Sharon wisely decided to wait for darkness before trying again. This time, quietly scaling the cliffs with blackened faces and muffled weapons, the paras fell on the Egyptian positions with sub-machine-guns and grenades and succeeded in dislodging them at last. The Mitla Pass was in Israeli hands at the loss of 38 killed and 120 wounded, while the Egyptians had lost over 260 dead. After a 48-hour pause for rest, Sharon led 202 Brigade on a long overland march down the eastern bank of the Gulf of Suez to Sharm el Sheik, two companies being parachuted in advance to capture the airfield at Tor. The brigade met up with the 9th Infantry Brigade on 5 November, the day before the ceasefire was agreed. Despite the comparatively heavy casualties (Israel only lost 181 dead in the whole Sinai campaign), the paras had vindicated their existence and would henceforth play a major role in the Israeli Defence Forces.

Since 1956, although fully trained in the parachute role, Israeli paras have not, so far as is known, made any more combat drops, being either heliborne, air-landed or serving as élite light infantry. Col Mordecai Gur's 55 Brigade was largely responsible for the capture of the Old City of Jerusalem in June 1967 during the Six Days' War while 202 Brigade acted as motorized infantry with Maj-Gen Israel Tal's armoured strike force. (By this time 202 Brigade was commanded by Eitan, Sharon having been promoted to command one of the three principal army groups used in the invasion of Egypt.) Other Israeli parachute companies were lifted by helicopter to take an Egyptian artillery battery from the rear at Umm Qataf, near Abu Agheila, during the first night of the war on 5/6 June, and similarly on the 8th were ferried by helicopter to capture Ras el Sudr airfield in advance of an armoured column. Other paras were dropped by helicopter in the Golan Heights to take out Syrian artillery positions, the men having to abseil down from the hovering machines because of the uneven and rocky terrain. A planned parachute drop on Sharm el Sheik was abandoned because an amphibious task force had already taken the town so the Noratlas transports were able to land before disgorging their troops, to the great disappointment of the men who were thus denied the distinction of a red flash on their uniform denoting a combat jump.

The paras are also known to have taken part in several daring raids into hostile Arab countries, but the usual and understandable Israeli paranoia about security means few details are available. In 1969 heliborne raiders destroyed the Egyptian Naga Hamady transformer station and a number of bridges over the River Nile in retaliation for Egyptian harassment over the Suez Canal. In another heliborne assault on 28 December 1968 a force of paras had landed on Lebanon's Beirut airport and destroyed all aircraft belonging to Arab airlines in reprisal for PLO attacks on El Al airliners. On another occasion, reminiscent of the Bruneval raid, heliborne paras seized an advanced Soviet radar installation deep inside Egypt and carried its components away before the Egyptian army — distracted by an air raid — could react. But all these exploits are overshadowed by the Entebbe raid which was a classic as both a hostage rescue and an air-landing assault.

Briefly, because the story has been well told many times, a man and a woman from the notorious Baader-Meinhof gang plus two men from the Palestinian Liberation Organization hijacked an Air France A300 Airbus on 27 June 1976. After refuelling at Benghazi in Libya the airliner was flown on to Entebbe in Uganda, the country's ruler at the time being self-styled Field Marshal Idi Amin Dada who was sympathetic towards the PLO cause. The hijackers demanded the release of 53 of their comrades held in various prisons on charges of terrorism. To begin with a rescue attempt was thought impossible because of logistics and the sheer number of hostages — 258. Playing for time, on 1 July the Israeli government announced that it was prepared to consider the release of the prisoners it held, and the hijackers consequently released all their hostages apart from 105 of Jewish nationality; the 12 courageous members of the French aircrew remained behind voluntarily.

This reduced the scale of the problem and Mordecai Gur, by this time the Israeli Chief-of-Staff with the rank of Lieutenant-General, began carefully planning a rescue operation. Some 200 volunteers from the 35th Para Brigade and the élite Golani Brigade were selected to form a task force under Brig-Gen Dan Shomron, and they began rehearsing the operation in great secrecy at Sharm el Sheik air base. On 3 July the Israeli cabinet gave the go-ahead for operation 'Thunderbolt', two new factors having further improved the chances of success. The Kenyan government had agreed to co-operate, and a strike by air traffic controllers in Sudan meant that Israeli aircraft could fly down the Gulf of Suez then head across Ethiopia with impunity. In addition, the American air force had donated satellite photographs of Entebbe. Six aircraft were used in the raid: four Lockheed C-130 Hercules to carry the assault party and return with the hostages, a Boeing 707 aerial command post and a second Boeing 707 fitted out as an emergency hospital which would land at Nairobi in case of need. They took off from Ophira air base at 16:00 on the 3rd and landed at Entebbe precisely at 00:01 on the 4th. The first group on the ground, entrusted with the principal task of rescuing the hostages from the old airport terminal where they were being held, raced down the Hercules' ramp in two Jeeps preceded by a black Mercedes limousine identical to that used by Idi Amin on his frequent unannounced visits over the preceding few days. This gained the paras precious moments of time before the guards reacted. Then, Uzi sub-machine-guns blazing, they stormed the terminal, shooting the hijackers and Ugandan soldiers who tried to interfere while shouting at the hostages to lie flat.

Meanwhile, a second assault party had seized the control tower and new terminal building while a third had deployed to block the road from Kampala, for there was an army barracks only 20 miles (32km) away housing tanks and armoured cars. A fourth group systematically destroyed the Ugandan MiG-17 fighters on the field to prevent them taking chase. Within seven minutes the hostages had been hustled from the old terminal. Two had been accidentally killed when they stood up in the middle of the crossfire and seven were wounded. Fortunately, the assault force included 33 doctors and medics who were able to render immediate first aid. Tension mounted as the minutes ticked away while the men refuelled the aircraft but at 00:45 they began taking off again for the long flight back to Israel, stopping first at Nairobi to transfer the two most seriously injured hostages to hospital and top up their fuel tanks again. The raid had been a momentous success, marred only by the death of the popular leader of the principal assault group, Lt-Col Jonathan 'Yoni' Netanyahu. Three other paras had been wounded but all four hijackers and about 20 Ugandan soldiers were dead.

Three years before Entebbe, 35 Para Brigade had also seen action in the Yom Kippur War during the assault on Egyptian positions on the east bank of the Suez Canal at the agricultural settlement of Chinese Farm but, as later in Lebanon, only in the infantry or heliborne role. Nevertheless, the Israeli parachute corps, which currently consists of three active brigades (50th, 202nd and 890th) and two reserve (35th and 55th) with their depot and principal training school at Eqron, is today one of the world's most highly trained and skilled rapid deployment forces in the world.

Following the Suez operation, Britain's 16 Para Brigade returned to Cyprus then 1 and 3 Para went back to Aldershot leaving 2 Para patrolling in the Troodos Mountains. Eighteen months later, in June 1958 a threat to the pro-British government of King Hussein of Jordan brought the brigade back together again on Cyprus before 2 and 3 Para were despatched to Amman to guard both the airfield and the royal family. The crisis died down and 2 and 3 Para returned to the UK in October followed by 1 Para in March 1959 just prior to Cyprus formally gaining independence. Reorganization followed, the 7th Parachute Regiment, Royal Horse Artillery (RHA), replacing the 33rd Parachute Light Regiment, Royal Artillery (RA). The brigade was also reinforced by the addition of the Parachute Squadron, Royal Armoured Corps (RAC), whose Ferret armoured cars equipped with Vigilant wire-guided missiles gave the brigade greatly improved anti-tank capability. At the same time the Guards Parachute Company lost the title 'Independent'.

The next assignment was Kuwait, where 2 Para joined 42 Commando Brigade, Royal Marines, in 1961 in response to an appeal from the country's ruler who feared an imminent invasion by Iraq. Again the British presence cooled the situation and the Iraqis pulled in their horns — only to return a quarter-century later. Then it was back to Cyprus in 1963 — where by arrangement with Archbishop Makarios Britain had retained military facilities at Akrotiri, Episkipi, Larnaca and Troodos, and married quarters at Limassol — when fighting flared up again between the Greeks and Turks. 1 Para had a tricky task trying to both keep the protagonists apart and protect British lives and property, but they were so successful that when a UN peacekeeping force was appointed in 1964, 1 Para remained as part of it.

There were no airborne assaults as such during these years, and the same was true of 3 Para's operations in the high, rugged and hot Radfan mountains of Aden from April to June 1964. Here, fierce Quteibi hill tribesmen, spurred on by the revolutionary left-wing government of Yemen and supplied with Soviet arms by Egypt, were attempting to take over the Protectorate by force. In a short, sharp campaign in which helicopters were extensively used in the resupply and casualty evacuation (casevac) roles, Lt-Col Anthony Farrar-Hockley's paras defeated the rebels and brought them to the peace table. But once again a military victory was to be thrown away by the politicians. In 1966 the Labour government declared that Aden should become independent in 1968 — much against the wishes of the majority of the South Arabian people who saw the British armed forces as their only protection against a communist takeover. Col Mike Walsh's 1 Para was sent out to Aden to cover the British withdrawal early in 1967 and from then until November saw some of the fiercest fighting around Sheik Othman, Khormaksar airfield and the Crater district while trying to keep the peace. Unfairly, as often happens in such cases, the paras also had to contend with left-wing criticism of their 'brutality' in the newspapers at home.

While 1 and 3 Para were thus engaged, 2 Para found itself on the other side of the world. In the early 1960s the island of Borneo consisted of Kalimantan, the eastern and largest section; the British provinces of Sabah and Sarawak which today form Eastern Malaysia; and the independent Sultanate of Brunei. Kalimantan was part of the Indonesian empire built up since 1949 by the ambitious President Sukarno, who now wished to add these territories — and, if possible, Malaya and Singapore — to his domain. He began in 1962 by fomenting an armed rebellion in Brunei, which the Sultan put down with the assistance of British troops by May 1963. In September that year the Federation of Malaysia was brought into being, comprising Malaya (West Malaysia), Singapore (until 1963), and Sabah and Sarawak (East Malaysia), Brunei remaining independent. And in 1964 Sukarno began intensifying the number and scale of cross-border raids designed to pull down the Federation.

British troops, including Gurkhas, intensified their own patrols and established a chain of strongpoints along the border, but patrolling in the dense, humid, mosquito-ridden jungles and swamps was an exhausting experience requiring both acclimatization and special training. It was into this inferno that the Guards Parachute Company was thrown in June 1964, to form an extra squadron for 22 SAS who were already active there. They were soon followed by 2 Para whose 'C' Company, alongside the Gurkha Parachute Company, also received training in SAS methods. (Ever since the Borneo confrontation, each of the three battalions in The Parachute Regiment has had an SAS-trained 'patrol company'.)

Unlike the earlier campaign in Malaya, in Borneo the British were not fighting irregular guerrillas but well trained and equipped regulars and there were several pitched battles in which helicopters again played a vital role, dropping patrols behind Indonesian forces to cut off their retreat. However, there were no parachute drops and the nature of the terrain precluded any large scale airborne operations. The troops were eventually brought home in August 1966 after President Sukarno was discredited for having illicit dealings with the Indonesian Communist Party and executive leadership passed to He Suharto, who relinquished all claims on Malaysia. It was the last taste of action for the paras until the present troubles began in Ulster in 1969, although 3 Para was deployed to British Guiana on peacekeeping duties in 1966 and 2 Para similarly to the Caribbean island of Antigua in 1969. Meanwhile, however, there were problems in other parts of the world, and to begin with we must return to Algeria in 1956.

Algeria was not a French colony in the normal sense, for since 1848 it had formed a part of Metropolitan France and Algiers was regarded just as much a French city as Paris. Nevertheless, the country was not immune to the wave of nationalism which swept the world after 1945 and in November 1954 the Moslem Front de Libération Nationale (FLN) had launched a guerrilla campaign to drive the Europeans out. The French armed forces, including the Foreign Legion (which had been first formed in 1831 to safeguard French interests in Algeria), fought back hard against the insurgents and by the middle of 1955 thought they had the problem licked. In August, however, the FLN massacred 123 white civilians at Philippeville (Skikda), provoking an even tougher French line and driving a wedge between the Moslems and families of European descent. In 1956 the renamed Armée de Libération Nationale (ALN) began a new campaign in Algiers itself. Shortly afterwards, the Suez affair discredited France in the eyes of the Arab world and aid began to flow to the rebels, particularly from Morocco and Tunisia which had gained their own independence in March of the same year, but also from Libya and Egypt.

The undeclared war in Algeria began with fighting in the wild country-side, sparsely populated, with a boulder and scrub-strewn interior and a thickly wooded region of crags and gullies closer to the coast; the struggle then moved to the urban areas, back to the country and finally back to Algiers itself during 'the putsch'. In the first phase the French army and Foreign Legion, making extensive use of helicopters — although there were few parachute drops, so far as I have ascertained — sought out the guerrillas on their own ground and were largely successful.

A typical minor parachute operation in support of what was basically a heliborne exercise took place in November 1957. On the 8th, army deserters sympathetic to the ALN cause wiped out a French convoy near Timimoun, which lies in the most hostile part of the Sahara. The Great Erg is a vast area of mountainous, constantly shifting sand dunes, barren and implacably hot and dry. It is a region where a man on foot, even travelling in the cool of the night, would be lucky to achieve a couple of miles a day in a straight line. And it was into the Great Erg that Col Marcel Bigeard's veteran 3e RPC was sent on a mission to search out and destroy the rebels. Arriving in Timimoun by truck on the 15th, Bigeard's men began questioning the locals and sending out patrols around the town. They eventually pieced together enough clues to be fairly certain that the ALN force was hidden out somewhere near Hassi Rhambou 50 miles (80km) to the north, a fact confirmed by aerial reconnaissance. The nearest patrol was the 3rd Company under Capt de Lamcy whom Bigeard ordered to the oasis at Tebelkoza where he would be reinforced by another squadron of men flown in by helicopter. Once the two forces were together they would be air-lifted to Hassi Rhambou.

Bigeard met up with de Lancy at 08:00 on the 21st and, flying low to avoid detection, the helicopters landed behind the shelter of a dune 15 minutes later. The regiment's 4th Company under Capt Douceur stood at readiness beside their Noratlas transports back at Timimoun airstrip, waiting Bigeard's signal. But the rebels had heard the helicopters' approach and, as the leading men of the 3rd Company surged over the crest of the dune, they were met by a hail of fire. The paras knew they could be easily picked off, silhouetted against the bright blue sky as they crossed the ridge 'Grenades!', shouted the popular Sgt-Maj Sentenac, and as they exploded on the far side of the dune he led his men in a wild charge. He was hit almost immediately and died shortly afterwards, but his men now had the rebels pinned down, their only hope to hold out for the rest of the day and escape at night. This was exactly what Bigeard had predicted and shortly after midday the parachutes of the 4th Company began blossoming in the sky behind the ALN positions. Encircled, the ALN fought back hard but the paras gave no quarter and by 16:30 the last rebel had been killed. A fortnight later another ALN hideout was discovered at Hassi Ali, further to the west. This time Bigeard reversed his tactics. The 2nd Company was parachuted in first to engage the rebels then the 4th Company was flown in by helicopter. And again, although they took their own casualties, the paras annihilated their foe. One of the dead was Si Yacoub, the ALN commander in the Sahara. Although small in scale, these two operations show the versatility of paratroops operating in conjunction with helicopters.

Following such successful forays as this, the ALN brought the war into the towns, provoking a violent reaction from European settlers who formed armed vigilante groups. There were atrocities on both sides, with prisoners being tortured before execution. The 10th Parachute Division, commanded by Gen Jacques Massu and including the re-formed and retitled 1er and 2e REP as well as the 2e and 8e RPC, played a major part in restoring order while army and civilian engineers completed the construction of electrified border fences supplemented by minefields and armed patrols along the borders with Morocco and Tunisia. Militarily, the French held the whip hand all along and ALN casualties were 10 times those of the army, but the war could have gone on — like that in Ulster — for decades were it not for political changes in France itself.

On 1 June 1958 Gen Charles de Gaulle, whom many Frenchmen regarded as the true victor of the Second World War, was returned to power. One of his principal platforms was that Algeria should remain French, and for this reason he had the enthusiastic support of the army. Once in power, however, de Gaulle realized the problems of an ongoing war of attrition in Algeria and began veering towards a policy of 'self-determination'. Many army officers were recalled or resigned when the trend became apparent, and the Algérie Française movement grew both within the army and the European population of the country, popularly known as *les pieds noirs* ('blackfeet'). This culminated in an armed revolt led by senior army officers such as Generals Maurice Challe, Edmond Jouhard, Raoul Salan and André Zeller in April 1961. They seized Algiers by force, demanding de Gaulle's resignation and a guarantee that Algeria would remain part of France, but failed to find the popular support they expected and gave up the struggle after just five days. Of the paras, only the Legion's 1er REP threw their lot in almost unanimously with the rebellion, 2e REP and the remainder of the 10th and 25th Parachute Divisions remaining loyal to de Gaulle and the army. One of the results of the collapse of the revolt, other than Algeria formally gaining independence in March 1962, was the third and final dissolution of 1er REP.

Subsequently, since 1967, 2e REP has been a principal constituent of the new 11th Parachute Division (11e Division Parachutiste) which replaced the old 10th and 25th and forms the strongest (14,000–strong) component in France's Force d'Action Rapide (Rapid Action Force), alongside the 4e Division Aermobile (4th Airmobile Division), 6e Division Légère Blindée (6th Light Armoured Division), 9e Division d'Infanterie Marine (9th

Marine Infantry Division) and 27e Division Alpine, which needs no translation. Apart from the légionnaires, the 11th includes the 1er, 3e, 6e and 8e Régiments Parachutiste d'Infanterie de Marine (RPIMa or Marine Infantry Parachute Regiments), the 1er and 9e Régiments de Chasseurs Parachutiste (RCP or Light Parachute Regiments) and a number of others on a rotation basis. 1er RPIMa is France's equivalent of the British SAS. The division is based at Tarbes while, since the withdrawal from Algeria, the Legion's parachute regiment has its headquarters and depot at Camp Raffali, outside Calvi on the island of Corsica. It was from here that they flew on one of the most daring and dangerous of all postwar parachute jumps.

The Shaba province of eastern Zaïre, briefly known as Katanga in the mid-1960s when it attempted to secede from the newly independent Congo, had been a thorn in the side of the Zaïrean government ever since. Tribal differences helped maintain the tension and when Cuban troops arrived in neighbouring Angola the dissidents had both a base in which they could train safely as well as access to Soviet arms. Trouble began on Saturday 13 May 1978, when a uniformed brigade of some 4,000 Katangese rebels from the Congolese National Liberation Front (FNLC) under Maj Mufu crossed the border clandestinely and, as a preliminary to an advance on the provincial capital of Lubumbashi (formerly Elisabeth-ville), seized the important copper mining town of Kolwezi. Some 2,300 Europeans lived in the town, mostly Belgian and French miners and their families who barricaded themselves into their bungalows. Although the FNLC troops behaved with discipline to begin with, they soon began looting the bars and liquor stores and went on the rampage, wantonly smashing shop fronts, molesting anyone who ventured on the streets and searching the Europeans' homes for suspected mercenaries. Several people were shot and when the Zaïrean army dropped a company of paratroopers into the town on the 16th they were massacred, survivors fleeing into the countryside.

The Belgians, former rulers of the Congo, were reluctant to intervene so in desperation President Mobutu appealed to President Giscard d'Estaing of France. At 10:00 on 17 May Lt-Col Philippe Erulin received a telephone call placing his 2e REP on six-hour alert. The order to move out came at 01:30 on the 18th and the paras boarded the trucks which would take them to Solenzara airfield where five DC-8 airliners were waiting. There was no room to pack their parachutes in addition to their weapons and ammunition, and their heavy support weapons and vehicles would have to follow on in C-141 Starlifters and C-5 Galaxies loaned by the United States Air Force. The 650 men of the regiment's four rifle companies plus headquarters, reconnaissance and mortar platoons, took off for the eight-hour flight to Kinshasa at 08:00.

When they arrived, the paras found they had another sleepless night ahead because the American T-10 parachutes which had been found for them were incompatible with their jump-bags. The légionnaires had to improve leg straps and tie their weapons on with string and tape. The machine-gunners were worse off: used to dropping with their weapons and ammunition belts carried in a valise dangling on a rope beneath them, they had to strap the guns across their chests and ammunition belts around their necks. To top it all, where Zaïre had agreed to provide seven C-130 Hercules transports *(Appendix 2)*, only four plus a single C-160 Transall were serviceable, so 80 men had to squeeze into fuselages designed for 60 and even at that a third of the men would have to remain behind to form a second wave. But the Legion's unofficial motto is *Démerdez-vous!* ('make do') and the paras did just that.

Eyes red-rimmed with fatigue, the paras pushed and shoved their way into the five aircraft on the morning of the 19th and finally took off for the four-hour flight to Kolwezi at 11:30. Two DZs had been chosen, 'Alpha', on the western outskirts of the Old Town and 'Bravo', on the eastern side of the New Town. The plan was for 1, 2 and 3 Companies to drop at 'Alpha' in the first wave, fanning out to retake the gendarmerie barracks, school, hospital, hotel, rail bridge and mine buildings, followed by the reconnaissance and mortar platoons in the second wave while 4 Company dropped at 'Bravo'.

Dropping from a cloudless sky at 15:30, the paras were fortunate to take the FNLC troops by complete surprise because they were badly scattered on landing and had trouble regrouping in the tall elephant grass which made visibility difficult (as the 503rd PIR had discovered at Nadzab in 1943). To begin with there was little resistance, and it later transpired that several hundred of Mufu's men fled into the bush the moment they heard of the légionnaires' arrival. As the paras entered the Old Town they encountered terrible sights: bodies, both black and white, lay in pools of blood in the streets, their corpses partially gnawed by mangy dogs. The stench of blood, decomposition and faeces lay thick in the air. As 3 Company raced for the Impala Hotel and the rail bridge, the FNLC massacred the hostages they had been holding there and retreated over the bridge. Shortly afterwards, they counter-attacked with three captured Zaïrean army AML armoured cars, but a well-aimed anti-tank rocket knocked out the leading vehicle and the other two pulled back out of range.

As 1 Company swept through the town, terrified and half-starved whites started venturing out of their homes to welcome them. Several fell to FNLC snipers and Erulin ordered the rest shepherded to the Lycée Jean XXIII for safety. Meanwhile, 2 Company headed for the mine company buildings to seize whatever trucks were there pending the arrival of the légionnaires' own transport. By dusk most of the northern part of the Old Town was in the paras' hands with over 100 FNLC troops killed, and when the aircraft carrying the second wave appeared overhead Erulin ordered them by radio to fly on to Lubumbashi because he did not want to run the risk of disorientated groups of paras accidentally opening fire on each other in the dark.

Sporadic fighting continued through the night as marauding FNLC patrols bumped into légionnaire positions but then at dawn the aircraft returned and, thus reinforced, Erulin commenced the task of clearing the New Town as well as completing the task in the Old Town. The FNLC did not give up easily, though, and had to be winkled from position after position. In the New Town, further hideous sights greeted the paras: in one house the bodies of 38 men, women and children were found in a pile. This fired the paras with cold, deadly determination and they ruthlessly shot anyone in FNLC 'Tiger' uniform even though many of them were mere 15 and 16-year-olds. Miraculously, though, there were 2,000 European survivors from the massacre.

By the 21st Kolwezi was secured and on the same day the rest of the regiment arrived in their own vehicles, having driven from Lubumbashi. The Europeans were evacuated by air from the strip outside Kolwezi which had been seized in a belated drop by Belgian Para-Commandos in support of the French operation. However, the légionnaires' task was not yet finished, and over the next few days they patrolled the surrounding countryside hunting down the remainder of Mufu's brigade, with further fierce firefights at Kapata and Luilu. Mufu withdrew his tattered survivors into Angola and on 28 May the paras thankfully drove to Lubumbashi for a well-earned rest. Many of them had not eaten for days. They finally flew back to Corsica on 4/5 June with President Mobutu's grateful thanks ringing in their ears.

The Kolwezi operation was not the first time that paratroops had been used in the Congo. In 1964 the left-wing politician Christopher Gbenye had formed a rival self-styled government, the République Populaire du Congo, in opposition to Moise Tshombe, and took over Stanleyville (Kisangani) as his operational base following the withdrawal of the UN peacekeeping force in June. Ever since independence on 30 June 1960 there had been a constant struggle for power which Tshombe, who favoured Katangese separation, had finally won after murdering Patrice Lumumba, but there were still many internal tribal differences and at the beginning of August 1964 Simba rebels of Gbenye's Popular Army under 'General' Nicholas Olenga took control of Stanleyville. Gbenye's idea was that the largely Belgian white population of the town could be held hostage against any action by Tshombe's brutal Armée Nationale Congolaise (ANC), but the Simbas ran amok and started slaughtering their prisoners. Gbenye proved powerless to control them and after fruitless diplomatic negotiations had dragged on for two months Tshombe appealed to Belgium to mount a rescue operation.

By this time — the end of October — ANC troops led by foreign mercenaries were advancing well into rebel country and there were genuine and well justified fears that the Simbas might execute the remainder of their hostages out of hand. Indeed, they had threatened to grill them alive and eat them if the ANC did not back off. The Belgians, with American and British backing and support, agreed to give it a go. The force chosen to undertake the mission was the 1st Battalion, plus elements of the 2nd, from Col Charles Laurent's Régiment Para-Commando. This was — and is — the direct descendant of the wartime Belgian parachute battalion which became part of the 1st Special Air Service Brigade (*Chapter 3*). The regiment has three battalions, but at the time only one was really combat-ready, the conscripts in the other two having had only between two and five months' or so of training. The regiment had already seen action in the Congo once before, when in July 1960 some 800 of its men were air-lifted out to Katanga province to safeguard European lives. Now they were to undertake a proper combat drop.

The plan was complicated by the need to use American C-130 Hercules aircraft which were then unfamiliar to the Belgians but were the only machines available with the range, and even then they would have to stage via Spain and Ascencion Island to refuel. But, like the French 14 years later, the para-commandos would 'make do'. The attack plan called for the rapid seizure of Stanleyville airfield (there were actually two, but the new one was still incomplete) so that armoured Jeeps could be air-landed to roar into the town and surrounding district rescuing hostages. These phases were to be undertaken by the 1st Battalion, after which the chosen volunteers from the 2nd would also be air-landed with fresh supplies.

The 545 Para-Commandos plus Jeeps and Fabrique Nationale AS-24 'trikes' (low slung, lightweight, parachute-droppable utility vehicles towing four-wheeled trailers) embarked in 14 C-130s (some sources say 12 and others 16) of the USAF 464th Troop Carrier Wing from Kleine Brogel airbase in Belgium on 17 November 1964 and, after staging through the British airbase on Ascencion, arrived at Kamina — just north-west of Kolwezi — at 10:00 on the 22nd. Despite media reports of a massive airborne 'exercise', no news seems to have reached the Simba forces, luckily, for some 1,300 hostages were still believed to be alive. By this time ANC and mercenary troops were rapidly approaching Stanleyville and, with the prospect of a wholesale slaughter vividly in mind, Laurent gave his men just a day's rest after their exhausting flight before re-embarking in the early hours of 24 November. They would fly in two waves, the first of seven and the second of five aircraft only 20 minutes apart, such was the Belgian commander's confidence that the airport could be secured quickly.

He was right. The first 320 men of the 1st Battalion jumped on to the golf course adjoining the airfield at 06:00 (some sources say 05:00, suggesting a mix-up in local time zones) and, after a brief firefight around the control tower, secured the area, taking a number of prisoners whom in the light of what was to follow, deserved any rough handling they received. The second wave of aircraft landed on schedule with no trouble and Laurent immediately sent a column of vehicles racing into Stanleyville. It was too late for some of the hostages. The Simbas, seeing the descending parachutes, had herded about 250 white men, women and children into Lumumba Square, where they systematically set about shooting them and stabbing them with spears. Twenty-two were killed outright, including two small girls; five died subsequently and another 35 were seriously injured before the paras started shooting and the surviving Simbas fled. The arrival of Laurent's force had been timely indeed, for at 11:00 leading elements of the ANC column began arriving. Given that three-hour respite, the Simba massacre would have been even more hideous. As it was, some 1,500 Europeans survived to be evacuated to safety, plus another 375 at the nearby town of Paulis where the paras jumped a second time on the 26th. The Belgian Para-Commandos had suffered just three dead and the regiment received a rapturous welcome when it paraded through the streets of Brussels on 1 December.

There were no such scenes to greet members of the United States airborne forces when they returned from tours of duty in Vietnam. This dirty and ultimately futile undeclared war dragged on for over a decade and, unlike the earlier and superficially similar conflict in Korea, almost totally failed to attract popular support either at home or abroad. Indeed, opposition was so fierce that the 82nd Airborne Division — being a volunteer formation and therefore considered more trustworthy than any unit made up of reluctant conscripts — spent most of the war in security duties within the continental United States, helping the police and National Guard keep order at protest rallies. Only one of its brigades — the 3rd, under Col Alex Bolling, Jr — saw service in south-east Asia, when it was hurriedly flown out to help contain the North Vietnamese Tet offensive in February 1968. Even then, it made no combat drops and, indeed, there was only one large-scale parachute operation in the whole of the war. There were two reasons for this: first, the largely unsuitable nature of the terrain: and second, the fact that the US army had, by the mid-1960s, almost totally gone over to the 'airmobile' concept.

8

Airmobile

Traditionally, it is often said with a lot of truth, armies prepare to fight the last war rather than the next. The Maginot Line is usually cited as the perfect example. But the Germans under Hitler had not fallen into the usual trap with the result that their combination of parachute and glider-borne forces acting in conjunction with fast-moving tanks supported by motorized infantry and Stukas in the aerial artillery role had swept virtually without check through Poland, Western Europe, the Balkans and North Africa during 1939–41. It was only the entry of Russia and then America into the war which sealed the fate of the Third Reich and even then victory was assured mainly through brute strength rather than finesse. Korea was, in most respects, just a continuation of the Second World War so far as weapons and tactics were concerned, although helicopters were used successfully in the casevac role. But by the mid-1950s it was evident to those with the eyes to see that a revolution was at hand, its impetus the guided missile and the helicopter. Three far-sighted men with the status and influence to capitalize on this were Generals James M. Gavin, Mathew B. Ridgway and Maxwell D. Taylor.

In April 1954 the influential magazine *Harper's* published an article by Gavin, by then a senior staff officer in the Pentagon, entitled 'Cavalry, and I don't mean horses!'. In this, and a subsequent, even more controversial article he wrote for *Army Quarterly*, 'Slim Jim' seemed to many outraged airborne veterans to be putting the kiss of death on the paratroop role on the modern battlefield. The helicopter, he said, was the key to future battle mobility. Helicopters, as we have seen, had been used operationally as early as 1944; the British army took them into battle in Malaya and later at Suez in the follow-up to 3 Para's assault, while the French used them with great effect in Algeria. Gavin and other like-minded officers saw in this the key to the future. Helicopters, operating in three instead of two dimensions but with the ability to hover, unlike a conventional fixed-wing aircraft, could take on most of the conventional cavalry roles of reconnaissance and pursuit. They could drop troops into the worst sort of terrain, inaccessible overland and fraught with hazard for paratroopers or gliders. They could ferry supplies and equipment in and casualties and intelligence reports out. Apart from the fact that they were vulnerable to small-arms fire, they could do almost anything a conventional armoured/mechanized force could — but more quickly and with greater flexibility. Hanging guns and missiles on them, already tried experimentally with varying degrees of success, only added to their versatility.

Details of heliborne operations are beyond the scope of this book and may be covered in a subsequent volume. Suffice to say that in Vietnam the helicopter reigned supreme and largely lived up to the promise Gavin foresaw. Apart from Special Forces ('Green Beret') drops to liaise with pro-western *montagnards*, operations involving fewer than half-a-dozen men just like SOE and OSS 'moonlights' in the Second World War, there was only one solitary parachute drop in the whole of the Vietnam conflict. Yet, as Gavin saw while many people missed the point, there was and remains a need for conventional airborne forces. Helicopters suffer from limited range and carrying capacity and are of principal value in the tactical role. A parachute division on the other hand can be transported very rapidly to any point in the world using giant modern multi-engine jet transports such as the Lockheed C-141 Starlifter or C-5 Galaxy each capable of carrying 150-plus fully kitted-out paratroopers or palletized vehicles, artillery pieces, anti-tank and surface-to-air missiles (SAMs). For this reason the 82nd Airborne Division remains the 'point' element of the United States' rapid deployment force with one battalion constantly at 18 hours' readiness. They were to prove their value in 1983, and again in 1990-91, but this is getting ahead of events.

In the late 1950s the 'air cavalry' concept began to take shape, influenced partially by the French introduction into service in 1958 of the world's first helicopter-borne wire-guided anti-tank missile, the Nord SS-10. Although primitive by modern standards, it showed promise when used in Algeria where operators found they could accurately steer their missiles into ALN hideouts in mountain caves. Similarly, Soviet helicopter gunships would later prove the bane of the *mujaheddin* in Afghanistan. In 1955 Ridgway, by then army Chief of Staff, had appointed a close friend and colleague as Director of Army Aviation. Maj-Gen Hamilton Howze was an enthusiastic wargamer and had play-tested the concepts of using battalion and brigade-sized formations fully equipped with attack, assault and logistics helicopters to give rapid battlefield mobility. In 1959 Howze served on the Army Aircraft Requirements Review Board and two years later, now promoted to Lt-Gen, as chairman of a new study panel commissioned by Secretary of Defense Robert S. MacNamara. This was specifically instructed to look forward rather than back, to welcome rather than shun the unorthodox. It was one of the clearest and most far-sighted briefs any military review board can ever have received.

The almost immediate result after Howze completed his report in August 1962 was the creation of an experimental airmobile brigade. It was none too soon, for American involvement in Vietnam was growing. To begin with the US presence in South Vietnam was purely advisory, helping the Army of the Republic of Vietnam (ARVN) devise and implement counter-insurgency tactics against the Viet Cong guerrillas, lineal descendants of Giap's Viet Minh. The first American military helicopters had arrived in Vietnam in December 1961 as a direct result of a report made to President John F. Kennedy earlier in the year by his Military Advisor — General Maxwell D. Taylor. Then, following the Howze report, in January 1963 the old 11th Airborne Division was reactivated as the 11th Air Assault Division (Test) while a new 10th Air Transport Brigade was also formed. They were commanded by Brig-Gen Harry W.O. Kinnaird, a veteran from the 101st Airborne and latterly its deputy commander.

His task was not an easy one but by the middle of 1964, drawing extensively on mission reports from helicopter crews already serving in Vietnam, he had six battalions ready for action. In October the 11th fought a full-scale mock action against the 82nd and despite their lack of experience performed creditably, although the vulnerability of helicopters to ground fire was again underlined. Next, with the situation in Vietnam steadily deteriorating and the ARVN almost at the point of collapse even before the People's Army of North Vietnam (PAVN) invaded the south, at the beginning of 1965 the then Chief of Staff, Gen Harold Johnson, authorized the expansion of Kinnaird's brigade-sized formation into a full division. Reinforcements came from the 2nd Infantry Division and the composite unit took over the title 1st Cavalry Division (Airmobile) on 3 July. It was 15,787 men strong, organized in eight rifle battalions with an artillery brigade, engineer and signals battalions, and the 10th Air Transport Brigade with 434 aircraft, mainly helicopters.

The division deployed to Vietnam, during August/September alongside the 1st Brigade of the 101st Airborne, joining the 173rd Airborne Brigade which had been there since May. (The 173rd had been formed on 26 March 1963 around a cadre of veterans from the wartime 503rd Regiment whose exploits were described in Chapter 6, and it was to the 173rd that the distinction of making the sole combat drop in Vietnam would go.) Later, in December 1967 the Screaming Eagles' other two brigades arrived and it was redesignated 101st Airborne Division (Airmobile). Finally, the last airborne unit to arrive in Vietnam was the 82nd's 3rd Brigade in February 1968. Earlier, the 82nd had been air-landed in the Republic of Dominica in April 1965 to stamp out the civil war then raging and protect American lives and property, staying for 17 months until peace was restored. Thereafter, the remainder of the 'All Americans' remained in the continental United States (CONUS) because, despite their involvement in Vietnam, the US could not shrug off its commitment to the North Atlantic Treaty Organization (NATO) and had to keep a rapid deployment force in reserve. (It must be remembered that the Cuban Missile Crisis of 1962 was still very clear in everyone's memory and international tensions ran high. Indeed, in 1962 the 101st Airborne had been alerted for a paratroop invasion of Cuba which, fortunately, proved unnecessary.)

Date: 22 February 1967. Codename: operation 'Junction City'. Objective: to close a roughly horseshoe-shaped cordon around a number of Viet Cong bases north of Saigon in a clearly defined operation to 'find, fix and destroy' the enemy in South Vietnam as part of a deliberate policy of attrition forming a prelude to a less clearly defined 'pacification' programme. The words sound good but by this time the PAVN was also engaged in its own deliberate war of attrition designed to wear down the American will to fight, which was already shaky. Despite promises of free elections in the autumn, the South Vietnamese regime was not only corrupt but was increasingly being seen to be so. Premier Ky was already being called a 'butcher' in public but President Lyndon B. Johnson had announced his decision to 'stand firm' in Vietnam and 'Junction City' was merely the latest and largest of the US armed forces' attempts to clear the south of opposition and drive the communists back behind the 1954 demarcation line. It was this policy, combined with the bombing of civilian targets around Hanoi and deliberate defoliation of large tracts of jungle, which was really stirring up the protest movement in the States and elsewhere. All of which was far from the minds of the 780 men (some sources say 845, which would make sense if aircrew and despatchers are included) of the 2nd Battalion, 503rd Parachute Infantry Regiment (II/503rd) as they checked their gear in the early hours of the morning prior to an 08:25 take-off in their 16 C-130 Hercules transport aircraft from Bien Hoa airstrip.

First out of the leading Hercules' rear ramp 35min later was Brig-Gen John R. Deane Jr, CO of the 173rd Airborne Brigade. The battalion's target was the furthest from the city of Tay Ninh, close to the Cambodian (Kampuchean) border. It was their task to seal off a crucial sector on the right flank of the Viet Cong and PAVN line of retreat, and the choice of a parachute drop had been made to free helicopters for other phases of the operation which involved the rest of the brigade as well as the 1st and 25th Infantry Divisions, 11th Armored Cavalry Regiment and several ARVN units.

The aircraft were closely staggered at 20 second intervals and the men jumped from 1,000ft (305m) towards a coloured smoke marker dropped by a pathfinder. Within 20 minutes the whole force, which had dropped neatly and with only 11 minor injuries, had formed up. They had achieved total surprise and there were no casualties from enemy fire. Fanning out into defensive positions, they awaited the arrival of the I/503rd an hour later. Unfortunately, this was the first time the US army had used helicopters in support of a parachute operation, and a number of the discarded 'chutes blew off the ground in the helos' downwave to get entangled in their rotors, damaging several. The rest of the brigade arrived, also by helicopter, later in the day. Operation 'Junction City' was a qualified success. In 12 weeks lasting into May the US and ARVN forces killed some 2,700 communists and destroyed huge stocks of supplies, including a precious 800 tons of rice. But in the long run it was as futile as, unfortunately, the whole of the Vietnam war, because as soon as the Americans moved on to fresh targets, leaving the ARVN to their village 'pacification' programme, the Viet Cong simply moved back. Vietnam was a conflict which could never be won because of the political climate which prohibited a positive invasion of the north and because, faced with fighting both a guerrilla action against the Viet Cong and a conventional war against regular Chinese-trained PAVN formations, the US armed forces were unable to deploy their superior technology and resources properly.

The Soviet Union, which has built up the largest airborne force in the world since 1945, encountered similar problems in Afghanistan. Considering their lack of success in conducting airborne operations during the Second World War, the priority the Soviet Union gives to its parachute, air-landing and heliborne troops initially comes as something of a surprise, but in fact is very pragmatic. Consider first that for decades the main strength of the Soviet army has been directed against Western Europe. If an attack were to be successful, it would depend above all on speed and surprise to effect a *fait accompli* before reinforcements could be brought in from America. In the increasingly unlikely event of such an attack, airborne forces would play a crucial role, particularly on NATO's northern and southern flanks in Norway and Turkey and in seizing airfields and bridges, etc, in advance of the tank and motorized divisions. Mercifully, this threat has so receded with the opening up of borders between Eastern and Western Europe and the slow but sure forging of closer economic and cultural links that even the most pessimistic observers now believe war between the 'super powers' to be virtually unthinkable.

Even in this changed climate, however, Soviet élite forces — which include the airborne, naval infantry and Spetsnaz (special forces) brigades — are maintained at a high state of readiness. But apart from possible operations in Western Europe, two other reasons account for the numbers and status of the Russian airborne forces. Consider the sheer size of the country and the length of its borders — particularly that with China. Add to this the instability and hostility towards Moscow of several of the Soviet republics, despite recent changes in their status, and the availability of a highly mobile quick reaction force becomes even more logical. The dramatic events of August 1991, when paras were deployed in Moscow, Tallinn and Riga by a hardline junta seeking — rather half-heartedly, as it turned out — to halt progress towards self-determination in the Soviet republics, demonstrated the high trust the army places in them. The cities of Leningrad, Kiev and Tbilisi would probably have seen paras on the streets as well if the coup had not collapsed so quickly.

The speed with which airborne forces can be rushed to the scene explains why the USSR can field eight full airborne divisions of some 6,500–7,200 men apiece, seven active and one training, plus a further eight 2–2,600-man assault brigades, three 1,700–1,850-man airmobile brigades,

10 500-man independent air assault battalions and 16 1,500-man Spetsnaz brigades. (Spetsnaz, the popular name for *Voyska Spezialnoye Naznachenia* or 'special designation troops', is analogous to the US army's Special Forces — 'Green Berets' — and is trained SAS-style in deep penetration reconnaissance and sabotage missions behind enemy lines. For further details readers are referred to my earlier book, *Operation Spetsnaz*, co-authored with Mike Welham and also published by Patrick Stephens Ltd.) It should be noted that a Soviet division is considerably smaller than its western counterpart: we have already seen that the French 11th Parachute Division is 14,000-strong, and similarly the US 82nd Airborne is some 15,000-strong with its ready brigade alone consisting of 4,000 men.

Soviet military theory postulates four types of mission for airborne forces: strategic, operational, tactical and special. Strategic missions would be controlled directly by the Soviet High Command and would involve the dropping of at least one division anything up to 300 miles (500km) beyond enemy lines. Because they would be expected to hold out without any prospect of prompt relief by ground forces, the Soviet airborne divisions are more highly mechanized than those of other nations, whose paras are principally 'leg' infantry. In recent years they have received the BMD air-portable and amphibious tracked armoured personnel carrier which mounts either a 30mm or a 72.6mm gun in a turret plus launchers for AT-3 'Sagger' or AT-5 'Spandrel' anti-tank missiles. (Names in inverted commas are the NATO designations.) This gives the Soviet paras greatly enhanced battlefield mobility and protection as well as formidable anti-tank capability. Man-portable anti-tank and anti-aircraft missiles are also carried in large numbers.

What the Russians call an 'operational' mission would involve regimental or brigade-size task forces operating just in front of ground or amphibious troops to block a retreating enemy or prevent him moving reserves up to the front. Tactical missions on a battalion scale could either form part of an operational mission or be carried out independently to seize bridges and other key terrain features. Finally, 'special' missions would, as noted above, be carried out by Spetsnaz teams, usually of four men apiece although larger interlinked formations were employed in Afghanistan on occasion.

The bulk of the Soviet army is manned by conscripts serving a two-year tour but officers, most NCOs and all members of the airborne forces are volunteers selected from the cream of each year's intake. (For this reason they are often said to be considered more politically 'secure' than most other units so are entrusted with sensitive operations abroad. This is also true at home, and it is no coincidence that paras were among the first troops deployed by the 'Gang of Eight' which attempted to topple Mikhail Gorbachev and Boris Yeltsin in August 1991.) Basic para training normally only lasts four weeks as most volunteers will already have had some parachute experience in DOSAAF, the Voluntary Society for Co-operation with the Army, Air Force and Navy, a paramilitary high school organization which also teaches weapons drill, unarmed combat, swimming, diving, canoeing and other skills obviously useful to a soldier. Once selected for the airborne, a recruit will normally serve four instead of the usual two years.

The deployment of the Soviet airborne divisions at the time of writing was as follows: 7th Guards in the Baltic Military District; 76th Guards in the Leningrad area; 98th Guards in Odessa; 103rd Guards — which took part in both the invasion of Czechoslovakia in 1968 and the war in Afghanistan — in Belorussia; 104th Guards in the Transcaucasus; 105th Guards — which helped spearhead the invasion of Afghanistan — in Turkestan; and 106th Guards in Moscow. The eighth division is the 44th Guards Airborne Training Division, also based in the Baltic District. Airlift is provided by the *Voyenna-Transportnaya Aviastsiya* (VTA or Military Transport Aviation) which has a huge fleet of over 1,700 aircraft including giant Antonov An-12 'Cub' and Ilyushin Il-76 'Candid' transports (*Appendix 2*) each capable of carrying some 140 paratroopers, with the even larger An-124 'Condor' just entering service.

Soviet airborne forces have taken part in two major operations since 1945, Prague in 1968 and Afghanistan in 1979. Both, however, were air-landed rather than parachute missions because the immediate objectives — both airfields — had already been secured by Spetsnaz units infiltrated covertly to clear the way. During the night of 20/21 August 1968 two Aeroflot airliners made unscheduled stops at Prague's Ruzyme airport. The Brezhnev regime had become increasingly disturbed at the liberal reforms in the Czech government introduced earlier in the year by Alexandr Dubcek and had finally decided upon military intervention. The aircraft disgorged a number of 'civilians' who, after reconnoitring the situation, returned to their aircraft then came back armed to take over the control tower. This done, the Spetsnaz team guided in two military transports from which emerged two companies of the 103rd Guards Airborne Division who quickly seized the whole of the airfield. The remainder of the division rapidly followed and moved into the city centre to take control, alongside the 35th Motorized Rifle Division which had driven from the border. The 'Prague Spring' would not re-emerge until 1989.

The year 1989 also saw the final withdrawal of the last Soviet troops from Afghanistan after nearly a decade of struggle, although the bulk had gone by the end of 1988. The Soviet Union had since Stalin's death in 1953 supported successive Afghan governments who were trying to drag the country into the 20th century. In April 1979, however, open rebellion broke out against the government, formented by Moslem fundamentalists inspired by the Ayatollah Khomeini's accession to power in neighbouring Iran in January of that year. Alarmed by this disturbance on their borders, and also fearing that the wave of fanaticism would spread to the Moslem republics in the south of the Soviet Union, the Russians responded by sending military aid to Nur Mohammed Taraki's government. Then, in

September, Taraki was murdered in a coup which brought Prime Minister Hafizullah Amin to the Presidency. As former head of the secret police, he was widely hated and Leonid Brezhnev regarded his accession to power with horror.

At the beginning of December, First Deputy Minister of Defence Gen Sergei Sokolov started mobilizing the 40th Army, some 100,000-strong, in Turkestan. This included the 105th Guards Airborne Division which, spearheaded by a Spetsnaz task force, was given the vital task as in 1968 of first securing Bagram airfield outside Kabul and then the capital itself. The operation began on Christmas Eve, 24 December 1979. As in Czechoslovakia, the Spetsnaz operatives arrived in civilian clothes aboard Aeroflot aircraft. Led, unusually, by a KGB officer, Col Byeronov (Spetsnaz actually falls under the aegis of the GRU, the Soviet military intelligence apparatus which is frequently at loggerheads with the much larger secret police organization), the men began by putting under house arrest senior Afghan officers who innocently attended a reception at the Soviet embassy. Then, now dressed in Afghan army uniforms, they secured the airport ready for the arrival of the first transports carrying men of the 105th Airborne on Boxing Day. Their arrival was timely, for the Spetsnaz team's next task was an assault on the presidential Darularnon Palace and Amin's bodyguard fought back with such ferocity that the assistance of a company of paras was needed. Amin was killed and there was only one survivor from his bodyguard, a Captain who later gave his story to the French newspaper *Le Figaro*.

After this, the 105th remained in Afghanistan, later reinforced by elements of the 103rd and 104th, but did not undertake any combat jumps. Their principal weapons and means of going into action were helicopters and BMD mechanized combat vehicles, the latter proving superior to tanks in beating off the frequent *mujaheddin* attacks on road convoys. The Soviet Union was early to recognise the potential of the helicopter and as long ago as 1956 startled western observers by staging a heliborne assault as part of the Air Force Day display at Tushino airport. Russian experts assiduously studied the French use of helicopters in Algeria and, of course, American use in Vietnam and have subsequently produced a wide range of machines as gunships, tankbusters, scouts, troop carriers and heavy lift transports. In Afghanistan they adopted the same techniques pioneered by British paras in their battle against hill tribesmen in Radfan, using helicopters to drop troops on crests and ridges along convoy routes. When a guerrilla force was sighted, gunships would pin them down by gun and rocket fire until the paras were in a position to engage. These tactics were very successful in the early stages of the war but Soviet casualties began to mount when the *mujaheddin* began receiving stocks of the American man-portable Stinger 'fire and forget' surface-to-air missile, allegedly through the auspices of the Central Intelligence Agency (CIA).

American reaction to the Soviet invasion of Afghanistan had been extremely hostile, not so much because it was seen as deliberate aggression against a neighbouring — and at least nominally unaligned — country, but because of the situation in Iran and fears that the Russians might exploit the general confusion and torn political and religious differences to take over the major Middle Eastern oilfields and refineries. Arms limitation talks were abandoned and there was a partial boycott of the Moscow Olympics; clandestine special forces teams were also sent in to aid and advise the *mujaheddin*, but in less than a year world attention became focused on the Iraqi invasion of Iran on 12 September 1980 and thereafter the Gulf War claimed the lion's share of public and military interest. Both conflicts 'ended' leaving many problems unresolved in 1988, neither — rather surprisingly — having seen any major use of airborne troops in the conventional assault role although helicopters had clearly arrived to stay.

Many countries have developed both paratroop and heliborne quick reaction forces in the decades since 1945 but, surprisingly, the United Kingdom almost abandoned airborne troops entirely in the years following the successful conclusion of the Borneo campaign. Once again a cost-conscious Labour government with an eye on a fickle electorate decided to make the armed forces suffer. Thus, in 1968 it was proposed that not just 16 Para Brigade but that The Parachute Regiment itself should be disbanded. Mercifully, a measure of common sense prevailed but the brigade was reduced to a mere two battalions in the airborne role, the third being relegated to overseas garrison duties. The brigade also lost its artillery and armoured cars. Shortly afterwards British paras became involved in the most difficult campaign they have ever had to fight, and one which still continues.

In January 1969 the violence which had never been far from the surface erupted in Northern Ireland when extremist Protestant followers of the Rev Ian Paisley disrupted a peaceful Roman Catholic civil rights march. Continuing clashes over the following months led to the army being sent in to restore order in August. The root causes of 'the troubles' go back hundreds of years to 1155 when Pope Adrian IV ceded Ireland to King Henry II. To cut a very long story as short as possible, the country was predominantly Roman Catholic — as was England at the time — but then came the Reformation, England shunned the Pope and the authority of the Church of Rome. King Henry VIII became head of the newly established Church of England and people generally adopted the new faith. Subsequently Queen Elizabeth I decreed that Ireland should follow suit, using the army to impose English law. The usual story of mismanagement and absentee landlords was the inevitable result, events coming to a head in 1688 when William of Orange replaced James II as King; Irish Roman Catholics ('Jacobites') supported James and Anglicans (or Protestants, later known as 'Orangemen') William. War followed and the result was the transfer of almost all land titles to Protestants, particularly in the north of the country. This inevitably caused a great deal of perfectly understandable resentment among the still predominantly Roman Catholic population, and it is the residue of this which we have inherited in the present day.

In 1798, inspired by the events of the French Revolution, Wolf Tone led an armed rebellion to throw the English out. The revolt was brutally quashed and the Act of Union made Ireland part of the United Kingdom in 1801. Catholic emancipation in 1829 did little to help the population because, although they were now freed to worship in their own way, few Roman Catholics could hope to rise to any position of responsibility or authority. Thus, in the wake of the famine caused by the failure of the potato crop in 1845–8 which caused a million deaths and drove another two million people to emigrate, there was a resurgence of popular demand for a return to home rule. Further intermittent violence followed and when William Gladstone — who was not unsympathetic to the aims of the Irish nationalists — attempted to pass a Home Rule Bill in 1886, it was defeated in the wake of the murder of Lord Cavendish in Dublin.

Next, in 1907 the journalist Arthur Griffiths started a newspaper entitled *Sinn Fein* ('Ourselves Alone'). This was originally dedicated to the creation of an autonomous Irish parliament in Dublin which would nevertheless owe allegiance to the English Crown, but after the brutal suppression of the Easter Rising in 1916 the nationalists, now led by Michael Collins, adopted a more extreme line demanding the formation of an independent republic. The militants within Sinn Fein had by this time formed the Irish Republican Army (IRA) whose guerrilla tactics forced the Anglo- Irish Agreement of December 1917 which established Eire as a Dominion and later (April 1949) as a fully independent republic but left unresolved the problem of the six northern counties which constitute Ulster. These by this time were mainly Protestant while the larger southern part of Ireland was, and is, Roman Catholic. And, undeniably, in Ulster the Roman Catholic minority suffered a surfeit of discrimination in jobs, housing and education. The evolution of a civil rights movement was thus inevitable, fomented by clashes throughout the 1950s and '60s between what was now called the Provisional IRA and the notoriously brutal thugs of the 'B Specials', the reserve force of the Royal Ulster Constabulary which was disbanded in 1970 because of its record of atrocities. This was a classic case of too little too late for the firing lines had already been established.

The tragic irony of the situation is that when British troops first began moving into Ulster in force in 1969, they were welcomed as much by the average Roman Catholic as by the Protestants, for both saw in their presence a return to law and order, to peace and normality. Unfortunately, the extremist elements on each side have refused to allow the army to fulfil its undemanded and unwanted task so the sectarian killings, the massacres of innocent bystanders including women and children, the bombings of 'soft' military and political targets, all continue under a spurious religious mantle which must make the founder of Christianity himself weep. This is the burden which the army bears with remarkable stoicism, restraint and amazing good humour.

The Parachute Regiment, by this time long versed in counter-insurgency warfare tactics and pacification of the civilian population, was inevitably involved in Ulster almost from the beginning of the current 'troubles', its battalions serving on rotation for tours lasting between 4 and 20 months. This puts an enormous strain on the regiment since its men have to be specially trained for an Ireland tour then retrained afterwards for their normal duties in Germany. (At the time this chapter was originally written, German reunification was just around the corner and Britain along with the rest of NATO and the Warsaw Pact was announcing significant defence cuts, but exactly who and what would be directly affected remained unclear. Actual reunification became a reality at midnight on 2 October 1990 but still left knotty problems, military, political, economic and social, which will take a long time to resolve.)

The British army's task in Northern Ireland, working alongside the Royal Ulster Constabulary, is to keep the peace and protect the innocent from cowardly attacks which no longer come just from the Provisionals but also from the Marxist Irish National Liberation Army (INLA) and the rival Protestant Ulster Volunteer Force (UVF) and Ulster Defence Association (UDA). This involves constant street patrolling with the ever-present threat of a thrown brick, a petrol bomb or even a bullet or grenade, while in the south Armagh countryside border patrols run the risk of a landmine or an anti-tank missile. Tracking down terrorist hideouts and using specially trained dogs to sniff out arms caches are equally vital jobs. As in any war, intelligence is a key factor and there is close liaison between the police, Special Branch, D15, the army's own Intelligence Corps and the specialists of the SAS who have scored many spectacular successes and earned themselves the particular hatred of the terrorists. The Parachute Regiment is almost as feared and hated as the SAS, largely as the result of an incident in 1972 in which 13 civilians were killed. Lt-Col Derek Wilford's 1 Para had been stationed in Belfast since September 1970 but on Sunday, 30 January 1972, they were in Londonderry as a reserve force for the police because of a protest march by civil rights demonstrators. The bulk of the 3,000-odd men, women and children involved were perfectly peaceful, law abiding citizens but their ranks included an estimated 150 'yobbos' (to use the army expression) who were clearly intent solely on causing trouble. The paras were well accustomed to having bricks and canisters of CS gas thrown at them but did not expect the shot which rang out at 17:55, directed at a group of soldiers in William Street. Seconds later two troopers shot and killed a young man spotted lighting a nail bomb.

The paras attempted to arrest the yobbos and converged in their armoured personnel carriers (popularly known as 'Pigs') on the block of flats from which the shot appeared to have been fired. As they dismounted they were met by a hail of sub-machine-gun fire and nail bombs from the Rossville Flats and Rossville Street. Three men, who looked in the gathering dusk as if they were carrying weapons, were shot as they ran in front of the flats. Another nine men were killed in the engagement, which lasted about half an hour. None of the paras were hit.

The incident, which the media with inevitable lack of imagination immediately began to call 'Bloody Sunday', provoked a rift in relations between the army and the Roman Catholic population of Ulster even after the early hysterical allegations that the paras had fired indiscriminately at women and children had been disproved. The facts that the paras operated strictly under the legal rules of engagement, only returned fire when they had themselves first been fired upon, and that all those killed were males between the ages of 18 and 26, combine to tell a very different story. The reader should be capable of working out the carnage which would have resulted if the paras had really loosed off their 7.62mm FN FAL L1A1 self-loading rifles 'indiscriminately' because each carried a full clip of either 20 or 30 rounds . . .

IRA retaliation was, of course, inevitable and three weeks later a bomb was planted in a Parachute Regiment mess in Aldershot. It went off at the wrong time and no soldiers were killed but five women staff, one civilian man and a Roman Catholic padre died. The Provisionals did not get their 'revenge' until seven years later, on 27 August 1979. At 16:30 that afternoon a three-vehicle convoy was patrolling along the road on the north bank of Carlingford Lough, which separates Ulster from Eire. As they passed a trailer parked at the side of the road, terrorists hidden safely on the other side of the 200yd (183m) stretch of water used a radio control device to detonate 500lb (227kg) of explosives hidden in milk churns in the trailer. Sixteen men from 2 Para died or were badly injured, along with other soldiers from the Queen's Own Highlanders whose CO, Lt-Col David Blair, had flown to the scene in a Gazelle helicopter the moment news of the atrocity reached him in nearby Warrenpoint.

Medics from an accompanying Wessex helo were attending to the wounded, under fire from the far side of the lough, when there was a second even larger explosion from the lodge gates of an adjacent house. Nothing apart from a single uniform badge was ever found of Blair's body, and altogether 18 soldiers died. The atrocity, compounded by the murder on the same day of the much loved and respected Lord Louis Mountbatten (commander of HMS *Kelly* during the battle of Crete, father-figure of Combined Operations and last Viceroy of India, uncle to The Queen and a most humanitarian if authoritative and outspoken statesman) provoked worldwide revulsion. It also hardened the attitude of British soldiers of all regiments to such an extent that the terrorists barely dare any longer to operate on their own territory, and seek 'soft' targets abroad. Wolf Tone and Michael Collins probably turn in their graves.

In the years between 1972 and 1979 The Parachute Regiment had gone through yet another of its transformations and was about to see still more. On 31 March 1974 the 16th Parachute Brigade finally ceased to exist thanks to yet more Labour government cuts and the regiment was only allowed to retain one of its three battalions in the airborne role. Fortunately they were allowed to rotate, so the para skills continued to be shared around. During the following years the battalions were shuffled between

Berlin and Belfast with the one currently designated 'airborne' forming the spearhead of 6th Field Force in the Federal Republic of Germany. This state of affairs fortunately changed when Mrs Margaret Thatcher was elected Prime Minister in 1979, one of her first acts in 1980 being to start the reinstatement of a proper, flexible, British rapid deployment force. This brought an initial return to two battalions in the airborne role, 1 Para remaining with 6th Field Force until it returned to Ireland in December 1981 while 2 and 3 Para became part of 8th Field Force until it too was renamed as 5th Infantry Brigade in January 1982, commanded by Brig M.J.A. Wilson, and the paras were rejoined with their old Gurkha friends of the 7th Duke of Edinburgh's Own Rifles. Thus it was that a very disgruntled 1 Para felt thoroughly left out of the 'real' action when 2 and 3 Para set sail for the South Atlantic in April.

The battle for the Falkland Islands did not involve any airborne assaults and the story has in any case been well told so many times that only a brief résumé can be given here. Lt-Col Hew Pike's 3 Para embarked aboard the P&O liner *Canberra* on 9 April, seven days after Argentine troops had invaded the islands. It formed part of Brig Julian Thompson's 3 Commando Brigade, alongside Nos 40, 42 and 45 Commando, Royal Marines. Men of the Marines' crack Mountain & Arctic Warfare Cadre and Special Boat Squadron (both parachute-trained) also constituted a vital part of the task force. A few days later, after SAS reconnaissance patrols had revealed the presence of some 10–11,000 Argentine troops in the islands, it was decided that the task force needed beefing up, so to their delight Lt-Col H. Jones' 2 Para were instructed to embark aboard the MV *Norland* and also head for the South Atlantic. Most of the battalion had been on leave prior to a tour of duty in Belize but, acting quite unofficially, 'H' had passed the word through the grapevine recalling his men and they were able to sail on 26 April. They also had 68 machine-guns, twice the normal number, thanks to wily scrounging by the battalion's deputy commander, Maj Chris Keeble.

The men were put ashore by landing craft in San Carlos Water on 21 May, 2 Para and 40 Commando plus a troop of Scorpion and Scimitar light tanks of the Blues and Royals in the lead, followed by 3 Para and 45 Commando, then finally by 42 Commando. By this time the rest of 5 Infantry Brigade was also at sea aboard the *QE II* (1st Battalion, 7th Gurkha Rifles, 1st Battalion, Welsh Guards and 2nd Battalion, Scots Guards); the submarine HMS *Conqueror* had torpedoed and sunk the *General Belgrano* to which the Argentines responded by attacking HMS *Sheffield* with air-launched Exocet missiles. Several more ships would be sunk in the war at sea despite the valiant efforts of the Harriers and Sea Harriers aboard HMSs *Hermes* and *Invincible*, one of the most serious losses to the ground forces being the container ship *Atlantic Conveyor* which was carrying the bulk of their Chinook and Wessex helicopters.

The first major land battle of the campaign, disregarding minor skirmishes, came on 28 May when 2 Para was tasked with taking out the

Argentine garrison in and around the settlements of Darwin and Goose Green. This was necessary to secure the right flank for further operations towards the islands' capital, Stanley. Unfortunately, the garrison which the SAS had reported to be about 600 strong had been substantially reinforced and actually outnumbered 2 Para by approximately three to one. The attack began at 02:30 and to begin with seemed to be going well, but then bogged down on Darwin Hill due to the fierceness of the opposition. The Argentine troops were mainly, contrary to popular rumour, both courageous and well armed, not poor underfed conscripts (indeed, Argentine rations were better than those the Brits had to endure).

At this point, about 09:30, 'H' personally led an outflanking attack against a line of enemy trenches but was hit by machine-gun fire and died shortly afterwards. But his example served as inspiration to his men, who swept over the Argentine positions. Lt-Col H. Jones was posthumously awarded the Victoria Cross. Command of 2 Para was temporarily assumed by Chris Keeble, who drove his men angrily on to such effect that by nightfall they had captured Darwin and surrounded Goose Green. A company from 42 Commando then joined them but Keeble was concerned about unnecessary civilian casualties if he launched a frontal assault, so at first light sent a pair of prisoners into Goose Green with a surrender demand, which was eventually accepted after a degree of negotiation. You can imagine the paras' consternation when they found the garrison had consisted of 1,350 men! The Argentines had lost 50 dead and 140 wounded; total British losses were 20 killed and 47 wounded, 18 of the dead and 35 of the injured being from 2 Para.

Meanwhile, lacking helicopters, 3 Para and 45 Commando had begun the gruelling cross-country march ('tab' in para jargon, 'yomp' in that of the Marines) across the peat bogs, coarse grass tussocks and stretches of loose-strewn boulders towards Stanley. The terrain was similar to that they had to endure in training in the hills and moorlands of the Brecon Beacons in Wales or on Dartmoor, but with temperatures dropping well below zero, high never-ending winds and boots still wet from wading ashore, it was a singularly uncomfortable and exhausting experience. (40 Commando had been left behind to safeguard the beachhead and 42 Commando would experience the luxury of following on by helicopter.) 3 Para made excellent time and had reached Teal Inlet when the news of 2 Para's victory reached them; they then pushed straight on to Mount Kent while the Mountain & Arctic Warfare Cadre fought a short, sharp engagement on their right flank at Top Malo House, an isolated Argentine forward observation post. (This battle has actually been recreated in an instructional video film for the armed forces as a classic small-scale infantry action.) 45 Commando then came up on their left flank and 42 Commando was air-lifted to join them.

Meanwhile, 2 Para had been ordered to take the southerly route from Goose Green towards Stanley. Reconnaissance by Scout helicopter revealed that, amazingly, there were no Argentine troops in Fitzroy or Bluff

Cove. Keeble took advantage of the last remaining daylight on 2 June to ferry 160 men forward in two trips by the battalion's solitary Chinook, 80 men packing into a space designed for 40! At Fitzroy, Keeble was joined by 'H' Jones' official replacement, Lt-Col David Chaundler, who had flown out from England, parachuted into the freezing South Atlantic alongside the carrier *Hermes* and then been taken forward by helicopter. 2 Para then settled in to await the arrival of the rest of 5 Infantry Brigade, sending patrols forward towards Mount Harriet while, to their north, 3 Para was doing the same in the vicinity of Mount Longdon. The Scots Guards came ashore safely by landing craft on 6 June but, tragically, the logistic landing ships *Sir Galahad* and *Sir Tristram* arrived in daylight two days later and were heavily bombed by the Argentine air force, resulting in heavy casualties among the Welsh Guards.

The campaign now moved rapidly towards its conclusion. During the night of 11/12 June Hew Pike's 3 Para moved forward against the well dug-in Argentine troops on Mount Longdon, who included men of the *Buzo Tactico*, or élite special forces. Even they proved no match for the paras in the end, but it was a fierce battle. The Argentine troops were securely entrenched and protected by minefields which channelled the paras' approach routes, but they took out position after position with 66 and 84mm rocket launchers, following through with grenades and bayonets. It was during one such foray that Sgt Ian McKay also won a posthumous Victoria Cross. With his company pinned down by heavy machine-gun fire and his company commander dead, McKay took charge and led three of his men in a frontal assault up the rocky slope. One man was killed and the other two badly wounded but McKay seemed to bear a charmed life as he raced towards the sangar. He was hit and killed as he reached the lip of the emplacement but his body fell blocking the gun and the rest of his men soon cleaned up. Heavy fighting continued throughout the night but by daybreak the Argentines had pulled back along Wireless Ridge. Pursuit was impossible because the paras now came under heavy artillery fire from Mount Tumbledown and had to take shelter in the abandoned enemy dugouts, which they found to their delight housed dozens of bottles of brandy and cartons of cigarettes!

In the meantime, 45 Commando had similarly secured the Two Sisters heights but again the arrival of daylight prevented them pressing on to Tumbledown. That prize fell to the Scots Guards during the night of 13/14 June. At the same time 2 Para, who had marched from Fitzroy round the rear of 3 Para's positions on Mount Longdon to the north of Wireless Ridge, launched their own assault. Supported by 3 Para's mortars, two batteries of 105mm light guns, naval gunfire support from HMS *Ambuscade* and a troop of Scorpions and Scimitars, 2 Para found Wireless Ridge a walkover compared with Goose Green. As day broke on the 14th the paras were rewarded with the sight of streams of Argentine troops scurrying back into Stanley; the same scene was repeated on the slopes of Mount Tumbledown. Rakishly slinging their helmets and donning their red berets, the paras chased into the town but were ordered to halt at the racecourse. Argentine troops threw down their arms and crews abandoned the armoured cars which had sat uselessly doing nothing throughout the campaign. Later that afternoon the Argentine commander, Brig-Gen Menendez, formally surrendered.

What the Falklands proved was the need for Britain to retain a ready, mobile, rapid deployment force, and recognition of the paras' crucial role in defeating the Argentines came in December 1982 when Defence Secretary Michael Heseltine announced personally to the paras in Aldershot that 5 Infantry Brigade was going to have its structure altered and would become 5 Airborne Brigade. This promise was ratified in October of the following year by an official name change and Brig Tony Jeapes — a former commander of the 22nd Special Air Service Regiment — became CO. At the time of writing the brigade's order of battle included 2 and 3 Para plus the 2nd Battalion, King Edward VII's Own Gurkha Rifles, in the air-landing role. Support services have returned in the shape of the Life Guards with Fox armoured cars and Scimitar light tanks (which the army designates 'combat vehicle reconnaissance [tracked]'), the Royal Horse Artillery whose 7th Field Regiment provides the 105mm guns, plus mechanical and electrical engineers, a transport squadron, medics, a squadron of helicopters and two dedicated squadrons of RAF Hercules to provide the airlift capability which had been lacking in the past.

It is about time the paras were given more modern aircraft with greater range, but with the decrease in East-West tension during 1989–91 the brigade's future has once again been thrown into doubt. However, the Iraqi invasion of Kuwait in August 1990 must surely show that while fanatics like Saddam Hussein continue to rule anywhere in the world, other countries need to retain a quick reaction potential both for their own defence and to go to the aid of others threatened by military aggression. The arrival of the US 82nd Airborne Division in Saudi Arabia, quickly followed by the 5,000 men of Egypt's two Independent Parachute Brigades as the spearhead of a multi-national deterrent force, demonstrated more clearly than anything else could have that paratroops, whether dropped, air-landed or heliborne, can play a key part in preserving the peace.

The 82nd Airborne regularly holds 'Bright Star' exercises in Egypt, parachuting from their C-141s over the open desert, so they are no strangers to the Middle East. Indeed, many 'All Americans' already wear Egyptian parachute wings alongside their own, a practice to which officialdom turns a blind eye. Similarly, many wear unauthorized 'Grenada' patches as a result of their rescue operation on that Caribbean island in 1983. However, it was to the Rangers that the kudos went of undertaking the actual parachute part of the assault, although two members of the 82nd accompanied them.

The US Army's Rangers are one of the finest light infantry formations in the world, tracing their inheritance back to the 18th century and with a demanding training second to virtually none. The original 'Rogers

Rangers' were formed in 1756 by Maj Robert Rogers as a light, fast-moving unit to fight for what were then the British colonies in North America against the French and Indians. The name was revived during the Second World War when Gen George C. Marshall authorized the young 34th Infantry Division Maj Orlando Darby to recruit volunteers from American servicemen then based in Ireland to form a US Army unit analogous to the British Commandos. This was in June 1942 but already Darby had a clear idea of what sort of man he should look for, and the basic criteria for commando-style troops, whether parachute trained or not, remain constant. Physical fitness and general toughness, courage and self-discipline were the obvious starting points, but to speed things up Darby also looked for volunteers who had already proved themselves good marksmen, who understood fieldcraft and could map-read and navigate, could swim and preferably had some experience of climbing and small boat handling. Darby also looked outside the infantry for a good cross-section of experts in ordnance, signals, engineering and motor maintenance and repair. Parachuting, at the time, was not seen as a Ranger requirement.

Unfortunately, Darby's Rangers did not have a happy war, suffering such heavy casualties at Anzio in particular that they were reduced from five to two battalions (plus one battalion in the Pacific) and at the end of hostilities they were disbanded. Reactivated to serve in Korea, they were again disbanded in 1953 but a cadre was retained at Fort Benning in Georgia as a leadership school to teach light infantry tactics. The Rangers were not revived during the Vietnam conflict but instructors at Fort Benning helped create and train the Special Forces and in 1975 it was decided to form a small new élite of two battalions which was given the title 75th Infantry Regiment (I/75th and II/75th Rangers). They were based respectively at Fort Stewart, Georgia, and Fort Lewis, Washington. A third battalion was added after the successful Grenada operation, in 1984. The 2,300-man regiment currently forms part of the US 1st Special Forces Operations Command whose headquarters is at Fort Bragg.

All members of the Rangers are triple volunteers. First they volunteer for the army then, before they will be considered for the arduous 58-day Ranger course, they have to take parachute training. The Ranger course itself, leading to award of the black beret, stresses survival skills in all types of different terrain as well as navigation, advanced weapons handling, close combat and the technique of abseiling from helicopters into jungles or mountains. The course is very tough but because each intake consists of only 10 to 30 men, the level of individual instruction is high with the result that nearly 70 per cent of volunteers succeed in making the grade. They normally serve for two years but this can be extended by up to six months under special circumstances. Rangers have to be fit, keen and 'on the bounce' so rarely remain in the line over the age of 22 although some will stay on as instructors while others will return to their original regiment or join a different one, thus helping to pass on Ranger skills throughout the army.

It was these attributes which caused the Rangers to be selected as part of the élite force sent in to Grenada in October 1983. On the 19th of that month a military junta headed by Gen Hudson Austin deposed and executed Prime Minister Maurice Bishop (who had himself usurped power in a bloodless coup four years earlier) and five of his government colleagues. The junta set up a new Revolutionary Council and Soviet-equipped Cuban troops began to flow in to reinforce those already on the island who, under the guise of consultants and engineers, had already started to extend the main runway at Point Salines airport to take large military transport aircraft. This caused a great deal of alarm among the other six members of the Organization of Eastern Caribbean States, and on the 23rd they appealed to President Ronald Reagan to intervene. The US government was already appalled at the thought of another Marxist state on the doorstep and particularly concerned for the welfare of the thousand American citizens, including 600 medical students, on the island.

Operation 'Urgent Fury', which was able to begin on the same day the appeal for help was received since special forces had already been alerted, involved all four branches of the US armed forces: the Rangers and the 82nd Airborne, US Navy SEAL Team 6, the Marine Corps' 22nd Marine Amphibious Unit (MAU) which was diverted while *en route* to Lebanon, and the USAF's 1st Special Operations Wing with C-130 transports and AC-130 Spectre gunships. Special Operations Detachment Delta (the dedicated counter-terrorist unit founded in 1977 by Col Charles A. Beckwith after he had observed SAS training methods) was also put on alert in case Austin's People's Revolutionary Army (PRA) attempted to hold any of the students or faculty members of St George's Medical College hostage. Twenty-two SEALs were first ashore, 11 of them parachuting in unobserved during the night of the 23rd/24th. They probably employed the high altitude, high opening (HAHO) technique, being dropped from some 30,000ft (9,150m) several miles offshore and using ram-air 'chutes with similar characteristics to hang gliders in order to fly to their destination. Their task was to reconnoitre the situation around Government House where the British Governor-General, Sir Paul Scoon, was being effectively held captive. On the following night the remainder of the SEALs landed by sea to scout out beaches for the Marines.

The main assault began at 05:20 on the 25th when 22 MAU was embarked by helicopter from the USS *Guam* to secure the island's second airport, Pearls, on the north-east coast. They began landing 16 minutes later, only encountering light anti-aircraft fire which damaged one helicopter, but this was rapidly suppressed by their Cobra gunships and within an hour the Marines had secured all their objectives. Meanwhile, the SEALs had moved in to capture Government House and ensure the safety of Sir Paul Scoon. They were pinned down by heavy Grenadian fire, particularly from three BTR-60 armoured personnel carriers which blocked the exits, but the SEALs returned the fire with vigour. They managed to hold out throughout the day and following night and Sir Paul was safely evacuated by helicopter early in the morning of the 26th, flying to the *Guam* to confer with the task force commander, Rear-Adm Joseph Metcalfe.

Following the SEALs and Marines, the C-130s carrying 550 men of the two Ranger battalions which had staged through Barbados, approached Point Salines at 06:00, flying at 1,000ft (300m). As the first stick of 12 men from 'A' Company of Lt Wes Taylor's 1st Ranger Battalion flung themselves from the leading Hercules, searchlights suddenly stabbed the air and a furious barrage of anti-aircraft fire whipped around them. The Hercules pilot took violent avoiding action, leaving the 12 men drifting down to a hot reception from Cuban and Grenadian troops, of whom there were about 600 at Point Salines. Discarding their 'chutes, the men took cover in the mass of rubble and earth-clearing machinery which littered the runway and began returning fire.

The remainder of the aircraft carrying the 1st Battalion veered away while AC-130s poured withering fire into the anti-aircraft positions. They decided to re-approach at 500ft (150m) so that the anti-aircraft guns would be unable to bear for so long and the Rangers would have less time in the air. This also meant they would be unable to deploy their reserve 'chutes if the main one failed to open properly, but fortunately there were no casualties from malfunctions. A radio signal alerted Lt-Col Ralph Hagler's 2nd Battalion to the situation. The original plan had been that they would land on the runway after the 1st Battalion had secured it, but the clutter on the runway prevented this so the Rangers prepared to jump instead; the Jeeps could be landed after they had secured the airfield and cleared the runway. Fortunately, one of the two members of the 82nd Airborne who was jumping with them was a skilled bulldozer driver. Because they knew in advance they would only be dropping from 500ft, Hagler's men abandoned their reserve 'chutes and loaded themselves up with extra ammunition.

The Rangers, helped by the gunships overhead, rapidly drove the Cuban and Grenadian troops from the airfield, killing several and taking a large number prisoner. A Cuban counter-attack by three BTR-60s was beaten back and by 07:00 Point Salines was safely in their hands; then the bulldozers quickly set to work clearing the rubble so that the first C-130 carrying the Jeeps, which mounted heavy machine-guns, could touch down at 07:15. The Rangers then moved out to the closest of the two college facilities, 'True Blue' campus, which was secured by 05:50. Later in the day the larger C-141s of the 82nd Airborne began to touch down, the II/325th landing first with the divisional CO, Maj-Gen Edward Trubboughs. They quickly assumed responsibility for airfield security and the Rangers headed inland. The Cuban and Grenadian troops put up a sporadic resistance, snipers being the main problem, but casualties were light.

Adm Metcalfe now moved the *Guam* around to the west coast and landed a further force of 250 Marines with six M-60 tanks and 13 LVTP-7 amphibious armoured personnel carriers in Grand Mal Bay. They moved into the island's capital, St Georges, and at 07:00 on the 26th reached Government House to relieve the SEALs; shortly afterwards a heliborne force of Rangers from Hagler's 2nd Battalion liberated the second campus, Grand Anse, losing one helicopter in the assault but suffering no fatalities. The last objectives, Fort Frederick and Richmond Hill prison, were stormed that afternoon, and by the end of the day Grenada was safely in US hands. Eighteen American soldiers had been killed for 24 Cubans and 16 Grenadians. Shortly afterwards the task force was pulled out and 400 troops from neighbouring Caribbean islands replaced them as a peacekeeping force until democratic elections could be held.

What operation 'Urgent Fury' proved beyond a shadow of doubt was the continuing efficacy of paratroop forces in the modern world. Their ability to be airlifted over thousands of miles at short notice and the quality of the officers and men who qualify for the coveted Wings mean that they can take control of a situation rapidly, minimising casualties by sheer speed, surprise, skill and controlled aggression. The motto of the British Parachute Regiment *'Utrinque Paratus'*, says it all: Ready For Anything.

Appendices

1: Parachutes

The title of this book is *Airborne Assault* and the emphasis is on operations, with technical details deliberately kept to a minimum. The following remarks were originally included as footnotes within each chapter but on the publisher's recommendation are now included as appendices to help the reader towards a greater understanding of the problems of airborne assault, without interrupting the narrative. They are not intended as a comprehensive survey of parachute designs and types but are included to illustrate some of the difficulties which arose in choosing and using parachutes for military operations. Only the principal wartime models and their descendants are described, but it is hoped that this will nevertheless prove informative and useful.

In Germany, responsibility for parachute design in the prewar years belonged to the Air Ministry's Technical Equipment Division at four research centres in Berlin, Darmstadt, Rechlin and Stuttgart. The first production design was RZ1 (RZ = *Rückenpackung Zwangauslösung* or 'rucksack packed to open') but user trials were unsatisfactory and in 1940 the improved RZ16 was introduced, followed by the RZ20 in 1941 which remained in service for the remainder of the war.

The circular canopy was 28ft (8.5m) in diameter and sewn from 28 gores (wedge-shaped pieces) of silk. To begin with the canopies were all white but by the time of the invasion of Crete they were being dyed in subdued camouflage colours, not to make them invisible in the air but to render them less obvious targets on the ground during the vulnerable seconds while a parachutist disengaged himself from his harness and freed his weapons. The parachute was packed in a cloth bag; a thin cord attached the apex of the folded canopy itself to the mouth of the bag, and the bag was firmly attached to the static line. The bagged canopy and the carefully coiled-down shrouds or rigging lines were packed in a stout canvas pack which clipped to the rear of the shoulder harness. The static line itself was coiled under the flap on the back of the pack.

As the Ju 52 transport aircraft *(Appendix 2)* approached its target the despatcher *(Absetzer)* ordered the men to their feet. Taking the end of the static line in their teeth to leave their hands free in case the aircraft was forced to manoeuvre suddenly, the men lined up in single file beside the cable high up on the fuselage side. On the command, each man would hook his own static line to this cable and check the comrade in front while the despatcher checked the last in line, making sure they were all hooked on securely. (Given the low height from which drops were usually made, carrying a reserve 'chute was pointless, so every care had to be taken to ensure safety at this stage.) The static line hooks ran freely along the cable as each man approached the door. The technique for exiting was determined by the parachute design and was, of course, thoroughly practised during training. On reaching the door, each man braced himself with feet spread and one hand either side of the door frame, then launched himself into space in a crucifix shape.

As he fell, his 29½ft (9m) static line unfurled and tugged the flaps of the backpack apart, almost simultaneously pulling out the bagged canopy. As the man continued to fall the bag was jerked off the canopy and the thin cord attaching the bag to the apex snapped. The static line and bag remained attached to the aircraft while the parachutist continued to fall freely, the canopy pulling the shrouds taut as it developed and bringing the man up short with a hard jerk.

The need for the head-first cruciform exiting configuration was caused by the design of the rigging which, as stated in Chapter 2, was based on the early Italian Salvatore model. Instead of the shrouds being attached to straps (called 'risers' or 'lift webs') on each shoulder, as in the case of the British 'X' type and later Allied parachutes, they came together at a single point behind the parachutist's shoulders, attached to a triangular rope arrangement at the top of the pack. This meant the man had to be in a flat, downward-facing position when the 'chute deployed, or risk being flipped over and fouling the canopy and shrouds. Other disadvantages of the design were that the parachutist was unable to control the direction of his descent other than by flailing his arms to twist his body in the air, and that he landed rather hard in a face-forward position, necessitating the wearing of strap-on knee pads filled with kapok (rather like a cricketer's) to prevent injury. The sole advantage the RZ types had over Allied parachutes of the time was that they deployed fully very quickly — within 120ft (36m) — so, despite the vicious jerk on opening, the Germans appreciated the low jump height this permitted, getting them on the ground faster.

The RZ parachutes were also something of a menace once a man was on the ground, for if there was a strong wind blowing and the canopy refused to collapse he could be dragged some distance across the ground before he managed to release the four clips on the harness — there was no central quick release button as on the British 'chute. In a jump over rugged terrain, this could and did lead to many injuries. In *extremis,* a para could use his gravity knife to cut himself free. This was a large jackknife carried in a special pocket on the right leg. It had a weighted blade which automatically opened when it was withdrawn and a single-handed locking catch. It was also, of course, used as a combat knife.

The early British 28ft (8.66m) diameter 'A' Type parachute was designed by the expatriate American stuntman Leslie Leroy Irvin and was adopted for aircrew by the RAF in 1925. Irvin established his own company in Letchworth, Hertfordshire, in 1926 but from 1934 the prime contractor to the RAF was the Gregory-Quilter (GQ) company in Woking, Surrey. The training parachute adapted for the paras was slightly larger than that worn by aircrew, giving a softer landing or, alternatively, permitting a greater weight of equipment to be carried, and had a 22in (56cm) hole in its apex to reduce stress on the canopy and help prevent oscillation. It was constructed from 28 gores of silk (later cotton and ultimately nylon) and differed principally from the German model in that the 28 shrouds converged on four 'D' rings at the end of the lift webs above each shoulder instead of to a single point behind the shoulder blades. Manipulating these webs gave the parachutist a measure of control over his speed and direction.

The Irvin 'A' Type parachute, being designed for aircrew, was fitted with a ripcord and worked perfectly well, saving thousands of lives. Unfortunately, the use of a static line was found on occasion to cause the shrouds to become entangled with the canopy, causing partial or total failure. In tests using dummies as part of the enquiry following the first fatality, three out of 24 'chutes failed to deploy properly, so something obviously had to be done. Mr (later Sir) Raymond Quilter of GQ found the answer. He combined the Irvin parachute with a GQ outer bag, the latter being firmly attached to the static line and remaining hooked to the aircraft. Inside this an inner bag contained the canopy with the lift webs and shrouds folded under a flap.

As the outer bag was pulled away at the end of the 12ft 6in (3.87m) static line, a cord dragged out the lift webs first, then the shrouds and finally the canopy. This opened with a clearly audible 'crack' but the shock to the parachutist's body was negligible compared to the rupturing jerk sustained with an RZ type. Further comfort was assured by the harness design, the webbing straps descending from the lift webs down the body and around the upper thighs to converge at a single quick-release box on the midriff, with an extra strap around the waist. The parachutist therefore literally sat underneath his canopy instead of dangling face-forwards as with the German design. Thus modified, the British 'chute was designated 'X' Type and remained in service until the 1960s. Its only disadvantage was that it deployed more slowly than the RZ, meaning that British paras had to be dropped from a greater altitude, leaving them more vulnerable to ground fire. In the postwar period a more refined version designated 'PX1' has been introduced which has material of decreasing porosity towards the rim; this helps damp out oscillation. The canopy also has a strip of gauze around the rim known as an anti-inversion ring, which prevents the 'chute turning inside out. The current PX1 Mk 4 is worn with a chest-mounted reserve 'chute, the PR7. This has a 22ft (6.7m) canopy and is spring-actuated after the ripcord is pulled. Two gores of nylon have been deliberately cut out so that the PR7 automatically pulls away from the main 'chute, a valuable safety feature.

After experimenting prewar with Irvin-style parachutes, the Soviet airborne brigades adopted a unique square-shaped rig which gave better lateral control. Its disadvantage was that it deployed slowly so minimum jump height was 1,000ft (309m), but this in turn permitted the wearing of a reserve, ripcord-operated 'chute on the chest. In the postwar period, the Soviet paras have reverted to a 'chute with circular canopy.

American paras also wore a reserve on their chests, so felt it unnecessary to alter the basic Irvin design from canopy first to canopy last as the British had done. Men who have used both the 'X' and the American T-7 rigs, however, generally report more favourably on the former, partly because of the relatively gentle canopy deployment and partly because of the quick-release box. Until the T-10 was introduced in the late 1950s, US parachutes were attached to the harness by three snap fasteners which were sometimes difficult to release in a hurry, particularly at night or in a strong wind. This flaw caused many unnecessary casualties, as at Corregidor for example. On the T-10 the fasteners were replaced by three quick-release snaps. The 'chute is also larger, with a 35ft (10.6m) canopy, and as a safety feature incorporates a semi-rigid anti-inversion ring around the rim to prevent a thrown line causing 'roman candling'. The T-10 can be opened safely at 150mph (240km/h) compared with 115mph (184km/h) for the T-7 and gives a softer landing; it is used in conjunction with a ripcord-operated chest reserve 'chute which has a diameter of 24ft (7.3m). Although the T-10 is still used, more recently the MC1-1B has also entered service. This has the same diameter but has cut gores and steering lines, making control in the air and landing on the right spot far easier. The parachutes of all other nations are simply variations of the American T-10 or British PX1.

2: Principal aircraft

As before, this is not intended as a comprehensive guide to all aircraft used over the years by airborne troops, but to the main types mentioned in the narrative. Again, since the Germans effectively started the ball rolling, we shall begin with them.

The DFS 230 (DFS standing for *Deutsches Forschungsinstitut für Segelflug,* or German Gliding Research Institute) was the principal German glider throughout the war. A relatively small aircraft with a wingspan of 68ft 5½in (20.87m), it could carry eight fully-equipped infantrymen plus its pilot. Construction was of fabric and plywood over a lightweight metal framework. It had belly-mounted skids for landing but for take-off was mounted on a small two-wheeled trolley which was dropped once the machine was in the air. It could sustain a towing speed of 130mph (210km/h) and had a maximum diving speed of 180mph (290km/h). After operational experience in 1940, a small hatch was fitted in the fuselage roof behind the cockpit through which a crew member could operate a pintle-mounted 7.92mm MG 15 machine-gun to lay down covering fire while the infantry jumped out of the side door. Other developments included a braking parachute on the B-1 variant and three retro rockets on the C-1 — the latter being the version used in the rescue of Mussolini from Gran Sasso in 1943.

Normal towing aircraft for the DFS 230 was the Junkers Ju 52/3m, a low-wing cantilever monoplane with fixed undercarriage usually powered by three BMW 132T 830hp engines, although other powerplants were sometimes fitted. The 'workhorse' of the *Luftwaffe,* the Ju 52 was built in thousands, first as an airliner then as a bomber during the Spanish Civil War (1936-9) and finally as a general cargo and troop-carrying aircraft, serving alongside the German army on all fronts during the war. Some versions were equipped with skis or floats instead of wheels, while others had a dorsal machine-gun position towards the tail and a second machine-gun in a ventral 'bucket' lowered just behind the main undercarriage after take-off. The Ju 52/3m had a wingspan of 95ft 11½in (29.25m), a top speed of 168mph (270km/h), a ceiling of 18,000ft (5,500m) and a range, fully laden, of 568 miles (915km). In addition to towing the DFS 230, the Ju 52 was also used to carry up to 18 fully-equipped infantry or 13 paratroopers. It was popularly known as the *'Tante Ju'* (Auntie Ju).

Other towing aircraft for the DFS 230 included the Junkers Ju 87 Stuka, Heinkel He 111H bomber and the weird five-engined He 111Z which was essentially a pair of standard He 111s with their wings joined together at the nacelle of the fifth engine. The latter, however, was principally used to tow the larger Messerschmitt Me 321 or Gotha Go 242 transport gliders.

The Me 321, aptly named *Gigant* ('Giant'), was a massive high-wing glider with a span of 180ft 5½in (55m) capable of carrying up to 150 troops, a PzKpfw IV medium tank, an 88mm gun or similar loads up to 48,500lb (22 tonnes). It took off on a four-wheel dolly which was then abandoned, the aircraft landing on its skids. Since none of its towing aircraft had sufficient power to get it off the ground when conditions were muddy, rockets were fitted beneath the wings. First entering service in May 1941, the Me 321 served almost exclusively as a transport aircraft on the Eastern Front, a total of 200 being built. Early versions only carried a single pilot, who had his work cut out to control such a heavy aircraft so, in later production models, room was made for a co-pilot to share the load. A powered version of the glider, with six Gnome/Rhône radial engines and designated Me 323, was also produced and saw service ferrying supplies across the Mediterranean to the Afrika Korps as well as in Russia.

Following the successful deployment of the DFS 230 in 1940, the German armed forces also became interested in a new glider being developed by Gotha which could carry 21 troops — nearly three times the capacity of the earlier design. Alternatively, it could carry a Kübelwagen 'jeep'. The Go 242 was an unusual and attractive twin-boom design with a wingspan of 80ft 4in (24.5m) which could be towed at up to 150mph (240km/h), usually by a He 111. Over 1,500 were produced, most seeing service in Russia as transports after Hitler abandoned the idea of airborne assault, and 133 were converted into Go 244s by the addition of a pair of Gnome/Rhöne engines and fixed tricycle undercarriage.

Shortly after Winston Churchill called for the creation of a British airborne force, in November 1940 the first prototype of the General Aircraft Hotspur glider first took to the air. Although never seeing action, it was the principal glider used for training throughout the Second World War, over 1,000 being built. With a wingspan of 45ft 10in (14.2m), it was directly comparable to the DFS 230 and could carry seven fully-armed troops. Its operational role was taken over by the Airspeed Horsa which first flew a year later, in November 1941, and saw its action debut during the tragic attempt to land a raiding party in Norway in 1942 *(see Chapter 3)*. Some 3,656 Horsas were built and the aircraft took part in the invasions of Sicily and Normandy as well as at Arnhem and during operation 'Varsity'. Considerably larger than the Hotspur, the Horsa had a wingspan of 88ft (27.23m) and could carry up to 25 soldiers plus its two pilots. Of all-wood construction, it had a jettisonable wheeled undercarriage and a landing skid, could be towed at 127mph (203km/h) and had a top gliding speed of 100mph (160km/h). As an alternative to troops, the Horsa could carry a Jeep, a 6 or 17pdr anti-tank gun, a 40mm anti-aircraft gun or a variety of other stores, although the principal British cargo glider was the General Aircraft Hamilcar.

This large aircraft, with a 110ft (34m) span, was commissioned in 1940 and first flew in March 1942. Designed to carry a light tank (the Tetrarch), it first saw action in Normandy and later in Holland and Germany. Like the Horsa, this was of wooden construction with jettisonable undercarriage, landing on its skids, but it differed in having a hinged nose to allow cargo to be wheeled in and out. Maximum speed was 150mph (240km/h), normal towing aircraft being the Short Stirling or Handley Page Halifax four-engined bombers.

The principal American glider was the Waco CG-4A, known by the US airborne forces as the Haig and by the British as the Hadrian. It was smaller than the Horsa with a wingspan of 83ft 8in (25.9m) and a capacity of 13 men or a Jeep in addition to its crew of two. The whole nose section folded upwards to allow stores to be loaded and unloaded, although the normal troop entrance and exit was through a door in the port side of the fuselage. This high-wing monoplane was built in greater numbers than any other glider before or since — 12,393 being produced up to December 1944. It was of plywood and fabric construction over a light tubular steel frame for rigidity and could be towed at 125mph (200km/h). The undercarriage was fixed for training purposes when using prepared airstrips but operationally the wheels were dropped on take-off and the aircraft landed on a skid.

By far the most important aircraft used by the Allied airborne forces as a transport for paras or air-landing troops and as a glider tug was the C-47 'Gooney Bird', often referred to as 'a collection of rivets flying in formation' because of the incredible din inside its fuselage! More officially known as the Skytrain by the Americans and the Dakota by the British, the C-47 is the most significant transport aircraft the world has ever seen. The civilian version (the Douglas DC-3) first flew in 1935 and the US Army Air Corps started receiving converted examples known as the C-53 Skytrooper in October 1941, quickly followed by the definitive C-47 which had more powerful

1,200bhp Twin Wasp engines. The C-47 was distinguished from the civil version by the provision of 28 bench seats for troops, large double doors, strengthened undercarriage and a glider towing attachment point. The low-wing cantilever monoplane's twin engines gave it a top speed of 229mph at 8,500ft (368km/h at 2,630m) although normal cruising speed was 185mph (298km/h); when towing a Horsa or CG-4A this had to be reduced still further. The C-47 had a range of 1,500 to 2,125 miles (2,414–3,420km) depending on load and atmospheric conditions. This venerable aircraft soldiered on until late in the 1960s with numerous air forces including the French in Indo-China, and a number were converted into gunships for use in Vietnam when they were designated AC-47s and popularly known as 'Puff the Magic Dragon'.

The Italians, among the first in the airborne field, were slow to develop a glider, the Caproni TM2 not making its first flight until the spring of 1943, just before the surrender. It crashed, and nothing more was done. The Japanese were also slow, and the Kokusai Ku-7 *Manzuru* ('Crane') did not make an appearance until August 1944 — too late by far. It had a twin-boom design like the Go 242 but was larger (wingspan 114ft 10in [35m]) and intended to carry 32 troops or a light tank. The Ku-7 was not deployed operationally but the smaller Ku-8 was, during the invasion of the Philippines. This had a span of 76ft 1in (23.2m) and could carry 20 men. Nor were the Russians successful with a glider design. In the early 1930s Marshal Tukachevsky — who was executed by Stalin in the great 1937 purge — had asked for a military glider and the eventual result was the Antonov A-7 which carried a pilot and seven troops. It was very similar to the DFS 230 or Hotspur, with a wingspan of 59ft (18m), but only 50 were built (in 1942) and they were used to help supply the partisans. After the war the military glider virtually disappeared from the scene entirely except for *ab initio* flying training and sport. The British disposed of the last of theirs in 1951 and the American Joint Airborne Troops Board declared them obsolete a year later, but the Russians kept the Yakolev Yak-14 in service for several years after its first appearance in 1947.

After the war there was a quick succession of almost uniformly unremarkable aircraft designed to replace the C-47. The earliest was the American Curtiss C-46 Commando, used successfully in the Pacific war as a transport but which proved a disaster as a paratroop machine during the Rhine crossings in March 1945 because it caught fire so easily when hit by flak. This led Matthew Ridgway to ban its future use despite the fact that it could carry more men and had jump doors on both sides of the fuselage. Then came the Fairchild C-82 Packet/C-119 Flying Boxcar, a twin-boom design with two rear doors which served the US paras reasonably well from 1949 until the arrival of the C-130 Hercules in 1956. The twin-engined C-119 had a span of 109ft 3in (33.3m) and could carry 46 paras (or 62 troops unencumbered by 'chutes) at 243mph (391km/h). By contrast the four-engined Lockheed Hercules, which has been constantly upgraded over the years with more powerful engines and improved avionics, can carry 64 paras at over 380mph (620km/h).

The Hercules is now used by the armies and air forces of most western and non-aligned nations and looks set almost to beat the C-47's record, but before its arrival on the international scene there were a variety of other 'home grown' designs for the airborne and air-landing roles, of which one of the most successful was the French Nord N2501 Noratlas. Another twin-boom design like the C-119, the Noratlas first flew in November 1950 and 200 were built for *l'Armée de l'Air* between 1952 and 1954; other customers included West Germany and Israel. Powered by a pair of French-built Bristol Hercules radial engines, the 106ft 8in (32.5m) wingspan N2501 could carry 31 paras or 45 air-landing troops at a cruising speed of 208mph (335km/h). Another twin-boom design was the much larger British Hawker Siddeley Argosy, which entered service as a replacement for the Vickers Valetta C1. The latter was a comparatively small twin-engined design which first entered service in 1948 as a troop and freight carrier and casualty evacuation aircraft, eventually replacing the C-47. It had a wingspan of 89ft 3in (27.2m), could cruise at 211mph (338km/h) and could carry either 34 troops or 20 paras. The Valetta remained in service until 1969.

The Argosy was a four-engined aircraft with a spacious fuselage capable of carrying 69 troops, 54 paras or 48 stretchers. It had clamshell doors at the rear through which the paras, or vehicles and supplies lashed to pallets, could be dropped. It had a span of 115ft (35m) and a cruising speed of 268mph (429km/h). Only 56 were built 1961–4, the last being replaced by the Hercules in 1974. Other interim British designs were the Hastings and Beverley. The Handley Page Hastings was a conventional low-wing four-engined aircraft which first flew in 1947 and remained in service until 1968 when it, too, was replaced by the Hercules. It had a span of 113ft (34.4m) and could carry either 30 paras or 50 ordinary troops at a cruising speed of 302mph (483km/h). The much larger Blackburn Beverley was specifically designed for the task of dropping paratroops and army equipment through its rear doors. It was an unconventional high wing, four-engined aircraft with twin tail fins and rudders, a bulbous fuselage and fixed undercarriage which, despite its ungainly appearance, had a remarkable STOL capability, being able to land in only 350yd (320m) and take off in 810 (740m). It had a span of 162ft (49.3m), a cruising speed of 173mph (277km/h) and could carry 94 ordinary or 70 paratroops. Only 47 were built though and, like the Hastings, the Beverley was finally retired in 1968.

The Lockheed C-130 Hercules was first ordered by the USAF in 1952 and has subsequently gone on to serve with over 40 air forces around the world, including the RAF who took delivery of their first in 1966. The Hercules was a vast improvement over all other military transport aircraft in existence in the 1960s and the aircraft still has plenty of life left in it. Powered by four Allison turboprops which have been progressively uprated to give a cruising speed of 386mph (621km/h) and a range without inflight refuelling of some 5,000 miles (8,000km), the 'Herk' has a wingspan of 132ft 7in (40.4m) and can carry either 64 paras or 92 ordinary troops, or 74 stretcher cases plus two medics in addition to its crew of four/five. The C-130 has been adapted for many other roles, including gunship and electronic warfare aircraft. In the paratroop guise, the men exit ('shotgun' is the American expression) out of two doors either side of the fuselage, while palleted stores, artillery pieces and vehicles can be offloaded from the large rear ramp. One specialized technique called parachute extraction involves the aircraft flying scant feet above a dropping zone; parachutes attached to loads too heavy for normal dropping are then deployed out of the rear door to pull the load out and on to the ground. This is a particularly useful technique for delivering heavy weapons to airborne forces when there is no runway available or the DZ is under enemy fire.

The Soviet Union had also developed a wide variety of transport aircraft for the airborne role since 1945, ranging from the tactical to the strategic. Earliest was the Ilyushin I1-12 which entered service in 1947. This was broadly similar to the C-47 but had a tricycle undercarriage. Powered by twin radial engines and with a wingspan of 107ft (31.7m), it could carry 32 troops at a cruising speed of 217mph (350km/h). After 1953 it was replaced by the I1-14 'Crate' which was basically the same but had a strengthened structure allowing heavier loads to be carried, and more powerful engines. It in turn was replaced from 1959 by the Antonov An-12 'Cub', the Soviet equivalent of the Hercules from which many features were copied. These included the high tail beneath which is a hydraulic door through which stores can be offloaded on the ground or by parachute while in flight, and the high wing, four-engine configuration. Unusually, though, the rear door opens upwards, so for on-loading a detachable ramp must be affixed. A feature retained on many postwar Soviet aircraft but abandoned as ineffectual in the west was a rearward-facing gun position. The An-12 has a span of 124ft 8in (38m) and can carry 100 paratroops at a cruising speed of 416mph (670km/h). Naturally, parachute drops cannot be carried out at this speed but the An-12 can stay in the air at just over 100mph (160km/h). Alternative loads include the BMD and other armoured fighting vehicles, missiles or artillery pieces.

Much smaller than the An-12 is the An-24/26 'Coke'/'Curl', a twin-engined turboprop utility aircraft which can carry up to 40 paras. It has a short field capability which makes it useful for special forces operations. The same is true of the An-32 'Cline' which appeared in 1977; this can carry 30 paras and has been purchased by the Indian Air Force who name it *Sutlej*. Another aircraft used for parachute training is the An-2, a single-engined cabin biplane which can accommodate 12 to 14 novices; nowadays it is principally used by DOSAAF.

Moving in to the jet age, the Soviet Air Force can deploy the An-72 twin turbofan design which can carry 32 paras, but much more significant are the An-124 'Condor' and Il-76 'Candid'. The latter is the earlier of the two designs, entering service in 1973–5, and greatly resembles the American C-141 Starlifter just as the former (which entered service circa 1985) resembles the C-5 Galaxy. The Ilyushin is a large aircraft with a 165ft 8in (50.5m) span powered by four turbofans which gave a cruising speed of 497mph (800km/h) at between 30–40,000ft (9,144–12,192m); maximum ceiling is even higher and the Il-76 has established a world record by dropping a stick of paras from 50,479ft (15,386m)! The aircraft can carry up to 140 troops or their equivalent in other loads and has exceptional STOL capability for such a large machine, landing in 490yd (450m) and taking off in 930 (850m). The even more massive An-124 can carry an estimated 175 paratroops, although its primary task is heavy lift of all Soviet weapons systems including Intercontinental Ballistic Missiles (ICBMs). Powered by four advanced turbofans delivering nearly double the thrust of those on the Il-76, it has a wingspan of 240ft 6in (73.3m) and can cruise at 537mph (865km/h).

The C-141 Starlifter, alongside the Hercules, is the principal aircraft of today's American rapid deployment forces, including the 82nd Airborne, Rangers and Green Berets. This was the principal aircraft used in the deployment of US airborne troops to Saudi Arabia shortly after the Iraqi take-over of Kuwait in August 1990. The C-141 came about as the result of a requirement specified in the late 1950s for a purpose-designed long-range transport and began entering service with the USAF in August 1961. It is a high wing aircraft with a span of 159ft 11in (48.7m) powered by four turbofans which give it a high cruising speed of 566mph (910km/h) at 30–40,000ft (9,144–12,192m) carrying 154 troops, 123 paras, 80 stretcher cases plus attendants, or a variety of vehicles, stores and munitions. It has a range with maximum payload of some 4,000 miles (6,400km), on paper nearly 25 per cent better than the Il-76 although such figures are subject to endless variations. The even larger Lockheed C-5 Galaxy also has four turbofans but again with nearly twice the thrust rating to power the 222ft 8in (67.9m) wingspan aircraft through the air at 518mph (834km/h) at 30,000ft (9,144m). It is not designed as a paratroop aircraft but as a heavy load carrier deployed in support of rapid reaction forces and has a range of nearly 8,000 miles (12,800km). Recent modifications introduced on both the C-141 and the C-5 further improve speed, maximum ceiling and range.

3: Other airborne forces

As mentioned in Chapter 8, many other countries around the world have developed their own airborne formations in the years since 1945, the principal ones of which are summarised below.

Australia   Formed in July 1957 as 1st Special Air Services Company and later expanded to the size of a regiment, the Australian SAS has seen service during the Borneo confrontation and in Vietnam from 1966 to 1971. In recent years it has developed a counter-terrorist capability to help in defending offshore rigs. It is trained and organised along British SAS lines with three Sabre squadrons plus headquarters, signals and training squadrons.

Belgium   The Belgian Para-Commandos *(see Chapter 7)* currently form part of the Allied Command Europe (ACE) Mobile Force.

Brazil   The Brazilian army has a single parachute brigade organized and trained along American lines, as well as sufficient transport aircraft to carry it into action — which is not always the case in other nations.

Bulgaria   The Bulgarian army began experimenting with airborne troops in 1948 and is currently believed to have a single regiment based in the Burgas-Plovdi region.

Canada   Like Britain's Parachute Regiment, the Canadian Airborne Regiment now forms part of the army's rapid deployment force. The regiment's origins lie with the 1st Canadian Parachute Battalion which was raised in July 1942, trained at Fort Benning and formed part of 3 Para Brigade within the 6th Airborne Division for the invasion of Normandy and the later Rhine crossing, as related earlier. A second battalion raised at the same time was re-designated 1st Canadian Special Force Battalion in May 1943. This saw action in Italy and was prominent in the breakout from the Anzio beachhead and the drive on Rome. It then briefly formed part of the US/Canadian 1st Special Force for the landings in southern France in August 1944. The 2nd Battalion was disbanded in December of that year and the 1st in September 1945.

The modern Canadian Airborne Regiment was raised at the beginning of 1968 and remains the spearhead of the Special Service Force, a mobile, go anywhere, anytime brigade created in 1972 which also includes armour (8th Canadian Hussar Regiment [Princess Louise's]), an air-landing infantry battalion (1st Battalion, Royal Canadian Regiment), artillery (2nd Royal Canadian Horse Artillery Regiment) plus engineer, signals, logistic and other supporting units including a helicopter squadron. An unusual feature of the 740-man regiment reorganised in 1978, is that its 1st Company has the title 1er Commando and is entirely French-speaking; the 2nd Commando is English-speaking and the 3rd is bilingual. The regiment specialises in mountain and arctic warfare, its members being as expert in skiing as in parachuting, but is completely flexible and has been deployed in Cyprus and the Middle East on United Nations peacekeeping duties.

Chile   Like Brazil, Chile has an independent parachute brigade, trained US-style, with special links to the Green Berets.

China   The People's Republic is known to have three airborne divisions modelled on Soviet lines; uncommonly, they fall under air force instead of army command.

Czechoslovakia   Prior to the Soviet invasion in 1968, the Czech army fielded one airborne brigade, the 22nd *Vysadkova Brigada,* but this has subsequently been reduced to the size of a regiment. Based near Prosnice, it has one active and one special operations battalion plus a reserve and a training battalion. As with all Warsaw Pact forces, the status may have changed by the time this book is read.

Denmark   Denmark has no dedicated airborne forces but its *Jaegerkorps* is fully parachute-trained. This is a company-sized special forces unit analagous to an SAS squadron.

Egypt   The Egyptian army has two parachute brigades totalling some 5,000 men who were deployed to Saudi Arabia in August 1990. In addition there are two heliborne air assault brigades and a 500-man counter-terrorist battalion, the 'Thunderbolt' Battalion, which is trained in advanced HAHO and HALO techniques.

Germany   With the reunification of Germany in October 1990, the future composition and status of the armed forces of both the former east and west republics is impossible to estimate, so the following résumé can only describe the situation prior to the miraculous tearing down of the Berlin Wall which gave the world such a marvellous Christmas present in 1989.

(West)   Two months after the Federal Republic was admitted into NATO on 8 May 1955, recruiting began for the newly constituted *Bundeswehr,* a force voluntarily restricted in size to 12 divisions in three corps. Having seen how successful the Allied airborne divisions were in Normandy and other operations, the Germans drew upon their own earlier experience to form a complete parachute division to act as the army's mobile reserve.

There was no shortage of volunteers, many of them wartime veterans, and the 9th *Fallschirmjäger* Division soon consisted of three full brigades, each of three battalions. Later renumbered 1st *Fallschirmjäger* Division, it has its headquarters at Bruschal with the 25th Brigade at Schwarswald, the 26th at Saarlouis and the 27th at Lippstadt. They fall under II Korps in Hanover. Each of the three battalions in each brigade consists of two airborne infantry and two airmobile anti-tank companies, the latter being helicopter-equipped. The reason for the heavy weighting in the anti-tank role was because of fears of the massive Warsaw Pact armoured superiority, fears which are now gradually just becoming memories. The *Fallschirmjäger,* unlike any other airborne force other than the British Parachute Regiment, also specialize in urban warfare, drawing on their wartime experience at Stalingrad and Cassino. Basic training takes 12 weeks, followed by four weeks' jump training at Altenstadt in Bavaria.

The *Bundeswehr* also has its equivalent of the SAS in the three *Fernspähkompanien* or long range reconnaissance companies, one of which is attached to each of the three corps. About 150 men strong, each of these companies is parachute trained at the army jump school at Altenstadt and in more advanced techniques including free-fall jumping at the Ranger school at Schöngau, also in Bavaria. In addition there is the dedicated counter-terrorist unit, GSG9. This was formed by Ulrich Wegener in the wake of the massacre of Israeli athletes during the 1972 Olympic Games at Munich, and subsequently achieved a remarkable success by rescuing all 87 passengers aboard a Lufthansa airliner hijacked in October 1977 and flown to Mogadishu in Somalia. This is not part of the army, its 60-odd men coming from the *Bundesgrenzchutz* or Federal Border Guard, hence its full designation *Grenzschutzgruppe* 9. It does, however, utilize army training facilities, including the jump and Ranger schools and the British SAS school at Weingarten.

(East)   The former Democratic Republic, part of the Warsaw Pact which was formed to counter the 'threat' posed by NATO, only had a single airborne unit, the 40th 'Willi Sanger' *Fallschirmjäger* Battalion. Based at Proro on the Baltic island of Rugen, this was formed in 1973 and would have had a wartime role analagous to the Soviet *Spetsnaz* brigades, with responsibility for behind the lines reconnaissance and sabotage. Its future is currently very much in doubt.

Greece   The Greek army includes a parachute regiment supported by three aviation battalions, and furnishes a counter-terrorist platoon on call to the police in Athens.

Holland   There are no airborne units in the Dutch armed forces although many of the men in the Marine Corps' two Amphibious Combat Groups undertake parachute training alongside the British Royal Marines, with whom they maintain very close links.

Hungary   Like Czechoslovakia, the Hungarian army found its airborne strength greatly reduced in the wake of the 1956 uprising which was brutally suppressed by Soviet troops and tanks. At that time it had a full division but at the time of writing it just had a single 400-man battalion.

India   With independence and the partition of India and Pakistan in 1947, the wartime 44th Indian Parachute Division was disbanded leaving just the 50th Parachute Brigade, four battalions strong. This saw action against Pakistan in Kashmir 1947-9 and later again in 1965. There are also two independent Para-Commando Battalions, the 9th and 10th, formed 1966-9.

Indonesia   On paper, Indonesia can field two airborne brigades, but lacks the transport aircraft to carry more than a few men at a time into action.

Italy   The wartime *Folgore* and *Nembo* Divisions were disbanded with the end of the Italian campaign, but in 1946 a Parachute School was re-established at Tarquina. Subsequent progress was slow and the first airborne units were not created until 1962. In 1978 these became the *Folgore* Brigade, based at Pisa. It has a two-battalion regiment of airborne infantry, a *carabinieri* (police) battalion, an artillery battalion plus an engineer company and aviation flight. In addition, many men in the five alpine brigades (*Cadore, Julia, Orobica, Taurinese* and *Tridentina*) are parachute trained, as is the *San Marco* Marines Battalion, a 1,000-strong force equally skilled in amphibious assaults and rock climbing. Finally there is COMSUBIN *(Commando Raggruppamento Subacqu' ed Incursori* or Special Sub-aqua Raiding Commando Unit). This is an élite 200-man penetration force, equivalent to Britain's Special Boat Service, and is highly trained in parachuting as well as in swimming and diving. Its personnel are all drawn from volunteers from the *San Marco* Marines.

Japan   The Japanese Self-Defence Force includes the 1st Parachute Brigade which, although para-trained, is really a helicopter-borne airmobile unit.

Jordan   The first Jordanian paratroop company, trained to British standards, was raised in 1963 and further expansion has resulted in the current establishment of three para battalions, each of some 500 men.

Korea (North)   The Democratic Republic of Korea fields 22 Special Operations Forces brigades, totalling some 80,000 men. They are organised and trained as light infantry and only a small proportion are parachute-trained.

Korea (South)   The Republic of Korea has seven Special Forces brigades trained by

US Green Beret and Ranger instructors in the parachute, heliborne and amphibious light infantry roles.

New Zealand   The only dedicated airborne unit in the small but efficient New Zealand army is the 1st Ranger Squadron, New Zealand Special Air Service. Descendants of the original squadron sent out to help the British in Malaya in 1956, which was subsequently disbanded in 1957 but resuscitated less than a year later, the squadron received its present designation in 1963 and saw service alongside the Australian SAS in Vietnam until 1971. Based in Auckland, the 1st Ranger Squadron has a headquarters and five Sabre troops.

Norway   Norway maintains one parachute-trained platoon of *Jägers* alongside a Marine platoon as the two principal components in its special forces counter-terrorist company which would double in time of war in the usual roles of deep reconnaissance and sabotage. The whole of the Norwegian army is specifically trained in mountain and arctic warfare and exercises regularly alongside American, British and other NATO partners.

Poland   Apart from the Soviet Union, Poland was the only member of the Warsaw Pact to have a complete airborne division, even if it was really just a reinforced brigade. Current status is unknown and the following remarks apply to 1989. In 1957 the 6th Pomeranian Infantry Division was reorganized along Russian lines as the 6th *Pomorska Dywizja Powietrzna-Desantowa,* or Pomeranian Air Assault Division, with its depot in Krakow. Little was known of its composition except that it was more heavily mechanized than western airborne forces (or those of the other Warsaw Pact nations). Although its personnel were parachute-trained, the division was almost entirely heliborne. It included a *Spetsnaz*-style special operations battalion for deep reconnaissance and sabotage missions.

Portugal   The Portuguese armed forces include one naval commando battalion, one from the army and one from the air force; the last two are both para-trained but more likely to be used in heliborne operations.

Romania   The Romanians, who fought on the German side during the Second World War, formed the 1st Parachute Battalion some time after 1941 but this was abolished when the Red Army overran the country in 1944. Romania, never more than nominally a member of the Warsaw Pact, has a single airborne unit, the 161st Parachute Regiment which is based at Buzau. No further details are available.

South Africa   The Republic of South Africa has a single parachute brigade, the 44th, which is independent of both the conventional and the territorial army chains of command and falls directly under the Chief of the Army. It saw extensive action in Rhodesia prior to Zimbabwe gaining independence in April 1980, as well as in Angola and Namibia. The brigade was reorganised in 1980 to absorb expatriate Rhodesian volunteers and now consists of three battalions (1, 2 and 3 Para) plus a pathfinder company. In addition there is the Reconnaissance Commando, a battalion-size formation of élite troops trained in deep penetration missions in the African bush, all of whose members are parachute-trained.

Spain   The Spanish army includes one parachute and one air-landing brigade in addition to the 4th *Tercio* (Regiment) of the Spanish Foreign Legion, three *banderas* (battalions) strong, plus the Special Operations Unit which is not only parachute-trained but also specialises in amphibious and scuba operations.

Sweden   The neutral Swedish army includes a Parachute Ranger *(Fallschirmjäger)* Company.

Switzerland   The Swiss army has a single para-commando company.

Syria   The Syrian army includes one parachute battalion of three companies and a commando battalion which is heliborne.

Taiwan   Because the descendants of Chiang Kai-Shek's wartime Nationalist Chinese army, which fought alongside the Allies against the Japanese, still consider themselves the rightful rulers of mainland China, the relatively small island previously known as Formosa maintains a standing army out of all proportion to its size. This includes two parachute brigades, a brigade of para-frogmen trained to jump into the sea and swim ashore underwater, and a long-range reconnaissance commando brigade which is also para-trained and maintains close links with Israeli and South African airborne forces.

Thailand   Virtually surrounded by potential enemies — Burma, Kampuchea, Vietnam, although none has a parachute assault force — Thailand also has a large army in proportion to its population. This includes two airborne 'divisions', the 1st and 2nd, each totalling some 3,000 men organized in three 1,000-strong regiments. They date back to 1963 when the 1st Ranger (Airborne) Battalion was formed and are subordinated to Thai Special Warfare Command. Highly trained and skilled in all aspects of jungle warfare and survival, they specialize in the art of unarmed combat.

Further reading

Angus, Tom, *aka* Powell, Geoffrey, *Men at Arnhem* (Leo Cooper, 1976; Buchan & Enright, 1986)

Bauer, Cornelius, *The Battle of Arnhem* (Hodder & Stoughton, 1966)

Davis, Brian L., *German Parachute Forces 1935–45* (Arms & Armour Press, 1974)

Fairley, John, *Remember Arnhem* (Pegasus Journal, 1978)

Ferguson, Gregor, *The Paras: British Airborne Forces 1940–1984* (Osprey, 1984)

Fitzsimons, Bernard (Ed), *The Illustrated Encyclopaedia of 20th Century Weapons and Warfare* (Purnell/Phoebus, 24 vols, 1967–77)

Gavin, Maj-Gen J.M., *Airborne Warfare* (Combat Forces Press, 1947); *On To Berlin* (Leo Cooper, 1979)

Gregory, Barry, and Batchelor, John, *Airborne Warfare 1918–1945* (Phoebus, 1979)

Hetherington, John, *Air-borne Invasion: The story of the battle of Crete* (Angus and Roberston, 1944)

Heydte, Obstlt Freiherr von der, *Daedalus Returned* (Hutchinson, 1958)

Hickey, Michael, *Out of the Sky* (Mills & Boon, 1979)

(HMSO), *By Air To Battle: The Official Account of the British First and Sixth Airborne Divisions* (His Majesty's Stationery Office, 1945; reprinted by Patrick Stephens Ltd, 1978)

Hoyt, Edwin P., *Airborne: The History of American Parachute Forces* (Stein & Day, 1979)

Kent, Ron, *First In! Parachute Pathfinder Company* (B.T. Batsford, 1979)

Kühn, Volkmar, *Deutsche Fallschirmjäger im Zweiten Weltkrieg* (Motorbuch Verlag, 5th edition 1985)

Lucas, James, *Storming Eagles: German Airborne Forces in World War Two* (Arms & Armour, 1988)

Millar, George, *The Bruneval Raid* (The Bodley Head, 1974)

Mitcham, Samuel W., *Hitler's Legions: German Army Order of Battle World War II* (Leo Cooper/Secker & Warburg, 1985)

Pöppel, Martin, *Heaven and Hell: The war diary of a German Paratrooper* (Spellmount, 1988)

Quarrie, Bruce, *Fallschirmpanzerdivision 'Hermann Göring'* (Osprey, 1978); *German Airborne Troops 1939–45* (Osprey, 1983); *German Paratroops in the Med* (Patrick Stephens, 1979); *The World's Elite Forces* (Octopus, 1985); *Special Forces* (Quintet, 1990)

Ryan, Cornelius, *A Bridge Too Far* (Hamish Hamilton, 1974); *The Longest Day* (Victor Gollancz, 1960)

Saunders, Hilary St George, *The Red Beret* (Michael Joseph, 1950)

Seymour, William, *British Special Forces* (Sidgwick and Jackson, 1985)

Smith, J.R., and Kay, Antony L., *German Aircraft of the Second World War* (Putnam, 1972 edition)

Tantum IV, W.H., and Hoffschmidt, E.J., *The Rise and Fall of the German Air Force* (W.E. Inc, 1969)

Thetford, Owen, *Aircraft of the Royal Air Force since 1918* (Putnam, 1976 edition)

Thompson, Julian, *Ready For Anything: The Parachute Regiment at war 1940–1982* (Weidenfeld & Nicolson, 1989)

Thompson, Leroy, *The All Americans: The 82nd Airborne* (David & Charles, 1988)

Tugwell, Maurice, *Airborne to Battle* (William Kimber, 1971)

Weeks, J., *Airborne Equipment* (David & Charles, 1976)

Windrow, Martin, and Braby, Wayne, *French Foreign Legion Paratroops* (Osprey, 1985)

Young, John Robert, *The French Foreign Legion* (Thames & Hudson, 1984)

Zaloga, Steve, and Loop, James, *Soviet Bloc Elite Forces* (Osprey, 1985)

Magazines and partworks

History of the Second World War (Purnell, 1966 ff)

Images of War (Marshall Cavendish, 1988–90)

The Elite (Orbis, 1986–8)

In Combat (Marshall Cavendish, 1991-)

NAM: The Vietnam experience 1965–75 (Orbis, 1987)

Video

Airborne Assault (Command Vision, 1989)

Elite Forces: Paratroops 1940–1945 (Castle/Lamancha, 1990)

Gulf Victory: The Nation's Finest (written by Bruce Quarrie and produced by Command Vision for Express Newspapers plc, 1991)

Index